FAMILY DAYS OUT
IN BRITAIN

Editor: Allen Stidwill

Art Editor: Glyn Barlow

Design Assistance by: KAG Design

Illustrations by: Peter Davies

Directory compiled by: Julia Cady, Lauren Cody, Julia Hynard, Daphne Jolley, Deborah Manley, Myrrhine Raikes

Children's London by: Deborah Manley
Illustrations by: Fran Griffiths

Maps: Prepared by the Cartographic Services Department of the Automobile Association

Filmset by: Tradespools Ltd, Frome, Somerset

Colour section produced by: J B Shears and Sons Ltd, Basingstoke, Hampshire

Printed and bound in Great Britain by: Blackmore Press, Shaftesbury, Dorset

Published by The Automobile Association, Fanum House, Basingstoke, Hampshire RG21 2EA

ISBN 0 86145 664 5

AA Reference 51033

Contents

Introduction

There are hundreds of places in Britain which make an ideal day out for both adults and children alike and this book will help you to choose where to go, whether you are on holiday or are looking for a day out from home.

The book is arranged in six regions and covers England, Wales and Scotland (see map on page 184). Within the regions, places to visit are listed in alphabetical order of towns, although some are too far away from any town or village and they are listed under their own name. We have also included some areas of particular interest where you might spend a day, such as the New Forest or Dartmoor, and they have a special write up, as do some of our more interesting towns. At the end of the book our location atlas will help you to pin-point the places you would like to visit and there is a complete index of towns and places of interest.

We give you as much information as possible about all of the places listed so that you can be absolutely sure of what you will find when you get there and how much it might cost. Every place has a full description and we tell you if refreshments are available, whether you can park right on the spot, whether there is a picnic area, whether your dog can go too and whether there is suitable access for wheelchairs – which will also, of course, give you an idea of the suitability for pushchairs and prams. Opening dates and times are given, together with admission charges, and these are as up-to-date as we could possibly make them. This kind of information is liable to change at short notice, though, so it is always advisable to check in advance of a visit.

We hope you enjoy your days out with our book and, if you find any attractions which we do not list, please let us know where they are.

The West Country

The West Country is an area that seems to have a limitless fund of beautiful and interesting places for people of all ages. Much of the 650 miles of coastline is designated an area of outstanding beauty with golden beaches, rocky coves, fine ports and picturesque harbours. Each of the counties that make up this region has its own special attraction. Gloucestershire has the beautiful cathedral city of Gloucester and many of the Cotswolds' prettiest honey-coloured villages, while Avon includes Bath – Britain's oldest and most famous spa town. Wiltshire is rural England at its best and is also the supreme county for prehistoric remains. Dorset is a varied county with lovely beaches backed by towering cliffs and the undulating countryside, studded with pretty villages, that is Hardy Country. Somerset boasts fine resorts, historic towns, exciting caves and the outstandingly beautiful Exmoor National Park. Then there is Devon – the land of cream teas – a county with two magnificent coastlines containing some of the best of British resorts. Inland is Dartmoor, a vast expanse of moorland, punctuated by granite tors. Last, but not least, there is Cornwall – a land that is steeped in legend and has some of Britain's most dramatic coastline, and prettiest fishing villages.

ABBOTSBURY, DORSET   Abbotsbury Gardens   Map 3 SY58

It's thanks to an extremely mild maritime climate here in Dorset that you'll see so many rare and exotic plants growing outdoors in these sub-tropical gardens at Abbotsbury. Set amid 20 acres of woodland, these formal gardens offer a constantly changing spectacle of interest and colour throughout the season. There is an aviary and a handsome collection of peacocks.

☎(0305) 871387
Located: In Beach Road.

Open: *mid Mar–mid Oct, daily 10–6.
Admission: fee payable, phone for details.
P. ⌷ & garden centre.

ABBOTSBURY, DORSET   Abbotsbury Swannery   Map 3 SY58

A visit to Britain's only herd of Mute Swans can be especially interesting during May, when you can venture quite close to the nesting swans and their cygnets. The carefully conserved natural environment attracts a great many species of wild birds, animals and fish to the reed beds, salt water lagoon and beach.

☎(0305) 871242
Located: In New Barn Road.

Open: mid May to mid Sep 9.30–4.30.
Admission: £1.20 (children 50p, senior citizens £1).
P. ⅂ & ✘

ARLINGTON, DEVON   Arlington Court   Map 2 SS64

Look out for the intriguing collections of model ships and shells inside this elegant 19th-century manor house. There is a large collection of horse-drawn vehicles in the stables and, from there, you can have a carriage ride around the magnificent 300-acre estate. You will see Jacob sheep and Shetland ponies grazing contentedly in the parkland, while the lake is sanctuary for a host of wildfowl. A two-mile circular walk from the lakeside leads through the beautiful oak woods and alongside the River Yeo.

☎Shirwell (027182) 296
Located: 7 miles north east of Barnstaple off A39.

Open: Apr–Oct, Sun–Fri 11–6 (last admission 5.30). Also open Bank Hol Sat. Garden & park also open Nov–Mar, daily until dusk.
Admission: £2.90. Gardens, grounds & stables £1.50 (children £1.45).
⌷ (licensed) & shop
National Trust

ASHTON KEYNES, GLOUCESTERSHIRE   Cotswold Water Park   Map 4 SZ09

Pits left from over 60 years of gravel extraction have been filled with water to produce an imaginative park with attractions to suit all the family – from paddling beaches for the little ones through to water sports such as sailing, skiing and windsurfing. Day permits are given for fishing, and sailing is allowed subject to evidence of boat insurance. Aquatic plants flourish in the exceptionally pure waters and, in winter, the lakes take on an additional role when they provide a refuge for thousands of wildfowl.

☎Cirencester (0285) 861459
Located: 4 miles south of Cirencester off A419.

Open: all year.
⅂

Symbols

☎	telephone number
P.	parking on the premises
⌷	refreshments available
⅂	picnic area
&	accessible to wheelchair-bound visitors
✘	no dogs
*	indicates 1987 details

BATH   Avon   Map 3 ST76

City of Georgian Elegance

Very special among British cities, Bath combines the country's finest Georgian townscape with an unrivalled collection of Roman remains. Today's visitors can explore not only these, but also a dazzling variety of museums, several fine parks and gardens, and shops and markets selling everything from antique buttons to hand-made dolls.

The spa waters that account for Bath's name and for much of its story were familiar to the Celts, but it was the Romans who built the first fine spa town here. It was the 18th-century, though, that saw the transformation of Bath into a fashionable resort. Architect John Wood and his son, designed the perfectly proportioned terraces, crescents and squares which still make Bath England's most elegant city.

Royal Crescent and The Circus are two of the Woods' showpieces, and No. 1 Royal Crescent, open as a museum, has been restored and furnished in period. Bath's other museums offer a great variety of experiences. The Postal Museum has a replica of a Victorian post office; Sally Lunn's Kitchen, named after the famous cook who worked here, is in Bath's oldest house; the Camden Works Museum reconstructs a Victorian family engineering works; there is even a Museum of Bookbinding.

The Arts flourish in Bath with three art galleries, the Theatre Royal, first opened in 1805 and recently refurbished, and the Bath Puppet Theatre near Pulteney Bridge.

Eight times winner of 'Britain in Bloom', Bath is well provided with pleasant parks and gardens. Royal Victoria Park has seven acres of botanical gardens, a lake, a boating pool and a good children's play area. Children and adults alike will enjoy the Bath Maze in Beazer Gardens.

☆STAR ATTRACTIONS

Roman Baths and Pump Room

Rediscovered in 1880, the Roman Great Bath is the centre-piece of this fascinating museum, which gives a vivid picture of life in Roman Britain. The bath, fed by a spring which rises at a constant temperature of 46.5°C, is still lined with its original lead sheets, now almost 2,000 years old. The museum contains many fascinating archaeological finds including mosaics, jewellery, tools and pottery.

☎(0225) 61111 ext. 327
Located: Abbey Churchyard.

Open: Mar–Jun & Sep–Oct daily 9–6; Jul & Aug daily 9–7; Nov–Feb Mon–Sat 9–5, Sun 10–5.
Admission: *£2 (children £1.15).
⌨ (licensed) & (ground floor only) shop ⍟

The adjacent Pump Room was the focal point of Bath's second Golden Age. Fashionable society gathered here to take the waters in the 18th-century. Today, tea and Bath buns (as well as lunches or morning coffee) can be enjoyed here to the genteel background music of the Pump Room Trio.

Museum of Costume

The elegant 18th-century Assembly Rooms, designed by John Wood the Younger, are now home to one of Britain's finest museums of costume. The theme is fashion down the ages, with displays ranging from Elizabethan embroidered jackets, caps and shirts to the work of leading 20th-century fashion designers.

☎(0225) 61111 ext. 425
Located: Assembly Rooms, Bennett Street.

Open: Mar–Oct, Mon–Sat 9.30–6, Sun 10–6; Nov–Feb, Mon–Sat 10–5, Sun 11–5.
Admission: *£1.40 (children 85p).
⌨ (licensed mid Jul–mid Sep) & shop ⍟

American Museum

This museum, the only one of its kind in Britain tells the story of America's history and its way of life. Lots of fascinating exhibits are on show and there are a number of recreated rooms showing various American styles. Outside is a re-creation of George Washington's Mount Vernon garden and lively special events are sometimes held.

☎(0225) 60503
Located: At Claverton Manor, 2½ miles east.

Open: Apr–Oct daily (except Mon) 2–5; Bank Hol Sun & Mon 11–5.
Admission: *£2.75 (children £2.25), grounds only £1.
P. ⌨ & (ground floor & gardens only) shop ⍟

BEER, DEVON   Pecorama   Map 3 SY28

This steam-operated ride through interesting scenic features and an exciting tunnel will appeal to garden-lovers and train enthusiasts alike. An exhibition of models continues the railway theme, as do souvenir and model shops, though some members of the family might prefer to visit the aviary, putting green, crazy golf course or children's corner.

☎Seaton (0297) 21542

Open: *Mon–Fri 10–5.30, Sat 10–1. Outside activities Easter, May Day, Spring Bank Hol weekend to early Oct & Autumn half term period. Also Sun during school hols & Spring Bank Hol. Indoor exhibition & shops all year round.
Admission: *Exhibition 70p (children 35p). Garden 80p (children 40p). Railway 45p (children 35p). Bargain ticket for all three (high season) £1.80 (children 80p).
P. ⊡ (licensed) ⊼ ₺ shop ⊁ (except in garden)

BICKLEIGH, DEVON   Bickleigh Castle   Map 3 SS90

This romantic medieval castle embraces 900 years of history, and the fine building houses many historical displays featuring the castle's connection with the *Mary Rose*, and an exhibition of maritime disasters including the ill-fated *Titanic*. There's a display of World War II P.O.W. escape gadgets, and younger children will enjoy the collection of 18th–20th-century artefacts and toys – particularly a ride on a period rocking horse!

☎(08845) 363
Located: Off the A396. Take the A3072 from Bickleigh Bridge, and follow signs.

Open: Easter week, then Wed, Sun & Bank Hols to Spring Bank Hol. Then daily (except Sat) 2–5 until early Oct.
Admission: *£2 (children £1, under 5 free). Family ticket £5.50.
P. ⊡ ⊼ ₺ (except Great Hall, Tudor Bedroom & Museum) shop ⊁

BICKLEIGH, DEVON   Bickleigh Mill–Devonshire's Centre   Map 3 SS90

A heritage farm with rare breeds worked by shire horses and oxen. Of special interest is the Otter and Fishing Centre and the Motor Museum. Enjoy a walk through the Exotic Bird Centre and a riverside picnic by the children's area. Craftwork produced at the enchanting old working watermill can be purchased in the showrooms.

☎(08845) 419

Open: Jan–Mar, Sat & Sun 10–5; Apr–Oct daily 10–6; Nov–Dec daily 10–5.
Admission: *£3 (children £2).
P. ⊡ (licensed) ⊼ ₺ (ground floor & gardens) shop.

BICTON, DEVON   Bicton Park   Map 3 SY08

At Bicton, among its 60 acres of historic gardens and pinetum, you can get lost in the magic of three 'Worlds'. There's the **World of Tomorrow**, where budding astronauts can take command in the space station or learn the intricacies of the flight deck on an SR2 simulator. Others might prefer to go back in time to the **World of Yesterday** with the help of original 'Penny in slot' machines and magic lantern shows. Finally, there's the action-packed **World of Leisure** complete with adventure playground, assault course, crazy golf and putting green. Also in the Park is the Woodland Railway, Countryside Collection and Bird Garden with its falconry displays, while the younger children will also enjoy a visit to Pet's Corner.

☎Colaton Raleigh (0395) 68074
Located: On A376 north of Budleigh Salterton

Open: Easter–Oct daily, 10–6. Apply for winter openings.
Admission: £2.25 (children £1.20–under 5 free, senior citizens £1.85).
P. ⊡ (licensed) ₺ shop

for BIRDLIP see page 10

Queen of the South Coast

Likened by Sir John Betjeman to a stately Victorian duchess, Bournemouth boomed during the second half of the 19th-century, at the height of the Victorian craze for the seaside. Much of the resort's character is derived from its planned Victorian townscape of fine villas, handsome churches and informal, tree-lined streets. Natural advantages such as seven miles of sheltered beaches, and sea-water that claims to be the warmest in Britain, have ensured that Bournemouth has never looked back. Today it lacks nothing that holidaymakers could wish for, from excellent shopping to all kinds of sporting facilities and from several museums to a great variety of evening entertainment.

Much of Bournemouth stands 100ft or so above the sea, separated from it by spectacular cliffs, broken at intervals by lush, wooded valleys. Parks and gardens account for as much as one-sixth of Bournemouth's total area – some 2,000 acres in all. They offer not only many attractive, traffic-free walks, but also a host of family leisure facilities. There is a miniature rifle range and a model boat pond, two 18-hole municipal golf courses, tennis courts, and bowling greens. Other fine-day pursuits might include a ride in an open-topped bus to Hengistbury Head, where stunning views over Christchurch Harbour are complemented by a nature trail and an important archaeological site. For wet weather there are several shopping arcades, amusements on two piers, an ice rink, and swimming pools including one with a wave-making machine. For the evenings, entertainment ranges from concerts by the prestigious Bournemouth Symphony Orchestra, to traditional holiday comedy shows at the Pier Theatre.

☆STAR ATTRACTIONS

The Beach

One of Britain's finest beaches, Bournemouth's long stretch of sand is sheltered by the Isle of Wight, the Isle of Purbeck and by its own 100ft cliffs, and enjoys above-average sunshine hours. Beach huts, deck chairs and small boats or sailboards can be hired, and the Piers offer traditional seaside amusements. There is even a free children's beach club, near Toft Steps, during the summer holidays.

Big Four Railway Museum

A large working model railway is among the attractions at this museum, a must for railway enthusiasts. More than 1,000 items are on display, including a large collection of locomotive nameplates and many static and working model locomotives.

☎(0202) 22278
Located: Dalkeith Hall, Dalkeith Steps, rear of 81A Old Christchurch Road.

Open: Mon–Sat 10–5. Closed Bank Hols.
Admission: £1 (children 50p). Family ticket £2.
shop

Russell-Cotes Art Gallery and Museum

Former lord mayor Sir Merton Russell-Cotes donated the original collection of Japanese and Burmese art around which this varied and popular museum grew. Set in a grand Victorian house, the museum features several period rooms with 19th-century furnishings, bric-à-brac and works of art. Other displays, include a room devoted to the great 19th-century actor Sir Henry Irving, a freshwater aquarium and a geological terrace.

☎(0202) 21009
Located: East Cliff.

Open: Mon–Sat 10–5.30.
Admission: 50p (children 10; under 5 free).
🖵 shop ✳

BIRDLIP, GLOUCESTERSHIRE   Crickley Hill Country Park   Map 3 SO91

There are 62 acres of beautiful Cotswold scenery to explore and enjoy here at Crickley Hill. The steep grassy slopes are rich in flowers and butterflies, while from the edge of the hill, there are commanding views across the Severn Valley to the Malverns, the Forest of Dean and the mountains of South Wales. It is a pleasant walking area with several trails including Scrubbs Trail to an excavation site, owned by the National Trust, which includes part of an Iron Age fort that was re-occupied during the 6th century AD.

☎Witcombe (0452) 863170 (seasonal) or 425675
Located: 1½ miles north east of Birdlip off B4070 near junction with A417 & A436.

Open: all year.
P. ⊟ ⊞ ዽ

BLACKMOOR GATE, DEVON   Exmoor Bird Gardens   Map 3 SS64

These unique and beautiful gardens are home to a varied and interesting collection of foreign birds, animals and waterfowl, many of which are at liberty within the extensive grounds. Some areas are formal while others are of outstanding natural beauty – all have magnificent views. Mum and Dad can relax too while junior lets off steam in Tarzan-Land.

☎Parracombe (05983) 352
Located: Off B3226 midway between Bratton Fleming and Blackmoor Gate.

Open: Easter–end Oct, daily 10–6.
Admission: *£2 (children 75p).
P. ⊟ ⊞ ዽ 补

BODMIN, CORNWALL   Pencarrow   Map 2 SX06

Situated down a mile-long drive through an ancient British encampment, this privately owned Georgian mansion houses a superb collection of paintings, furniture and china. There are fifty acres of woodland gardens with an internationally re-nowned collection of conifers and rhododendrons, signed trails, a children's play area and pets' corner.

☎St Mabyn (020884) 369
Located: At Washaway (4 miles north on an unclassified road off the A389).

Open: Easter–May & mid Sep–mid Oct, Sun–Thu 1.30–5; Jun–mid Sep & Bank Hol Mon, Sun–Thu 11–5. Garden daily during season.
Admission: *House and garden £2 (children £1). Garden only 50p (children 25p).
P. ⊟ ⊞ ዽ (ground floor & gardens only) plant & craft shop

for BOURNEMOUTH see page 9

BOVEY TRACEY, DEVON   Parke Rare Breeds Farm   Map 3 SX87

Conservation is an important part of education today and, here at Parke children can see for themselves the ancient breeds of goats, cattle, sheep, pigs and poultry that are being saved from extinction by the Rare Breeds Farm. Youngsters will enjoy the pets corner and play area. There are also some lovely walks through woodland alongside the River Bovey.

☎(0626) 833909

Open: Apr–Oct daily, 10–6 (last admission 5pm).
Admission: £1.80 (children 3–14 £1, senior citizens £1.40).
P. ⊟ ⊞ ዽ shop 补
National Trust

BOVINGTON CAMP, DORSET   The Tank Museum   Map 3 SY88

Fans of tanks, and all things military, will have a field day here. There are over 200 examples of armoured fighting vehicles (wheeled and tracked) dating from 1915 onwards. Three new exhibition halls cover Evolution, World War One and Inter-War years. Children will especially enjoy seeing the working models and video films. A Tank and Militaria jumble will take place on the 11th and 12th June 1988 whilst Battle Day is to be held on the 31st July 1988.

☎Bindon Abbey (0929) 462721 Ext 463 & 463953.
Located: Off A352 at Bovington Camp.

Open: daily, 10–5 (closed 10 days over Xmas and New Year).
Admission: £2 (children, senior citizens & disabled £1). Family ticket £4.
P. ⊟ (licensed) ⊞ ዽ shop 补

BRISTOL AVON   Map 3 ST57

Maritime Capital of the West

The statue of Neptune – god of the sea – presiding over the harbour is a fitting mascot for Bristol. Seafaring has been in the city's blood since its beginnings in Saxon times, and today popular events like the Powerboat Grand Prix and Bristol Regatta, held every summer, continue the maritime tradition.

A stroll round Bristol's streets will reveal more of the legacy left by centuries of successful trading. Various conducted walking tours are available daily in summer, starting at Neptune's statue at 11am. A different tour of discovery might be a visit to one of several museums. The Bristol Industrial Museum on Prince's Wharf has all kinds of horse-drawn and motorised vehicles, aircraft, railway exhibits and machinery, displayed in a converted dockside transit shed. There is a fully furnished Georgian house in Great George Street; John Wesley's chapel; or, returning to the inevitable nautical theme, the National Lifeboat Museum, or the Maritime Heritage Centre, devoted to Bristol's shipbuilding industry over two centuries. Past and present are fused in the Theatre Royal, where the prestigious Bristol Old Vic company performs in Britain's oldest working theatre, opened in 1766.

For outdoor pastimes in the city, try St George Park, where there is a new wheel park for roller-skating, skateboarding or riding BMX bicycles, as well as tennis courts and a boating lake. For a really memorable waterside experience, do not miss the Illuminated Water Carnival, the weekend before Christmas, when decorated floats and carol singing lend a festive atmosphere to the Historic Harbour.

☆ STAR ATTRACTIONS

Blaise Castle Estate

Though some distance from the city centre, Blaise Castle Estate offers a family day out in itself. Blaise Castle, is a Gothic-style folly standing in extensive landscaped grounds, with surprises like the Robber's Cave, the Butcher's Cave, and even the 'footprints' of the giant, Goram, embedded in a rock. Old farm and kitchen implements, dolls, toys and costumes are on display in the 18th-century Blaise Castle House.

☎(0272) 506789
Located: At Henbury (4 miles north-west of city centre, off B4057).

Open: Blaise Castle House; Sat–Wed 10–1 & 2–5. Closed Xmas and New Year.
Admission: Free.
P. & (ground floor only) shop ✴

Bristol Zoo

Some 400 mammals and 500 birds from all over the world can be seen, in 12 acres of gardens, here at Britain's fourth most popular zoo. Many of the creatures, including Europe's only white tigers, belong to rare or endangered species. There is a specially built house where nocturnal animals can be observed.

☎(0272) 738951
Located: At Clifton Down.

Open: Mon–Sat from 9am, Sun from 10am. Closing times vary with season. Closed Xmas.
Admission: ✴£3 (children £1.50).
P. ⌑ (licensed) & (most animal houses) shop ✴

SS Great Britain

Brunel's famous ship was built here in this dock and launched by Prince Albert in 1843. One of the largest vessels of her day (at 322ft long), she was the first ocean-going ship to have an iron hull and be driven by a propeller. She plied the oceans until 1886, when she was abandoned in the Falkland Islands. Towed back to Bristol in 1970, this remarkable ship is now being restored and is open to visitors. Her story is told in the dockside museum.

☎(0272) 260680
Located: At Great Western Dock, Gas Ferry Road.

Open: daily, summer 10–6, winter 10–5. Closed Xmas.
Admission: ✴£1.50 (children & senior citizens 70p).
⌑ (licensed) shop ✴

BRIXHAM, DEVON   Berry Head Country Park   Map 3 SX95

Be sure to bring your binoculars along to Berry Head, for this is an area rich in birdlife and flora. Guillemots, shags, cormorants and kittiwakes are at home on the towering cliffs whilst wrens, stonechats and linnets can be seen on the plateau. Rare and beautiful flowers such as orchid and rock rose thrive in the lime-rich environment. Nature trails will help you to appreciate this 100-acre park set within an area of outstanding natural beauty. Although man has had forts here since the Iron Age, the remains you'll see today date only from the 19th century.

Located: Directly east of Brixham via Gillard Road.

Open: all year, daily.
P. ⌕ ⩱

BROKERSWOOD, WILTSHIRE   Woodland Heritage Museum   Map 3 ST85

Eighty acres of natural woodland, still operated as a working concern, contain nature trails, a lake with wildfowl, a children's adventure playground and a wildlife and forestry museum. A woodland Fayre will take place on 4 June 1988.

☎**Westbury (0373) 822238**
Located: Off A361.

Open: Park daily 10–sunset. Museum Mon–Fri 9–6 (5.30 in winter), Sat & Sun 10.30–6.
Admission: £1 (unaccompanied children under 14 70p, accompanied children under 14 free).
P. ⌕ ⩱ shop

BROWNSEA ISLAND, DORSET   Poole Harbour   Map 4 SZ08

No boy scout should miss a trip to the island where Lord Baden-Powell had his first scout camp in 1907. These 500 acres of heath and woodland, with nature reserve and two lakes, are just as unspoilt today. There is also a mile-long bathing beach and fine views of the Dorset coastline.

☎**Canford Cliffs (0202) 707744**
Access: By boat from Poole Quay & Sandbanks – parking facilities at both.

Open: Apr–Sep, daily 10–8 (or dusk, if earlier).
Admission: ✳£1 (children 50p).
⌕ ⩱ & shop ⑂
National Trust

BUCKFASTLEIGH, DEVON   Dart Valley Railway   Map 3 SX76

Relive the golden days of steam in a scenic seven mile trip from Buckfastleigh to Totnes following the River Dart. At Buckfastleigh Station a miniature railway runs for half a mile around the picnic area, locomotives and Great Western rolling stock are on show in the steam park, and there is a three-dimensional cinema spectacular.

☎**(0364) 42338**

Open: Jun–Aug daily 10–5.30. Selected days early & late season, please enquire.
Admission/Fare: £3.40 (children £2.40 & senior citizens £3.10). Includes entry to station, steam park & train fare.
P. ⌕ (licensed) ⩱ & shop

CALNE, WILTSHIRE   Bowood House and Gardens   Map 3 ST96

Capability Brown's Pleasure Gardens cover some 100 acres and here the children can use up excess energy in an enormous adventure playground. Inside the elegant Georgian house, one can view the laboratory where Dr Joseph Priestly first discovered oxygen gas, superb watercolours, costume and sculpture, and a special exhibition outlining the history of the gardens.

☎**(0249) 812102**
Located: Two miles West off the A4.

Open: Apr–Oct daily 11–6 Rhododendron Gardens open mid May–mid Jun, 11–6 (separate entrance off A342).
Admission: House & grounds ✳£2.50 (children £1.30, senior citizens £1.80). Rhododendron Gardens £1.
P. ⌕ (licensed) ⩱ & (ground floor & gardens) gift shop & garden centre ⑂

CALSTOCK, CORNWALL   Cotehele   Map 2 SX46

The Earls of Mount Edgcumbe owned this handsome granite house from the 14th-century and it remained in the family until 1947 when it was given over to the National Trust. Interesting collections include tapestry, armour and furniture. The attractive tiered garden has a medieval dovecote. There is a restored watermill in the valley below, as well as a small museum of shipping. A restored barge, *The Shamrock*, can be seen from the quay.

☎Liskeard (0579) 50434
Located: 2 miles west of Calstock, on the west bank of the Tamar, 8 miles south west of Tavistock off A390.

Open: Apr–Oct daily, 11.6 or dusk (last admission 5.30). House only closed on Fri. Nov–Mar garden only open during daylight hours.
Admission: House, garden & mill £3.20. Garden & mill only £1.60.
P. ⬜ ⚹ (ground floor of house only) shop ✝
National Trust

CANFORD CLIFFS, DORSET   Compton Acres Gardens   Map 4 SZ08

Explore some fifteen acres of delightful gardens laid out in a series of contrasting styles, follow winding paths, negotiate stepping stones or cross bridges over streams and carp-filled pools and discover priceless bronzes and marble statues brought from all over the world.

The exquisite Japanese garden, with its original tea house, is particularly fascinating for children and there are fine views too over Poole Harbour and the Purbeck Hills.

☎(0202) 700778
Located: On the B3605 Canford Cliffs Road.

Open: Apr–Oct daily 10.30–6.
Admission: *£2 (children 95p, senior citizens £1.50).
P. ⬜ ⚹ shop & garden centre ✝

CHEDDAR, SOMERSET   Cheddar Caves and Museum   Map 3 ST45

Whilst older children (12 and over – must book) enjoy a spot of adventure caving, complete with helmets, lamps and boiler suits, younger brothers and sisters will have fun at Fantasy Grotto with its high-tech lighting effects. All will marvel at Gough's cave, the most beautiful cave in Britain. The museum is located on the cliffs and specialises in archaeology and zoology including finds from the Ice Age, the Iron Age and the Romano British occupation. Exhibits include flint and bone implements which were found in Gough's Cave.

☎(0934) 742343
Open: all year. Easter–Sep 10–5.30, rest of the year (except Xmas) 10.30–4.30.
Admission: Gough's Cave £1.70 (children 85p, senior citizens £1.10). Cox's Cave & Fantasy Grotto (incl. Hologram exhibition) £1.50 (children 75p, senior citizens £1); Jacob's Ladder 50p (children & senior citizens 25p). Exhibition & Museum 50p (children & senior citizens 25p). Combined ticket £2.95 (children & senior citizens £1.60). Adventuring Caving £3.95, Orienteering 70p (children & senior citizens 45p).
P. ⬜ (licensed) ⚹ (ground floor only) shop ✝ (in museum)

CHOLDERTON, WILTSHIRE   Cholderton Rare Breeds Farm   Map 4 SU24

Almost all the animals are endangered species so visitors are fortunate and privileged in being allowed to touch and feed them. All types of farm creatures can be seen here; pigs, goats, cattle, sheep, horses, poultry and ducks. Youngsters will love the giant rabbit section, not to mention the adventure playground and children's yard. There is a woodland walk, as well as some beautiful formal gardens and orchard. Education is the keynote and history and conservation the topics.

☎Cholderton (098064) 438
Located: In Amesbury Road.

Open: Apr–Oct daily, 10–6 (last admission 5pm).
Admission: £1.60 (children 80p, senior citizens £1).
P. ⬜ ⊼ ⚹ (ground floor only) shop

CLEARWELL, GLOUCESTERSHIRE Clearwell Caves Ancient Mines Map 3 SO50

See how iron ore has been mined over the last 3,000 years at this mining museum with eight large caverns and engine rooms to explore. For the more adventurous, deep level caving trips are available by appointment. There are exhibits of local mining and geology and several vintage stationary engines.

☎Dean (0594) 23700

Open: Mar–Oct daily 10–5.
Admission: £1.50 (children 80p & senior citizens £1.20).
P. ☞ 🛆 shop 🐾 (except guide dogs)

COMBE MARTIN, DEVON Bodstone Barton Working Farm Map 2 SS54

Children will delight in the animals at this beautiful country park, they can get really close to goats, sheep, pigs, rabbits, ducks and turkeys and even try their hand at bottle feeding lambs and kids. An adventure playground and a nature trail through streams and woodland will ensure that even the most active of youngsters has an enjoyable visit.

☎(027188) 3654

Open: Mar (Sun only); Apr (Sun, Wed, Thu); May–Sep daily (Closed Sat), Oct (Sun, Wed & Thu); 10.30–6 (last admission 4pm).
Admission: £2 (children & senior citizens £1, under 3 free, disabled 80p). Family ticket £6.
P. ☞ 🛆 & (grounds only) shop 🐾

COMBE MARTIN, DEVON Combe Martin Wildlife Park Map 2 SS54

A most attractive Wildlife Park with acres of gardens and forest complete with waterfalls, streams, tropical plants and rare trees. You'll find seals and otters enjoying the water whilst six species of monkey are at home among the trees and bamboo. There are wallabies and racoons too and a large collection of birds of prey. Native domestic animals can be found in the Children's Zoo, and don't miss the parrots, the Model Railway or the Adventure Playground.

☎(027188) 2486
Located: 5 miles west of Ilfracombe on the A399.

Open: all year daily, 10–dusk.
Admission: ✻£2.20 (children 5–12 & senior citizens £1.20).
P. ☞ (licensed) shop 🐾

CRANHAM, GLOUCESTERSHIRE Prinknash Bird Park Map 3 SO81

A wonderful selection of swans, geese and waterfowl in nine acres of beautiful parkland and lakes. Watch out for peacocks, Pygmy goats, cranes and fallow deer. Ornamental pheasants strut around the Golden Wood where ghosts reputedly haunt a fishpond built by 16th-century monks.

☎Painswick (0452) 812727

Open: Easter–Oct, 10–6.
Admission: ✻£1.50 (children & senior citizens 80p).
P. & shop 🐾

CRANMORE, SOMERSET East Somerset Railway Map 3 ST64

Even non-railway buffs will enjoy an outing to Cranmore Railway Station. For, apart from an excellent exhibition of steam locomotives and rolling stock, engine shed and work-shops, and a steam-hauled passenger train, you can enjoy a visit to the signal-box art gallery, museum, and wildlife information centre. There's even a children's play area, and they'll love to ride the Santa train in December. Watch out for special events such as the vintage vehicle rally and jazz concerts.

☎(074988) 417

Open: Apr–Oct, daily 10–5.30 (closes 4pm Apr, Sep & Oct); Nov–Dec & Mar, weekends only 10–4. Phone for details of Steam Days.
Admission: Steam Days incl. train ride (unlimited travel) £2.20 (children under 16 & senior citizens £1.10). Non-steam days 90p (children under 16 & senior citizens 45p).
P. ☞ (& restaurant car on Steam Days) 🛆 & (ground floor only) shop

for CRICKET ST THOMAS see page 16

In the heart of Devon between Okehampton, Tavistock, Ivybridge and Christow lie the 365 square miles of outstandingly beautiful countryside known as Dartmoor. Designated a National Park for over 30 years this is one of the few wide open spaces left in the south of England and its wild, rugged and dramatic scenery is freely available for public enjoyment. This is an area of sharp contrasts that encompasses high tors, deep valleys, vast expanses of bleak moorland and even towns and villages.

Although Dartmoor is farmed, most of the actual farmsteads are to be found around the edge of the moor or in the valleys. Higher up the terrain becomes more rocky and dramatic, great granite tors rise up from the ground in weird and wonderful shapes and it is here that evidence of pre-historic communities have been found.

The high and remote north and south plateaux that lie at the heart of Dartmoor are the source of the majority of Devon's rivers which criss-cross their way across the moor, past the pretty towns and villages below on their way to the sea. The Becka Brook is one such stream, which tumbles down a boulder-strewn valley to form the popular Becky Falls, just off the B3344. Probably better known is the White Lady waterfall in the Lydford Gorge which noisily falls 100 feet into the fern-clad ravine. Nearby there are remains of a 12th-century castle.

Wild Dartmoor ponies have roamed freely in this area for centuries and each year are rounded up by their owners so that the new foals can be branded. For lovers of the outdoors this is a place that provides infinite enjoyment for casual and experienced walkers as well as for those who prefer to find a beauty spot, sit down, have a picnic and simply absorb the glorious views. The National Trust has provided a nature walk through the beech and oak woods of the Teign Valley and a forest trail through Fernworthy Forest gives excellent views of the reservoir and the rest of Dartmoor. Dartmoor also has some of the best of Britain's riding and pony trekking country – a great way to gain access to and explore the remoter parts of the moor. For those who prefer their horse power in a motorised form, the Transmoor Link, a bus service which operates between Plymouth and Exeter during summer weekends, travels through the heart of this National Park offering wonderful views.

For places to visit in the area check the location atlas at the end of the book.

The tower of the parish church of Wide-combe-in-the-Moor stands nobly against the Dartmoor sky.

CRICKET ST THOMAS, SOMERSET   Wildlife Park   Map 3 ST30

A wide range of attractions to please all age groups, featuring a variety of birds and animals from many countries. A scenic miniature railway terminates at Flamingo Junction where passengers can enjoy views over the lake. There's a working dairy farm, shire horse centre and country life museum, and a 'Taste of Somerset' shop. An adventure playground, with a life size American fort, and assault course obstacles set along woodland pathways will challenge even the most energetic youngsters. You may recognise the house from BBC TV's 'To the Manor Born'.

☎Winsham (046030) 755

Open: daily Apr–Oct 10–6; Nov–Mar 10–5 (or dusk, whichever is earlier).
Admission: ✳£3.50 (children £2.50, under 3 free, senior citizens £3).
P. ⌨ (licensed) ⅗ shop garden centre

for DARTMOOR see page 15

DOBWALLS, CORNWALL   Dobwalls Theme Park   Map 2 SX26

This exciting theme park is set around an extensive miniature railway. Based on American railroads this two-mile-long track offers steam or diesel trains. You can take the Rio Grande through the Prairies or the Union Pacific through forests. When you get off the train you can visit Adventureland – five action-packed play areas filled with Swedish-designed equipment including aerial cableways and two tube slides.

☎Liskeard (0579) 20325/21129
Located: Just off A38 close to Liskeard.

Open: daily Easter–early Nov 10–6 (last admission 5pm). Adventureland open all year (winter 11–5, last admission 4pm). Some trains on fine days (winter).
Admission: ✳Global ticket £3.50 (children £1.99). Family ticket £9.99 (2 adults, 2 children). Stroller ticket £1.99 (children 99p).
Note: Global & Family tickets include two Railroad rides, Adventureland, Thorburn Museum (see following entry), picnic areas and almost all other facilities.
Stroller tickets do not include Railroad rides or Thorburn Museum entrance.
P. ⌨ 🎋 shop

DOBWALLS, CORNWALL   Thorburn Museum   Map 2 SX26

Mr Thorburn's Edwardian Countryside is the only audio-visual art gallery in the world. More than 200 original paintings by world-famous wildlife artist, Archibald Thorburn (1860–1935), are seen here in a setting which recreates his studio and the countryside that inspired him.

☎Liskeard (0579) 20325/21129
Located: Dobwalls Theme Park.

Open: daily Easter–Oct 10–6 (last admission 5pm); Oct–Easter 11–5 (last admission 4pm).
Admission: ✳£1.99 (children 99p). See previous entry.
P. ⌨ 🎋 ⅗ shop

DORCHESTER, DORSET   Dinosaur Museum   Map 3 SY69

The world of the dinosaurs comes alive among life-size reconstructions, skeletons, fossils, computerised and electronic displays. Children particularly will be enthralled by the 'interactive' exhibits where they can really get to grips with the prehistoric creatures. Displays are frequently changing so there is usually something new to see.

☎(0305) 69880
Located: In Icen Way.

Open: All year 9.30–5.30 (except Xmas & New Year's Day).
Admission: ✳£1.75 (children £1.25, senior citizens £1.50). Family ticket £5.50
⅗ (ground floor only). gift shop

for EAST HUNTSPILL see page 19

Devon's Cathedral City

Probably more often by-passed than visited, Exeter is well worth exploring. Excellent shops, a variety of fine museums, and historic attractions spanning almost 2,000 years make it a city that has something for everyone.

In its day Exeter has been a Roman walled town, a Norman stronghold, a prosperous centre of the cloth trade and a flourishing port. Each of these has left its legacy – though Exeter suffered terrible bomb damage during World War II which destroyed many of the older buildings. Nevertheless, in many parts of the city old and new stand companionably cheek by jowl.

Like many cities, Exeter is best explored on foot. That way you will not miss the quiet backwaters where the feel of bygone days remain. For example, tucked away not far from the Exe Bridges is cobbled Stepcote Hill and, near it, St Mary Steps Church, whose remarkable 17th-century clock has colourful moving figures which strike the hours. The Cathedral Close also demands leisurely exploration. Notice the fine Elizabethan building known as Mol's Coffee House, said to have been a rendezvous of famous seafarers like Drake and Hawkins.

A quiet street off Fore Street is where you will find St Nicholas' Priory, with a 15th-century kitchen and Norman undercroft. By contrast, the Royal Albert Memorial Museum is a large and splendid Victorian building whose varied collections range from Red Indian costumes to a stuffed giraffe.

☆STAR ATTRACTIONS

The Cathedral

Exeter Cathedral is a remarkable survivor of the wartime destruction, standing largely unchanged since it was completed some 600 years ago. Among its most notable features are the long stretch of exquisite rib-vaulting in the nave, and the beautifully carved roof bosses, now brightly painted again as they would originally have been. The huge, pinnacled Bishop's Throne is a masterpiece of medieval craftsmanship.

Located: Cathedral Close.

Maritime Museum

Allow plenty of time for a visit to this marvellous collection of the world's boats. Many of the larger vessels – which children are encouraged to explore – are moored in the Canal Basin, reached from the quay by a special passenger ferry for visitors. Smaller craft, including a boat in the shape of a swan, a Welsh coracle, and many kinds of canoe, are displayed in two large waterside warehouses.

☎(0392) 58075
Located: At Town Quay & Canal Basin.

Open: daily; summer 10–6; winter 10–5 (closed Xmas).
Admission: ✱£2.50 (children £1.30). Family tickets available.
P. ▭ ⛱ ♿ (ground floors only) shop

Underground Passages

Exeter was uniquely fortunate among England's medieval cities in having a man-made system of underground aqueducts to supply its citizens with pure water. Houses above the water conduits had holes in the floor through which buckets were lowered. Some of the vaulted passageways (now dry, of course) have been restored and can be explored on guided tours – though the passages are small and narrow, so this is not a pastime for the claustrophobic!

☎(0392) 265858
Located: In Princesshay.

Open: Tue–Sat, 2–4.30.
Admission: ✱50p (children 25p).
✶

The 265 square miles that make up Exmoor form one of the smallest but also one of the most beautiful and varied of our ten National Parks. Dunkery Beacon, at 1,705 feet, is the highest point and the walk to its summit is an easy one from the nearby unclassified road. The reward will be panoramic views in all directions, which can extend as far as Bodmin Moor in Cornwall and the Black Mountains of Wales, across the Bristol Channel.

Exmoor lies partly in Somerset and partly in Devon and from its magnificent towering coastline there are also commanding views over the Bristol Channel. Inland the vast expanses of heatherclad moorland are cut by deep wooded valleys through which course sparkling rivers: the Exe which flows southwards to Exeter; the Barle, across which the mysterious Tarr Steps stand near Ashway – possibly of prehistoric origin; the Lyn which meets the Bristol Channel at Lynmouth. This picturesque village has a narrow main street with some thatched cottages and a lovely little harbour, while its sister-town, Lynton, is a Victorian creation on the cliff-top to the west.

Within this National Park is 'Doone Country' the beautiful hilly area that forms the backcloth to the Victorian best-seller written by R.D. Blackmore – *Lorna Doone*. To the east of 'Doone Country' are the heavily forested Brendon Hills on the edge of which lie some of the prettiest and historically interesting of Exmoor's villages such as Dunster, with its fine old 17th-century castle and the eight-sides Yarn Market which presides over the wide main street.

There is much to occupy the family holidaying in this area whether the aim is relaxation or activity. There are safe, sandy beaches from which to bathe, good sea and river fishing, excellent facilities for riding and pony trekking with many stables in the area catering for the needs of novice and experienced riders alike. For walkers, Exmoor has countryside rugged enough to challenge the most energetic and experienced rambler as well as gentle and beautiful footpaths for individuals who prefer their walk to be more of a stroll. There are also many guided walks organised within this National Park which aim to cater for all tastes, ages and energy levels ranging from short ambles to all day excursions to study special subjects such as archaeology or ornithology. As this is an area that also abounds in wildlife there is a good chance of getting close to the red deer, wild moorland ponies and many different varieties of birds that have made their home here.

For places to visit in the area check the location atlas at the end of the book.

Picturesque Malmsmead, in the Doone Country.

EAST HUNTSPILL, SOMERSET   New Road Farm   Map 3 ST34

Modern and traditional methods are combined on this typical Somerset lowland dairy farm. Here historic outbuildings house many varieties of animals (including some rare breeds), together with agricultural machinery both old and new. Such seasonal activities as incubation and haymaking are made as visual as possible, and a new Somerset County Council Moor and Levels Centre is opening on the farm this year. Three play areas are provided for children.

for EXETER see page 17   for EXMOOR see opposite page

☎Burnham-on-Sea (0278) 783250

Open: Easter–mid Oct Tue–Sun 10–6.
Admission: £1.50 (children & senior citizens £1).
P. ⊞ & (except fields) shop, garden centre.

FARWAY, DEVON   Farway Countryside Park   Map 3 SY19

The kids will love the donkeycart rides (parents can lead the donkey if they wish), pony rides, animal sanctuary, pets' enclosure and 'Tarzan's Leap'. The 189 acres of natural countryside offer beautiful nature trails where many animals roam freely. Look out for the prehistoric mounds. Covered farm barn for rainy days.

☎(040487) 367
Located: 1½ miles south on an unclassified road, AA signposted on B3174.

Open: Easter–Sep Sun–Fri 10–6. Last admission one hour before closing.
Admission: ✳£1.80 (children & senior citizens £1.30).
P. ⌖ (licensed) ⊞ (though visitors can picnic anywhere) gift shop

---

FEOCK, CORNWALL   Trelissick Garden   Map 2 SW83

A product of Cornwall's mild climate, Trelissick boasts a fine collection of exotic plants from such faraway places as New Zealand and Chile. Colourful rhododendrons grow in abundance and there is a large shrub garden. Superb views of Falmouth harbour and the Fal Estuary can be enjoyed from the immaculate lawns.

☎Truro (0872) 862090
Located: 4 miles south of Truro, on B3289.

Open: Mar–end Oct, Mon–Sat 11–6 (or dusk if earlier), Sun 1–6 (garden & shop), 12–6 (restaurant). Woodland walk also open Nov–end Mar; shop & restaurant Nov & Dec.
Admission: £1.80.
P. ⌖ & shop
National Trust

GOONHAVERN, CORNWALL   World in Miniature   Map 2 SW75

See all the famous sights of the world in one afternoon. The Leaning Tower of Pisa, the Statue of Liberty, the Taj Mahal – they're all here; more than 20 models, built to perfect scale and standing amid 11 acres of landscaped garden. The excitement of foreign parts continues as you enter Tombstone, the Wild West Town. You can stroll down the boardwalk past the Saloon, the Barber's shop and the Wells Fargo Office – but watch out the Goonhavern Kid is on the loose! Don't expect to relax in the Adventure Dome either, for there you'll find Cinema 180, a 3D film experience where you'll feel as if you're part of the action as the camera takes you surfing off Waikiki Beach or pitching down the Chattanooga River on a raft.

☎Truro (0872) 572828

Open: late Mar–mid Oct, daily, 9.30–dusk.
Admission: ✳£2.80 (children £1.60, senior citizens £2.40).
P. ⌖ & shop & garden centre

GUITING POWER, GLOUCESTERSHIRE　Cotswold Farm Park　Map 4 SP02

Set amid beautiful Cotswold Scenery, the park contains the most comprehensive collection of rare breeds of British farm animals on display in this country. Whilst those too young to fully appreciate its scope are well catered for with adventure playground, farm trail and pets corner. In April there is a special undercover exhibition of lambing, which provides a unique opportunity to see lambs being born on the farm.

☎(04515) 307
Located: 3½ miles north-east on an unclassified road.

Open: Apr–Oct daily, 10.30–6.
Admission: £2 (children £1, senior citizens £1.50).
P. ⌂ ⊼ ₺ shop ⊁ (in exhibition)

HAYLE, CORNWALL　Paradise Park　Map 2 SW53

Free 'Save the Otter' badges are given to children who visit the Cornish Otter Sanctuary at Paradise Park – a new conservation project to help restore the otter to the Cornish countryside. At Bird Paradise you can see thirty endangered species such as the St Vincent Parrot and the Cornish Chough. Cuddly baby animals can be fed and photographed at Paradise Farm, and a first-class falconry display takes place at the Eagles Paradise.

☎(0736) 753365
Located: Follow A30 to Hayle, signposted from St Erth roundabout.

Open: daily 10–dusk (Last admissions; Oct–Mar 4pm, Apr & Sep 5pm, May–Aug 6pm).
Admission: £2.50 (children £1.20, senior citizens £2).
P. ⌂ (licensed) ⊼ ₺ shop ⊁ (in Bird Garden)

HELSTON, CORNWALL　Flambards Triple Theme Park　Map 2 SW62

A breathtaking array of children's amusements and rides, such as the Hyperglyde, Demon Dropslide, Bumper Boats or the spinning Major Orbit, will provide hours of fun, while parents can slow the pace with a visit to one of the three main themes here.

Flambards Victorian Village is an authentic life-size village with shops, carriages and fashions of the period. 'Britain in the Blitz' – how did we survive? The recreation of a real street offers a stunning Blitz experience. The final theme, Aero Park, includes a Battle of Britain War Gallery, helicopters, Concorde Flight deck and an SR2 simulator. The new giant 180° screen at Superscreen 3D offers a unique and exciting dimension to film, and the space-age Gyrotron takes you on a spin with a difference! Altogether it's a day out with a difference at this award-winning Park.

☎Helston (0326) 573404/574549

Open: Easter–Oct daily, 10–5 (last admissions). Last admissions 8.15pm (with evening entertainment), late Jul & Aug only.
Admission: £3.20 (children £1.60, senior citizens £2.60).
P. ⌂ (licensed) ⊼ ₺ shop & garden centre ⊁

ILFRACOMBE, DEVON　Watermouth Castle　Map 2 SS54

Amusement for all the family is to be found in one of Devon's finest castles. Children will especially enjoy the dungeon with its animated scenes. Demonstrations include a variety of subjects, such as mechanical music, handcarts of days gone by and rural artefacts. A more recent attraction is a display named 'Dancing Water'.

☎(0271) 63879
Located: 3 miles north-east of Ilfracombe, off the A399.

Open: Easter–Spring Bank Hol & Oct, Sun–Thu from 2.30pm. Spring Bank Hol–May & Sep. Mon–Fri from 11am, Sun from 2pm; Jul & Aug Mon–Fri from 10am. Last admission 4pm.
Admission: £3 (children £2).
P. ⌂ ⊼ ₺ (ground floor only) shop ⊁

LAND'S END, CORNWALL   Map 2 SW32

See the most westerly point of the English mainland, and explore this 200-acre site with its fascinating insight into Celtic cultures, and life as it was here thousands of years ago. Detailed exhibitions show the origins and natural history of Land's End, and its relationship with man through the ages.

☎**Penzance (0736) 871501**

Open: Site & exhibitions all year 10–dusk.
Admission: £1 (children free). Free access to headland.
P.(£1) ☐ (licensed) ⊞ & (ground floor & grounds only) shop

LAUNCESTON, CORNWALL   Launceston Steam Railway   Map 2 SX38

Enjoy a three-mile round trip hauled by a steam locomotive over 100 years old. Special coaches permit passengers to watch the engine in action, and afford an unobstructed view of the passing scenery. Items sure to interest transport buffs of all ages include a motor and motor cycle museum, a model railway and transport bookshop.

☎**(0566) 5665**
Located: At Newport.

Open: Good Fri, Easter Sun & Spring Bank Hol, then Jun–Sep daily 11–5. 'Santa' specials Dec weekends 2–5.
Admission: ✳£2 (children & senior citizens £1.20). Family ticket £5.90.
P. ☐ ⊞ & (ground floor only) shop

LONGLEAT HOUSE, WILTSHIRE   Map 3 ST84

There's more than just the world-famous lions at Longleat. Apart from the Safari Park and the magnificent 16th-century mansion, you'll find a host of other attractions in these beautifully landscaped grounds. For *Dr Who* fans there is a special exhibition complete with daleks, or, perhaps Mum might prefer a trip through the Victorian Kitchens. The whole family can get lost in the world's largest maze or relax on a Safari boat on the lake. Pets corner is sure to attract and the performing parrots will make everyone laugh. Lord Bath's VIP Vehicles include a Daimler owned by King George VI and Sir Winston Churchill's wartime car. Latest attraction is the Children's Adventure Castle.

☎**Maiden Bradley (09853) 551**
Located: Entrance on the Warminster to Frome road A362.

Open: House Easter–Sep daily 10.6; Oct–Easter daily 10–4 (closed 25 Dec). Safari Park, Boat Ride & Pets Corner mid Mar–end Oct 10–6 (last cars admitted 5.30). Other attractions Easter–Oct 11–6 (last entry to Maze & Railway 5.30). Closing times may vary in Mar, Oct & Nov.
Admission: All-inclusive discount ticket £7 (children £5, senior citizens £6). Safari Park £3.50 (children £2.50, senior citizens £3). Attractions can be payed for separately if preferred.
P. ☐ (licensed) ⊞ & Shop & garden shop

LOOE, CORNWALL   The Monkey Sanctuary   Map 2 SX25

A unique chance to meet the rare Amazon Woolly monkeys that make their home here in this pleasant wooded sanctuary. You can not only see the monkeys in the trees but meet mother monkeys with their babies in the grounds. Talks are given mornings and afternoons with indoor meetings in rainy weather. Children under 4 on dry days only please.

☎**(05036) 2532**
Located: 3 miles east-north-east off B3253.

Open: Easter (except Sat); Jul & Aug, Sun–Thu; May, Jun & Sep, Sun, Tue–Thu; 10.30–5.
Admission: ✳£2.50 (children £1 senior citizens £1.30).
P. ☐ & ✻ (car park only)

Symbols	
☎	telephone number
P.	parking on the premises
☐	refreshments available
⊞	picnic area
&	accessible to wheelchair-bound visitors
✻	no dogs
✳	indicates 1987 details

LOWER ASHTON, DEVON　Canonteign Falls and Farm Park　Map 3 SX88

Spend an unforgettable day at this spectacular waterfall, the highest in England, and only recently opened to the public. Set in 80 acres of ancient woodland, a Secret Garden and Grotto will enchant children, also the Ninety Steps, Devil's Leap and Wishing Pools. Scenic lakeside picnic area and large farmyard/patio with restaurant provides the perfect setting for a picnic or meal.

☎Christow (0647) 52666
Located: At Canonteigh.

Open: Apr–Sep daily 10–9.30; Mar–Oct weekends only.
Admission: £2 (children & senior citizens £1). P. ▱ (licensed restaurant) ⚘ shop

LYDFORD, DEVON　Lydford Gorge　Map 2 SX58

One of the loveliest spots in the West Country is this awe-inspiring gorge. Scooped into a succession of potholes by the River Lyd, it emerges into a steep, oak-wooded valley. Its two most exciting features are the 100ft White Lady Waterfall and the Devil's Cauldron, whose bubbling waters can be viewed from a path of wooden planks suspended just above.

☎(082282) 320
Located: At west end of Lydford, halfway between Okehampton and Tavistock.

Open: Apr–Oct daily, 10.30–6; Nov–Mar same times but from waterfall entrance as far as waterfall only.
Admission: £1.50 (children 75p). ⚘ shop ⚓
National Trust

LYDNEY, GLOUCESTERSHIRE　Dean Forest Railway　Map 3 SO60

Especially for railway enthusiasts! A collection of locomotives, coaches, wagons and other related equipment on display at Norchard, not far from Lydney. Take tea in the restaurant coach on steam days, or ride the Santa Specials in December. Guided tours available by arrangement.

☎Dean (0594) 43423
Located: 1 mile north of Lydney at New Mills on the B4234.

Open: daily for static display. Steam days; Bank Hol Sun & Mon; Sun Jun–Sep & Wed afternoons Jun–Aug.
Admission: £1.50 (children & senior citizens £1). P. ▱ ⚘ ♿ shop

LYME REGIS, DORSET　Dinosaurland　Map 3 SY39

The evolution of our planet from its birth, some 4,600 million years ago, to the extinction of the Dinosaur, is the major subject of this fascinating museum. There's a Fossil Collection, a Children's Grotto and an exhibition of life-size dinosaurs in their natural habitat.

☎Lyme Regis (02974) 3541/4
Located: In Coombe Street.

Open: Easter–Oct, daily 9–5 (or dusk).
Admission: £1.20 (children & senior citizens 60p).
▱ (licensed) ♿ (ground floor only) shop

MARLBOROUGH, WILTSHIRE　Savernake Forest　Map 4 SU26

A rare glimpse of forest as it was in medieval times can be had at Savernake Forest. Massive sessile oaks, some of the largest sweet chestnuts in the country and beeches, are the main forest trees. This is exactly the type of ancient deciduous forest that the birds and insects are happiest in, likewise mosses, lichens and fungi. Therefore, young naturalists will find much to interest them here, while the forest also offers a magnificent place to picnic or perhaps just to stroll around one of its lovely forest trails.

Located: Lies just to the south-east of Marlborough between the A4 & A346 roads.

Open: all year.
P. ⚘ forest trails

MINEHEAD, SOMERSET West Somerset Railway Map 3 SS94

The romantic age of steam is still alive at Minehead. You can ride on steam and railcar trains to various points, including Watchet and Bishops Lydeard, up to a distance of 40 miles.

☎(0643) 4996

Open: *Apr–late Oct, daily 9.30–7 & other days in off season (ring for details).
Admission: Fare payable.
P. ☐ (at Minehead & on most trains) & shop

MORWELLHAM, DEVON Morwellham Quay Open-Air Museum Map 2 SX46

Ride underground into a copper mine at the site of what was once the greatest copper port in the Empire. Blacksmiths, quayworkers, servant girls and coachmen all dressed in authentic period dress recreate the atmosphere of the great boom years, and visitors can enjoy a ride in a heavy horse-drawn wagonette. Beautiful countryside setting.

☎Tavistock (0822) 832766
Located: Off A390 between Tavistock & Gunnislake.

Open: all year, (except Xmas week). 10–5.30, (5pm in winter). Last admission 4pm, (2pm in winter).
Admission: *£3.95 (children £2.45, senior citizens & disabled £2.95).
P. ☐ (licensed) ☍ & (ground floor & gardens) gift shop

NEWENT, GLOUCESTERSHIRE Falconry Centre Map 3 SO72

The Falconry Centre is devoted to the breeding and protection of birds of prey, and a marvellous collection can be seen here. Birds are flown daily, weather permitting, and trained birds can be watched at the 'Hawk Walk', brooder room and the breeding aviaries.

☎(0531) 820286
Located: 1 mile south-west of Newent on unclassified Clifford's Mesne Road.

Open: Feb–Nov daily (except Tue) 10.30–5.30 or dusk if earlier.
Admission: *£2 (children £1.50).
P. ☍ & shop ✶

NEWENT, GLOUCESTERSHIRE Newent Butterfly Farm Map 3 SO72

You can imagine that you are in a tropical jungle here at Newent. Palm trees and other exotic plants surround you while giant gaily coloured butterflies flutter by freely in this replica of their home environment. The Centre stands amid some of the most attractive Gloucestershire countryside with superb views across the Malvern Hills.

☎(0531) 821800
Located: At Springbank, Birches Lane.

Open: *Easter–Oct, daily 10–5.
Admission: *£1.50 (children 90p, senior citizens £1.25).
P. ☐ ☍ shop ✶

NORTHLEACH, GLOUCESTERSHIRE Cotswold Countryside Collection Map 4 SP11

Discover how life was lived in the Cotswolds many years ago. Northleach 'House of Correction' was once a country prison, but now houses a number of fascinating displays and exhibitions. A specially designed gallery has life-size reconstructions of a blacksmith's and wheelwright's workshops. 'Below stairs' shows a laundry, kitchen and dairy complete with furnishings and utensils.

☎(0451) 60715
Located: At Fosseway.

Open: daily Apr–Oct 10–5.30, Sun 2–5.30.
Admission: *60p (children 30p & senior citizens 40p).
P. ☐ ☍ & (ground floor only) shop

PADSTOW, CORNWALL   Padstow Tropical Bird Gardens   Map 2 SW97

Enjoy a leisurely walk through two acres of beautifully landscaped gardens, and see the wonderful collection of tropical and sub-tropical birds. Butterfly World houses insects from all over the world, including moths, dragonflies and spiders – sure to appeal to the younger members of the family. Don't miss the jungle atmosphere of the Tropical House, with its free-flying birds.

☎(0841) 532262
Located: In Fentonluna Lane.

Open: daily 10.30–8 (5pm in winter). Closed Xmas day. Last admission one hour before closing.
Admission: *£1.90 (children 90p, under 4 free, senior citizens £1.50).
▱ (Easter–Sep) ⊼ & (ground floor & gardens) gift shop

PAIGNTON, DEVON   Torbay and Dartmouth Railway   Map 3 SX86

Take a steam train journey from Paignton to Kingswear on seven miles of former Great Western track. Minimum of four trains per day, stopping at Goodrington Sands and Churston for the Dartmouth ferry. Buffet at Kingswear Station serves light lunches and snacks.

☎(0803) 555872

Open: daily peak season, selected days early & late season; 9–5.30. Please enquire for specific details.
Admission/Fare: *£3.40 (children £2.40, senior citizens £3.10).
P. ▱ & shop

PAIGNTON, DEVON   Zoological and Botanical Gardens   Map 3 SX86

Over twelve hundred animals live here in England's third largest zoo. Special attractions include the baboon rock, monkey house, reptile house and a breeding colony of Lar gibbons on an island in the lake. A family centre, aptly named 'The Ark' has a children's adventure playground and a miniature railway.

☎(0803) 527936
Located: In Totnes Road.

Open: daily (except Xmas Day) 10–6.30 (4.30 in winter). Last admission 5pm (4pm in winter).
Admission: £2.90 (children £1.90, under 3 free, senior citizens £2.50).
P. ▱ (licensed) ⊼ & shop, garden centre
🐾 (kennels available)

PENDEEN, CORNWALL   Geevor Tin Mines   Map 2 SW33

A guided tour of the tin treatment plant and fascinating exhibits in the museum provide an insight into the methods and equipment used in the mining of tin. A video film illustrates the techniques used, both on the surface and underground.

☎(0736) 788662

Open: Easter–Sep. Museum 10–5.30, plant 10.30–4.
Admission: *£2.50 (children £1). Museum only £1 (children 50p).
P. ▱ ⊼ shop

PLYMPTON, DEVON   Dartmoor Wildlife Park   Map 2 SX55

The park features falconry displays (weather permitting) and contains a wide variety of wildlife – waterfowl, reptiles, seals, deer, wolves, bears and a large big cat collection (including the new Enclosure 2000 for jaguars). There are indoor facilities too, and displays emphasise learning through close contact with living things. Pony rides are available during weekends and holidays, and there are special events during Zoo Month (July).

☎Cornwood (075537) 209

Open: all year daily 10–dusk.
Admission: *£3.20 (children & senior citizens £2).
P. ▱ (licensed) ⊼ & shop

PRAZE-AN-BEEBLE, CORNWALL   Peloe Dairy Farm   Map 2 SW63

You'll find out all there is to know about dairy farming down on the farm at Peloe. Meet Daisy, the cow, and the Calf, Buttercup. See Demelza, the sheepdog, in action and cuddle Woolly, the lamb. The farmer will give you a tour in his tractor trailer and explain the technicalities of milking. After all of that you'll be ready to enjoy one of Peloe's special cream teas!

☎Praze (0209) 831284

Open: *May–Sep. Mon–Fri, 12–6.
Admission: *£1.20 (children 60p, senior citizens 90p).
P. ☐ ⊼ (grounds only) shop ⋔

PRISTON, AVON   Priston Mill   Map 3 ST66

Surrounded by beautiful countryside and farm animals, this watermill is one of the few commercially working Domesday Mills still left in England. A nature trail and children's play area sharpen appetites for the cream teas served in the tithe barn!

☎Bath (0225) 23894 or 29894

Open: Easter–Sep daily 2.15–5.30, Sun & Bank Hol 11–1 & 2.15–5.30.
Admission: 85p (children 50p, senior citizens 60p).
P. ☐ ⊼ ♿ (ground floor & gardens only) shop

RODE, SOMERSET   Tropical Bird Gardens   Map 3 ST85

A bird-lover's paradise with over 180 species of colourful birds in a beautiful 17-acre park complete with trees, shrubs, ornamental lake and ponds. For children, there is a play area and pets corner. There is also a tree trail and a clematis collection. Children under 14 must be accompanied by an adult.

☎Frome (0373) 830326

Open: Gardens open all year except Xmas day. Summer 10.30–7, (last admission 6pm), winter 10.30–sunset (last admission 1hr before sunset).
Admission: *£2.15 (children 14 £1.15, senior citizens £1.75).
P. ☐ (summer only) ♿ (gardens & grounds only) shop ⋔

ST AGNES, CORNWALL   St Agnes Leisure Park   Map 2 SW75

You'll need plenty of time at St Agnes, for there are no less than five major attractions within this beautifully landscaped Leisure Park. Cornwall in Miniature is a masterpiece of scaled-down models of Cornwall's most famous buildings. Truro's magnificent Cathedral is here, as is Restormel Castle, the Royal Naval air station – Culdrose, and there is even a working tin mine, all complete with sound effects. Turn a corner and you are into the Lost World of the Dinosaurs with prehistoric creatures as large as the miniature models are small. Then there's a recreation of the greatest show on earth with an animated Grand Circus. Nervous visitors might prefer not to visit the spooky Haunted House, but all will be entranced by the wonders of Fairyland. Floodlit at night.

☎St Agnes (087255) 2793

Open: late Mar–mid Oct daily, 9.30am–10pm.
Admission: *£2.80 (children £1.60, senior citizens £2.40).
P. ☐ (licensed) ♿ shop

ST AUSTELL, CORNWALL   Wheal Martin Museum   Map 2 SX05

This open air museum is based on a completely restored china clayworks. See the working water wheels, wooden slurry pump and the massive granite walled settling tanks. The transport side of the industry is illustrated by horse drawn wagons, a fully restored 1914 Peerless lorry, and two steam locomotives. Magnificent views can be seen from the viewing point of a modern working claypit.

☎(0726) 850362
Located: 2 miles north of St Austell on the A391.

Open: Apr–Oct 10–6 (last admission 5pm).
Admission: fee payable.
P. ☐ ⊼ ♿ (ground floor only) shop

ST NEWLYN EAST, CORNWALL   Lappa Valley Railway   Map 2 SW85

A round trip of over two miles through scenic countryside gives you access to a five-acre pleasure area with boating lake, maze, crazy golf, children's railway and play area with giant slide – all included in the fare. The 15″ gauge steam railway also has a stop at East Wheal Rose Halt, where you can explore the site of a famous old silver and lead mine.

☎Mitchell (087251) 317

Open: Easter–Sep. Easter for 2 weeks from Good Fri, daily 11–5; rest of Apr & Oct, Wed & Thu 11–5; May–mid Jul daily 10.30–5.30; mid Jul–early Sep daily 10–6; rest of Sep daily 11–5.
Admission: ✳£2.60 (children £1.40).
P. ⌂ (licensed) ⊼ shop

SHEBBEAR, DEVON   Alscott Farm Agricultural Museum   Map 2 SS40

North Devon's agricultural past is cleverly recreated with the help of this remarkable collection of vintage farm equipment, dairy and household implements, photographs and other memorabilia. The Wallis and Steevens traction engine is a handsome specimen. Circus-lovers will enjoy the delightful scale model of an Edwardian travelling fair, as well as contemporary photographs and original circus posters.

☎(040928) 206

Open: ✳Easter–Sep, daily 12–dusk.
Admission: ✳80p (children 40p).
P. & (ground floor only) shop

SHERBORNE, DORSET   Sherborne Castle   Map 3 ST61

Beautiful grounds of park and woodland rolling down to a lake are the setting for the magnificent home of the Digby family, which is filled with fine examples of furniture, porcelain and paintings. The old castle, now in ruins, can be seen to the rear of the present castle; almshouses and an ancient abbey are also worth a visit.

☎(0935) 813182

Open: Easter Sat–Sep, Thu, Sat, Sun & Bank Hol Mon, 2–6. Grounds open Easter Sat–Sep Sat, Sun & Bank Hol Mon 12–6, also Thu 1.30–6.
Admission: £2.50 (children £1.25 & senior citizens £2). Grounds only £1 (children 50p).
P. ⌂ & (ground floor & grounds) shop ✸ (in house)

SHERBORNE, DORSET   Worldwide Butterflies   Map 3 ST61

Spend a delightful day among butterflies from throughout the world. A natural jungle and tropical palmhouse provide the habitat for exotic species of butterfly seldom seen living in this country. The Lullingstone silk farm produced unique English-reared silk for the last two coronations and the wedding gowns of the Queen and the Princess of Wales.

☎Yeovil (0935) 74608
Located: At Compton House (entrance on A30, 2½ miles west of Sherborne).

Open: Apr–Oct 10–5.
Admission: ✳£2.50 (children £1.35 & senior citizens £1.95).
P. shop ✸

SLIMBRIDGE, GLOUCESTERSHIRE   The Wildfowl Trust   Map 3 SO70

'Conservation in action' that's how they describe themselves at The Wildfowl Trust, which was founded by Sir Peter Scott to help the world's largest and most varied collection of wildfowl survive the perils of the modern world. Swans, ducks, geese and, no less than six flocks of flamingos, can be studied here, at close quarters, from first-class viewing facilities. In winter, towers and hides ensure remarkable views of hundreds of wild swans and thousands of wild geese and ducks. Visually handicapped can enjoy special facilities and a nature trail with taped commentaries. There is also a Tropical House and an Exhibition Hall.

☎Cambridge (Glos) (045389) 333
Located: Off A38 and M5 (Junction 13 or 14).

Open: ✳daily 9.30–5, or dusk if earlier (closed Xmas).
Admission: ✳£2.50 (children under 4 £1.20, senior citizens £1.80).
P. ⌂ (licensed) ⊼ & shop ✸

SOUDLEY, GLOUCESTERSHIRE   Dean Heritage Museum   Map 3 SO61

Camp Mill, once a scrapyard, is now the centre of a range of exhibitions of Cotswold life and traditional industrial and agricultural methods including a reconstructed cottage, coal mine and watermill. Local wood has been used to build a magnificent adventure play area, complete with a tower and suspension bridge.

☎Dean (0594) 22170
Located: At Camp Mill.

Open: daily (except Xmas Day). Apr–Oct 10–6; Nov–Mar 10–5.
Admission: £2 (children & senior citizens £1.25).
P. ⌂ 🔥 ᶂ (except top floor of museum) shop

SWINDON, WILTSHIRE   Great Western Railway Museum   Map 4 SU18

Every would-be engine driver will find much of interest here. The locomotives include the 'Lode Star', 'Dean Goods' and a fine replica of the 'North Star', a broad guage locomotive. Plenty of displays relating to the Great Western Railway, and the temporary exhibitions change monthly.

☎(0793) 26161 ext 3131
Located: At Faringdon Road.

Open: Mon–Sat 10–5, Sun 2–5. Closed Good Fri, 25 & 26 Dec).
Admission: *90p (children, senior citizens & unemployed 45p).
ᶂ (ground floor only) shop ⚑

SYMOND'S YAT (WEST), HEREFORD & WORCESTER   Jubilee Maze   Map 3 SO51

Meet Edward and Lindsey Heyes, the men who built this superbly intricate maze – and then, go get lost in it for a while! If you ever find your way out of the maze, you'll be ready to relax in the fine gardens, designed by Julian Dowle. All that you ever wanted to know about the history of mazes, can be found here too, in the world's first museum of mazes.

☎(0600) 890655

Open: *Easter weekend–Oct daily, (except Fri) 11–6 (last admission 5.30). Illumination of Maze & Garden Easter Sat & Sun, & twice weekly during Jul & Aug from 7.30.
Admission: fee payable.
P. 🔥 ⚑

TIVERTON, DEVON   Grand Western Canal Country Park   Map 3 SS91/ST01

It's 100 years since this canal was used to transport local stone but, thanks to recent restoration, visitors can now travel more than 11 miles between Tiverton and Holcombe Rogus by horse-drawn barge. The delightful Devon countryside alongside the canal is a haven for wildlife, and the waters are popular with anglers, (fishing permits available at local tackle shops). For 'landlubbers', walking by the canal is a joy, particularly in summer when dragonflies and butterflies cast their spell.

Located: Terminus at Canal Basin, Canal Hill, Tiverton.

P. (at Tiverton Basin) 🔥

for TORQUAY see page 28

TRURO, CORNWALL   Killiow Country Park   Map 2 SW84

Woodland walks, a nature trail, pets corner and an adventure playground are just some of the delights on offer in this magnificent Country Park. There are extensive gardens, with a lake, and some beautifully preserved Georgian and Elizabethan buildings. Killiow is also home to many rare breeds of farm animals and there is a horse power farm museum as well as coach, carriage and harness displays. Country craft displays include pottery and weaving.

☎(0872) 72768/741412
Located: At Kea, 2 miles south west of Truro off A39.

Open: *mid Apr–mid May daily, 12.30–6 (except Sun, Bank Hol & mid May–early Oct when open 10.30–6).
Admission: fee payable.
P. ⌂ 🔥 shop garden centre ⚑

for VERWOOD see page 29

The English Riviera

Those who have savoured Torquay's kind climate, seen the palm trees and other exotic plants that flourish there, the beautiful harbour bedecked with bobbing boats and the villa-studded hills that rise up sharply behind the bay have no difficulty understanding why this town is often referred to as the English Riviera. The holidaymakers and locals to be seen strolling along the light-fringed seafront in the evenings, the inviting shops that stay open late to cater for this trade and the exciting nightlife that abounds here complete the 'Mediterranean' scene. Torquay's main streets – The Strand, Union and Fleet streets – which lead off from the harbour, have the best of departmental stores as well as boutiques, souvenir shops, restaurants and cafes.

Out of Torbay's three seaside resorts (Torquay, Paignton and Brixham) Torquay is the largest. It has all the very best of British seaside attractions, including pleasure boat and fishing trips which leave from the harbour, and some of the finest hotels to be found anywhere in Britain. Due to its gentle climate which seems almost unaffected by extremes of temperature, Torquay has become a resort for all seasons.

☆ STAR ATTRACTIONS

Kents Cavern

Visitors to Kents Cavern are guided through a magical, illuminated labyrinth of passageways and caves, complete with stalagmites and stalagtites. Apart from being very beautiful the caves are also of great historic interest. Here pre-historic man is known to have lived and many interesting finds have been discovered including implements made from flint and skulls, bones and teeth belonging to both prehistoric man and animals. Most of these finds are exhibited in the new Natural History Gallery within Torquay's Museum.

☎(0803) 24059
Located: At Wellswood, 1¼ miles north east off B3199.

Open: all year (except Xmas day); mid Jun–mid Sep 10am–9pm (6pm Sat); closes at 6pm spring and autumn; 5pm from Nov–Mar.
Admission: ✳£1.50 (children 75p).
P. ☞ (during summer) shop

Aqualand

The largest aquarium in the West Country, Aqualand specialises in exotic fish taken from tropical seas as well as locally found marine life. It also takes an active part in the conservation of marine and other wildlife found around our own coastline. There are Piranha fish to be seen, as well as Sea Turtles from the Cayman Islands and an enchanting pair of otters brought to this aquarium as part of a long term breeding programme and which are kept in a specially constructed enclosure. A wonderful chance for visitors to find out about life in 'the deep' without actually having to go deep sea diving.

☎(0803) 24439
Located: At Beacon Quay, Torquay Harbourside.

Open: all year daily from 10am; closes at 10pm Apr–Sep; 3pm Oct–Mar.
Admission: ✳£1.20 (children 60p).
P. ♿ shop

Babbacombe Model Village

Set in four acres of beautiful and typically English landscaped gardens is this delightful miniature village created from over 400 models. At dusk the village lights are switched on and the whole tiny valley springs to life with twinkling lights. As well as street lighting many of the houses have their own lights too, and their curtains are left slightly apart so that visitors can peep through the windows. Through the gardens, planted with a magnificent display of dwarf conifers, trees and flowering shrubs, runs 1200ft of railway track on which model trains operate daily during the summer months.

☎(0803) 38669

Open: all year daily from 9am, closes at 10pm Easter–mid Oct, dusk in winter. Closed Xmas day.
Admission: £2 (children £1).
P. ♿ shop & garden centre

VERWOOD, DORSET   Dorset Heavy Horse Centre   Map 4 SU00

Shire, Suffolk Punch, Percheron and Clydesdale are all breeds of heavy horses, and you'll meet and touch some of the champions of these 'gentle giants' at the Centre. There are demonstrations of plaiting and grooming for show, and of driving, in the arena. Farm wagons and implements are also on show.

☎(0202) 824040
Located: At Brambles Farm (1¼ miles north west) signposted from Verwood.

Open: Apr–Oct, daily 10–6. Parades at 11.30, 2.30 & 4.15.
Admission: £1.95 (children 3–14 & senior citizens £1.40). Family ticket £5.70.
P. ⌂ ⊓ & shop

WENDRON, CORNWALL   Poldark Mine   Map 2 SW63

A one-hour tour explores three levels of an old Cornish tin mine, and you are given an insight into this traditional industry by films and museum displays. At the surface are restaurants, shops, gardens and children's amusements, together with the West Country's largest collection of working antiques, which includes a forty-foot high beam engine. On Sunday afternoons in season there is music on the lawns, with music evenings in July and August.

☎Helston (0326) 573173

Open: Jul–Aug 10–10 (last tour 8pm). Apr, May, Jun, Sep & Oct 10–6 (last tour 5pm).
Admission: £3 (children £1.80) including tour of mine.
P. ⌂ (licensed) ⊓ & (ground floor & gardens only, mine not suitable) shop garden centre

WEST PUTFORD, DEVON   The Gnome Reserve   Map 2 SS31

Children and the young at heart should flock to this enchanting place. The world's first Gnome Reserve, there are over 1,000 gnomes and pixies living here in a woodland garden. You may borrow a hat while you're here – so that the gnomes will accept you as one of them! Admission also includes entry to a further two-acre pixie-inhabited Nature Trail and to the Pixie Kiln – where visitors can see tiny pottery pixies being made.

☎Bradworthy (040 924) 435
Located: Signposted from A388 at Milton Damerel.

Open: Apr–Oct 10–1 & 2–6 (also 7–9 Jun–early Sep). Closed Sat (except Bank hols).
Admission: 75p (children 4–15 & senior citizens 50p, children 2–3 20p).
P. ⊓ shop

WEYMOUTH, DORSET   Sea Life Centre   Map 3 SY67

You can explore the mysteries of the deep here at Britain's largest and most exciting marine life display. You'll see hundreds of sea creatures from the tiniest molluscs to the giant Blue Whale. Even the viewing areas are an experience; there's Ocean Tunnel, Cliffwalk and Island walkway. Rockpool Touch Tanks offer hands-on experience, but you'll have to be content to view from a distance the Blue Whale's Splash Pool. There is also a Theme Unit which explains Man's involvement with the oceans.

☎(0305) 770209
Located: In Lodmoor Country Park.

Open: ✳daily from 10am.
Admission: fee payable.
⌂ & shop ✗

WEYMOUTH, DORSET   The Great Shire Horse Centre   Map 3 SY67

Kids will enjoy a day out with these gentle giants. They'll see magnificent shires in their stables and in the washing and grooming area – they can even take a wagon ride around the complex pulled, of course, by a shire horse. There are harness displays, exhibitions of drays and wagons and videos, and you'll usually find a mare with her foal in the paddock. Children's play area, aviary and pets corner are more reasons to make this a day-long family outing.

☎Weymouth (0305) 75315
Located: In Lodmoor Country Park.

Open: Easter–end Sep, daily 10–5 (reduced opening times early & late season).
Admission: ✳£1.40 (children & senior citizens 90p), family ticket (2 adults & up to 4 children) £4.
& shop

WILTON, WILTSHIRE   Wilton House   Map 4 SU03

A delight for parents and children in the shape of 7,000 model soldiers, the palace dolls' house, a 400 sq ft working model railway, and a tableau of dolls and toys through the ages. Exhibits are to be found in this fine 16th–19th-century house famed for its collections of paintings, furniture and sculpture. There are lovely grounds too and a well-equipped adventure playground.

☎Salisbury (0722) 743115

Open: late Mar–mid Oct Tue–Sat & Bank Hols 11–6, Sun 1–6. Last admission 5.15. *Admission:* £2.50 (children £1.25, senior citizens £1.70). Grounds & adventure playground only £1 (children 70p). P. ☞ (licensed) & (not railway) shop, garden centre ✻ (except guide dogs)

WINCHCOMBE, GLOUCESTERSHIRE   Sudeley Castle and Gardens   Map 4 SP02

Castle buildings date from the 15th century, and house an interesting display of Victorian letters and photographs, and paintings by Turner and Constable. Craft workshops are held in the eerie dungeon tower, and a children's log fortress will captivate many a youngster. There are falconry displays and historical theme events in season.

☎(0242) 602308

Open: Apr–Oct daily; grounds 11–5.30, castle & museum 12–5. *Admission:* £3.25 (children £1.75). P. ☞ (licensed) ⊼ gift shop, craft gallery, garden centre ✻

WOOKEY HOLE, SOMERSET   Wookey Hole Caves and Mill   Map 3 ST54

Two thousand years ago, early man lived in the famous Great Cave, which is haunted, so legend says, by a wicked 'witch of Wookey'. So keep your eyes peeled! A canal path from the caves leads to a paper mill, still producing paper from cotton as was done in the 17th-century. The mill also houses Madame Tussauds' Cabinet of Curiosities and a delightful re-creation of a fairground at night. One of the largest collections of vintage slot machines can be viewed in the 'Old Penny Arcade'.

☎Wells (0749) 72243

Open: Mar–Oct daily 9.30–5.30; Nov–Feb 10.30–4.30 (except week before Xmas). *Admission:* £3.25 (children £2.25 & senior citizens £2.85). Family ticket £9.90. P. ☞ ⊼ & (mill & exhibitions only) shop ✻ (in caves or mill)

YEALMPTON, DEVON   National Shire Horse Centre   Map 2 SX55

Here's a chance to get close to these noble giants, the Shire horses, and to meet some adorable new foals. They'll display their strength and skill by transporting your family (and several others!) around the Centre in a cart, and, three times a day, will perform a stunning display in the arena. But, it's not all horses here! There's a Craft Centre, featuring traditional crafts such as pottery and glass engraving, a Falconry Centre, an Animal Farm and Adventure World.

☎Plymouth (0752) 880268
Located: at Dunstone

Open: daily 10–5 (closed Xmas). *Admission:* ✳£3.25 (children £2, senior citizens £2.75). P. ☞ (licensed) ⊼ & shop & garden centre

YEOVILTON, SOMERSET   Fleet Air Arm Museum   Map 3 ST52

All boys (and some girls?) will thrill to the story of action-packed drama that is the history of naval flying from 1908 to present-day battles. Famous aircraft of two World Wars are here, together with a special exhibition on the Falkland Islands, including four captured Argentinian aircraft. The Royal Navy in the jet age is covered in full with planes such as the Scimitar and the Buccaneer, capable of supersonic speeds. A special feature is the Concorde 002 – Britain's first assembled prototype.

☎Ilchester (0935) 840565
Located: At Royal Naval Air Station Yeovilton, just off the A303 near Ilchester.

Open: daily (except Xmas) 10–5.30 (4.30 Nov–Feb). *Admission:* ✳£3 (children & senior citizens £1.50). P. ☞ (licensed) ⊼ & shop ✻

South and South East England

The south of England can probably offer the greatest variety of things to see and do in the country and it certainly includes some of Britain's most visited tourist attractions including Windsor Castle and Beaulieu. There are ancient cities to explore, such as Winchester, Canterbury, Oxford and Cambridge – all having their own particular charm; there are pretty thatched villages, popular resorts such as Brighton and Eastbourne, the busy yachting and water-sports centres of the Solent and Chichester Harbour. Although the south has the highest concentration of population in the country, there are large tracts of unspoilt countryside. Chalk downland is a feature – the North and South Downs and the racehorse country of Berkshire. Great forests remain from former royal hunting preserves at Epping, Hatfield and, of course, the New Forest. The Thames flows through the heart of the area, providing lots of recreational facilities and some delightful riverside towns. One of the most popular holiday destinations is the Isle of Wight, its resorts frequently claiming the annual sunshine record. Historically, the south has always been important and its heritage can be explored through the huge number of historic houses, castles, Roman remains and ancient sites open to the public.

ALDERSHOT, HAMPSHIRE   Airborne Forces Museum   Map 4 SU85

A fascinating collection for all military buffs! Enemy arms and equipment captured during the Falklands conflict, as well as parachutes, scale models and weapons from other wars are on display here. Look out, too, for the fine array of medals, especially the Victoria and George Crosses.

☎(0252) 24431 ext 4619
Located: In the Browning Barracks on Queens's Avenue.

Open: Mon–Fri 9–12.30 & 2–4.30, Sat & Sun 10–12.30 & 2–4.30.
Admission: 50p (children, senior citizens & members or ex-members of the Airborne Forces 25p).
P. & shop ⌀

ALFRISTON, EAST SUSSEX   Drusilla's Zoo Park   Map 5 TQ50

Collections of small mammals and rare breeds of farm animals, penguins, a flamingo lake, butterfly house and Japanese garden offer a breadth of interest that makes this one of the best small zoos in the south. The adventure playground and railway offer further diversion for children, whilst their elders might prefer to explore a cottage bakery, wine centre, pottery and leathercraft shop. The English Wine Fair takes place here during the first weekend of September, and there is an Antique Fair on the third Wednesday in each month from May to September.

☎(0323) 870234

Open: late Mar–Oct daily 11–5.30. In winter zoo open daily till dusk (excluding Xmas).
Admission: Adults £2.50 & senior citizens £1.75 (including zoo & railway ride). Children £2.50 (including zoo, playland & railway ride). Grounds free.
P. ⌗ (licensed) ⊼ & (ground floor & grounds only) shop & garden centre ⌀ (in zoo or playground)

ALRESFORD, HAMPSHIRE   Mid Hants Railway   Map 4 SU53

Re-live the romantic days of steam on the Watercress Line as the train puffs through some of Hampshire's finest scenery between Alresford and Ropley. You'll still see the watercress beds that give the line its name. Steam locomotives in various stages of restoration can be seen at Ropley. You can even drive in style on the special Wine & Dine train on alternate Saturday evenings during the season (booking essential) or watch out for the special events, like the trips to Santaland around Christmastime.

☎(096273) 3810 or 4200
Located: At Alresford Station.

Main operating periods: *end Mar–Oct weekends; also Tue–Thu late May–mid Jul; daily (except Mon) mid Jul–Aug.
Leaflet available giving times of trains and special events or phone for details
Fare: details on application.
P. ⌗ ⊼ & shop

AMBERLEY, WEST SUSSEX   Chalk Pits Museum   Map 4 TQ01

Industrial history springs to life in this old chalk quarry as you watch traditional craftsmen at work, examine pumping and bricklaying exhibits or enjoy one of the many special events staged by the centre – an AA 'Best Museum' regional award winner. The 36-acre open-air site also features original lime-kilns, stationary engines, displays of tools, machine and industrial relics, and a narrow gauge railway.

☎Bury (0798) 831370
Located: At Houghton Bridge (off B2139).

Open: Apr–Oct Wed–Sun & Bank Hol Mon. Also Mon & Tue in school summer hols. 10–6 (last admission 5).
Admission: £2.20 (children £1, senior citizens £1.70). Family ticket (2 adults & 2 children) £6.
P. ⌗ ⊼ & shop

Symbols
☎   telephone number
P.   parking on the premises
⌗   refreshments available
⊼   picnic area
&   accessible to wheelchair-bound visitors
⌀   no dogs
*   indicates 1987 details

ANDOVER, HAMPSHIRE   Finkley Down Farm   Map 4 SU34

A comprehensive selection of different breeds of farm animals and poultry are on display here, many rearing their young in natural surroundings. The Barn of Bygones and a Romany encampment offer much of interest, whilst young children will particularly enjoy Pets' Corner, with its tame, hand-reared baby animals, and the adventure playground.

☎(0264) 52195

Open: Apr–Oct 10.30–6 (last admission 5).
Admission: ✱£1.50 (children & senior citizens 75p).
P. 🚻 & Shop

ARUNDEL, WEST SUSSEX   Arundel Castle   Map 4 TQ00

This grand Norman castle, greatly restored during the 18th and 19th-centuries overlooks the beautiful River Arun and is set in splendid grounds. Its furnishings include fine pieces from the 16th-century, tapestries, clocks and some important portraits. A special Naval exhibition to mark the 400th anniversary of the Spanish Armada is being staged during 1988.

☎(0903) 883136
Located: Entrance at Lower Lodge in Mill Road.

Open: Apr–last Fri in Oct, Sun-Fri 1–5 (from 12 noon during Jun, Jul, Aug & Bank Hols). Last admission 4pm.
Admission: £2.80 (children £1.70, under 5 free, senior citizens £2.40).
P. ⌑ shop

ARUNDEL, WEST SUSSEX   Museum of Curiosity   Map 4 TQ00

Children will love this unusual museum which features the life work of Victorian naturalist and taxidermist, Walter Potter. There are fascinating animal tableaux such as Kittens' Wedding, Rabbit's Village School, Death of Cock Robin and Guinea Pigs' Cricket Match. Also to be seen are collections of dolls, toys and curios from around the world.

☎(0903) 882420
Located: At No.6 High St.

Open: ✱Mar–Oct 10.30–1 & 2.15–5.30, Sat & Sun 11–1 & 2.15–5.30. Winter weekends & occasional weekdays 11–1 & 2.15–4.30 or dusk.
Admission: Fee payable
P. shop

ARUNDEL, WEST SUSSEX   Toy and Military Museum   Map 4 TQ00

A wonderful collection of toys that will surely appeal to all ages is housed in a Georgian cottage in the centre of town. See the toys which the children of yesteryear played with: dolls, dolls houses and prams, rocking horses, and a superb collection of toy soliders. There is also a collection of famous teddy bears.

☎(0903) 883101 or 882908
Located: At 23 High Street.

Open: daily Jun–Aug, Bank Hols & School Hols 10.30–5. Most days in Spring & during Sep & Oct. Also every weekend 12–5 (excluding Jan).
Admission: £1 (children, senior citizens & students 75p).
shop

ARUNDEL, WEST SUSSEX   Wildfowl Trust   Map 4 TQ00

See over 1,000 of the world's most colourful ducks, geese and swans amid 55 acres of attractively landscaped grounds. Conservation is the name of the game here, and the Wildfowl Trust has set up spacious observation hides so that visitors might enjoy the sight of rare, normally shy birds, at close quarters. There is also an indoor viewing gallery and an education complex.

☎(0903) 883355
Located: In Mill Rd.

Open: ✱daily. 9.30–5.30 (closed Xmas day).
Admission: Fee payable.
P. ⌑ (licensed) & shop

ASHURST, HAMPSHIRE   New Forest Butterfly Farm   Map 4 SU31

Walk among banana trees and passion flowers surrounded by exotic butterflies and moths, identify native species in the British Garden, admire the dragonflies hovering over the outdoor breeding ponds or shudder at the sight of scorpions and tarantulas (safely under glass!) in the insectarium. The Butterfly Farm forms part of a 2,000-acre estate, and on certain days rustic wagon ridges offer a view of surrounding woodlands not otherwise accessible to the public.

☎(042129) 2166

Open: late Mar–Oct daily 10–5.
Admission: ✱£2.20 (children £1.30, senior citizens £1.95).
P. ⌨ ⅌ ⅋ shop & garden centre ⅏

BASILDON, BERKSHIRE   Child Beale Wildlife Trust   Map 4 SU67

Child Beale is a wildlife park in a classical setting complete with elegant statues and strutting peacocks. Highland cattle and rare sheep, pheasants and flamingoes are just a few of the creatures you'll find here. Central to the park is the mansion which houses a quality craft centre. There is also a magnificent children's play area with a log and rope obstacle course, two paddling pools and a sandpit. There is also a new information/education facility, riverside trips and walks.

☎Upper Basildon (0491) 671325 or Pangbourne (07357) 5171

Open: Easter Sat–end Sep, daily 10–6.
Admission: Car £4, motor-cycle £2, pedestrian £1 (children 50p).
P. ⌨ ⅌ ⅋ shop ⅏ (ex in car park)

BEACONSFIELD, BUCKINGHAMSHIRE   Bekonscot Model Village   Map 4 SU99

The oldest model village in the world, Bekonscot's miniature wonderland enchants each generation anew. Churches, hotels, shops and houses line its two thousand feet of tarmac roadway, whilst a Gauge One railway – with twenty locomotives and a good range of coaches and rolling stock – meanders its way through pleasant 'countryside' wooded with eight thousand tiny conifers!

☎(0494) 672919
Located: In Warwick Rd, Beaconfield New Town. 2 miles from M40 Junction 2; 4 miles from M25 Junction 16.

Open: Mar–Oct daily 10–5.
Admission: £1.30 (children 70p, senior citizens & students £1).
P. ⌨ ⅌ ⅋ (access limited to max. width 21″ – wheelchairs available) shop

BEAULIEU, HAMPSHIRE   National Motor Museum   Map 4 SU30

Beaulieu's attractions – Motor Museum, Palace House and Abbey ruins – are set amid beautiful New Forest scenery. A hundred years of motoring are covered by the Motor Museum's spectacular display, and 'Wheels', an exciting automated ride, whisks you from Mini to Silver Ghost, from the first petrol-driven car of 1895 to one of the most recent Formula One racing models. There are also collections of motor cycles and commercial vehicles, and from a window in the motor cycle gallery visitors can view the restoration workshops next door. A monorail trip will take you to Palace House, once the gatehouse of the Abbey but now the home of Lord Montague, where displays with costumed figures depict the history of the family. Behind the house stands the ruined Cistercian abbey (founded in 1204 and largely destroyed by Henry VIII), including an Exhibition of Monastic Life.

☎(0590) 612345
Located: On B3054.

Open: May–Sep 10–6; Oct–Apr 10–5. Closed Xmas Day.
Admission: ✱£4.40 (children £3, students £3.40, senior citizens £3.60).
P. ⌨ (licensed) ⅌ ⅋ (ground floor & gardens) shop ⅏ (in building)

BEKESBOURNE, KENT   Howletts Zoo Park   Map 5 TR15

Lovers of the big cats will enjoy a visit to Howlett's, for here are John Aspinall's tigers – one of the largest collections in the world, including the magnificent Siberian tigers. The Gorillararium houses the largest collection of gorillas (what else!) outside America. There are lots more animals waiting to see you, including chimps, cheetahs and elephants.

☎**Canterbury (0227) 721286**
Located: Off A257.

Open: *daily, 10–5 (or dusk). Closed 25 Dec.
Admission: Fee payable.
P. ☐ ⤙ & shop ⑂

BELTRING, KENT   Whitbread Hop Farm   Map 5 TQ64

Enjoying a picturesque setting, the Hop Farm provides an interesting and educational day out for all the family. You can see the largest group of Victorian oast and galleried barns in the world and visit two award-winning museums, one devoted to rural crafts, the other on the history of hop farming. There are also nature trails, a working craft centre and a children's play area. You may even have the chance to pat one of the famous Whitbread shire horses.

☎**Maidstone (0622) 872068 or 872408**
Located: On the B2015.

Open: Easter–late Oct 10–5.30. Closed Mon except Bank Hol).
Admission: *£2 (children £1).
P. ☐ ⤙ &(ground floor & gardens) shop

BOGNOR REGIS, WEST SUSSEX   Butlins   Map 4 SZ99

Here's the chance to enjoy all the fun of a 'Leisure World' for only a day. Special daybreak tickets allow the family to enjoy all the facilities for one fixed price. Attractions include boating, roller skating, dodgems and other funfair rides and use of the heated indoor pool with wave machine, slides, whirlpool and other amusements.

☎**(0243) 820202**
Open: Early Apr–early Oct daily 10am–10pm.
Admission: Fee payable.
P. ☐ (licensed)

BRENTFORD, GT LONDON   Syon House and Park   Map 4 TQ17

The house, founded in 1415 as a monastery, was remodelled in the eighteenth-century with fine interiors by Robert Adam; the superbly coloured anteroom and the gallery library are particularly noteworthy, and the house contains fine portraits and furniture. Overlooking the Thames, it has fifty-six acres of grounds laid out by Capability Brown and said to be the first place in which trees were planted purely for ornament. The nineteenth-century Great Conservatory was the first large glass and metal construction of its kind in the world, and the inspiration for the Crystal Palace. The park has a six-acre rose garden and one of the largest garden centres in England; it is also the site of the British Motor History Heritage Trust, whose museum spans a hundred years of motoring, and the London Butterfly House.

☎**01-560 0881/3 (Motor Museum 01-560 1378)**
Located: Park – Follow A315 to Bush Corner & enter via Park Road, Isleworth; House – via Park Road off Twickenham Road.

Open: House Apr–Sep, Sun–Thu; Oct Sun only 12–5pm (last tickets 4.15pm). Park Apr–Oct daily 10–6; Nov–Mar 10–dusk (closed Xmas). Conservatory closed during Winter months.
Heritage Museum daily 10–5.30 (4pm Nov–Mar). Closed Xmas.
Admission: House *£1 (children & senior citizens 80p).
House & gardens *£1.50 (children & senior citizens £1).
Park *£1 (children & senior citizens 80p).
Rose Garden 10p.
£1.75 Heritage Motor Museum (children & senior citizens £1). Family rate £4.
☐ (licensed) & (with assistance) shop and garden centre ⑂

BRIGHTON   East Sussex   Map 4 TQ30

Playground of the Prince Regent

It seems hardly credible today that this famous and popular resort was once the unassuming fishing village of Brighthelmstone. The transformation began in the 1750s, and when George, Prince of Wales – later Prince Regent and finally King George IV – joined the trend. An elegant Regency townscape evolved which remains a characteristic of much of the resort. But, no museum piece, this stylish setting is now the backdrop to a host of up-to-the-minute facilities and entertainments.

Exploring Brighton as a visitor could not be easier: guided tours both on foot and by bus are available in summer, and open-topped buses provide an excellent way to see both the town and outlying places such as Rottingdean village, or Devil's Dyke on the breezy South Downs. Those who prefer a stroll might start with The Lanes, a maze of narrow streets and brick-paved alleyways that was once part of Brighthelmstone. Many of the former fishermen's cottages are now pubs, cafés or little shops.

Brighton offers a dazzling array of entertainment, from West End shows at the Theatre Royal to Punch and Judy on Palace Pier. A more sedate pastime might be a visit to the excellent Museum and Art Gallery, whose permanent displays include an award-winning fashion gallery and a fascinating seaside exhibition highlighting Brighton's history.

☆STAR ATTRACTIONS

Aquarium and Dolphinarium

Established more than a century ago, this is Britain's largest aquarium. Visitors can see seals, turtles and sealions, as well as some 10,000 fish from all over the world, displayed in a series of remarkable underground galleries. The dolphinarium, opened in the 1960s, seats up to 1000 spectators for its regular performing dolphin shows. There is a children's indoor play centre, too.

☎(0273) 604233
Located: Madeira Drive.

Open: daily, 10–5.15 (4.15 in winter) Closed Xmas.
Admission: ✳£2.70 (children £1.80). Family ticket £7.20.
P. ⌷ (licensed) & Shop ✻ (except guide dogs)

Royal Pavilion

One of England's most famous buildings, this great Indian-style extravaganza began life as a small farmhouse, rented by the Prince of Wales on his early trips to Brighton. In 1787 he commissioned Henry Holland to rebuild it as a demure neoclassical villa, and some 30 years later it was transformed again, by John Nash, to its present exotic appearance, with domes and minarets at every turn. The inside is as fantastic as the outside, its décor Chinese in style. Some fine Regency silver-gilt ware can be seen in the lavish banqueting room, and there are equally fascinating displays 'below stairs', where the great French chef Antonin Carême was among those who cooked for the Prince Regent.

☎(0273) 603005 ext. 3250
Located: Old Steine.

Open: daily, Jun–Sep 10–6, Oct–May 10–5. Closed Xmas.
Admission: ✳£2 (children £1).
⌷ & (ground floor and grounds only) Shop ✻ (except guide dogs)

Volk's Railway

Britain's first public electric railway, named after its founder, local engineer and inventor Magnus Volk, celebrated its centenary in 1983. This delightful legacy of the Victorian seaside now provides a most convenient link between the town centre (the terminus is near the Aquarium) and Brighton's new Marina. Moorings for some 200 yachts make this Europe's largest such complex.

☎(0273) 681061
Located: Madeira Drive/Brighton Marina.

Open: Volk's Railway daily, Apr–Sep.
Fare: payable.

BUCKLER'S HARD, HAMPSHIRE   Buckler's Hard Village   Map 4 SZ49

Here on the banks of the Beaulieu River wooden warships, including some for Nelson's fleet, were built from New Forest oak. The 18th-century homes of a shipwright and labourer still stand in the picturesque, historic village, whilst a typical inn scene and master-shipbuilder's office have been reconstructed in original buildings and are brought to life by appropriately costumed figures. The Village Festival takes place on 24 July 1988.

☎(059063) 203
Located: Off B3054.

Open: Easter–Spring Bank Hol 10–6; Spring Bank Hol–Sep 10–9; Oct–Easter 10–4.30. Closed Xmas Day.
Admission: £1.50 (children 90p, senior citizens £1.20).
P. ⌷ ⟟ shop ⴹ (in buildings).

BURFORD, OXFORDSHIRE   Cotswold Wildlife Park   Map 4 SP21

Opened in 1970, this wildlife park is set in 120 acres of lovely gardens and parkland. A good collection of animals from all over the world includes rhinos, zebras and ostriches, their paddocks enclosed by unobstrusive moats. Tigers and leopards have spacious grassy enclosures, while the old walled garden is home to the monkeys and many tropical birds. There is also a tropical house, a reptile house, an aquarium and a butterfly house. As if that wasn't enough to amuse the children, there is also an adventure playground and a narrow gauge railway, whilst in the old house is an unusual animal brass rubbing centre.

☎(099382) 3006
Located: 2 miles south of Burford, off A40 & A361.

Open: daily (except Xmas Day) 10–6 or dusk if earlier.
Admission: £2.70 (children over 4 & senior citizens £1.60).
P. ⌷ ⟟ ⅋ shop

BURNHAM BEECHES, BUCKINGHAMSHIRE   Map 4 SU98

Many of the great beech trees that gave their name to this attractive area of wood and common are over 450 years old. The rich variety of vegetation plays host to a wealth of animal, bird and insect life. Listen for the woodpecker, and see if you can spot a muntjac deer.

for CANTERBURY see page 38

Located: 3 miles north of Slough on west side of A355, 3 miles south of Junction 2 on M40.

Open: All year.
⟟

CASTLE HEDINGHAM, ESSEX   Colne Valley Railway   Map 5 TL73

Take a nostalgic day trip to the past as you ride on this reconstruction of a typical Essex branch line. The original station offices have been rebuilt, and stock includes seven steam locomotives and a variety of rolling stock. Care has been taken to integrate the railway into its natural surroundings, and the picnic area is designed as a small nature reserve.

☎Hedingham (0787) 61174

Open: Feb–Xmas daily 11–5. Steam Days Easter–Oct, 1st & 3rd Sun of month & Bank Hol Sun & Mon; Jul every Sun; Aug every Sun & Wed; 12–5. Santa Specials on Dec weekends.
Admission: Steam Days £2.50 (children £1.25). Family ticket (2 adults & up to 3 children) £7.50. Non-Steam Days £1.30 (children 70p).
P. ⌷ ⟟ ⅋ (most areas) shop ⴹ

CHALFONT ST GILES, BUCKINGHAMSHIRE   Chiltern Open Air Museum
Map 4 SU99

This marvellous open-air museum of buildings and everyday objects reflect 500 years of life in the area. Its forty five acres of parkland include a nature trail and give scope for the numerous special events which take place here during the year – Children's Day and the Transport Festival in May, Sheepdog Trials and a Living History event in August, and the Craft Fair in September.

☎(02407) 71117
Located: at Newlands Park off B4442.

Open: Apr–Oct Wed, Sun & Bank Hols; Aug Wed–Sun inclusive; 2–6.
Admission: £1.40 (children 70p, senior citizens £1).
P. ⌷ ⅋ (ground floor & grounds only, no purpose-built toilets) shop

for CHARLWOOD see page 39

Cradle of English Christianity

A wealth of narrow streets and historic buildings give Canterbury an old-world atmosphere which makes it a delight to explore. Dominated by its great cathedral, England's mother church, the compact town centre – much of it pedestrianised – offers plenty to see in a small area. Canterbury has attracted visitors ever since the time of Chaucer's pilgrims, but perhaps never more than today. Tourists can be sure of being well provided for and guided tours are readily available on foot, by bus or even by river.

The Romans made this their regional capital and ringed it with a town wall whose foundations underlie the sections of medieval city wall that survive today. An underground museum in Butchery Lane shows the remains of a Roman house, with a well-preserved tessellated pavement and other finds from Roman Canterbury.

There were several Christian churches here during the Roman occupation, but it was not until AD602 that St Augustine built the church that was to be the predecessor of the great cathedral. The first cathedral was begun around 1070 by the Normans, who also built a castle. Its keep – one of the biggest and oldest in England – can still be seen. Many of Canterbury's other medieval buildings had monastic origins, including the abbey that St Augustine had founded – now largely in ruins – and the buildings of the famous King's School, next to the cathedral.

☆ STAR ATTRACTIONS

Canterbury Heritage

There is no better introduction to Canterbury's story than this new museum, housed in a fine medieval building which was originally a hospice. Beginning with Durovernum, the Roman town, visitors are guided through displays illustrating many aspects of Canterbury through the ages. One features the *Invicta*, one of the earliest railway engines. Built in 1830, it pulled trains on the world's first regular steam-driven passenger service, which ran between Canterbury and Whitstable.

☎(0227) 452747
Located: Poor Priests' Hospital, Stour Street.

Open: Apr–Sep, Mon–Sat 10.30–4. Oct–Mar, reduced opening hours.
Admission: *70p (children 30p). Family ticket £2.
& (ground floor only) shop ¥

Christchurch Cathedral

One of the world's great churches, Canterbury Cathedral has been famous ever since Thomas Becket was dramatically murdered here in 1170. Much of the cathedral has been rebuilt since, though the crypt – the oldest part – is Norman. The magnificent nave dates from about 1400, whilst the distinctive tower, known as Bell Harry, was added a century later. The stained glass is among the finest in the country. Some 13th-century windows in the Trinity Chapel depict miracles that took place here at Thomas Becket's shrine. The shrine itself was visited by countless pilgrims until the time of Henry VIII, when it was destroyed. Tombs still to be seen in the cathedral include those of Henry IV and his queen, and of Edward, the Black Prince.

CHARLWOOD, SURREY   Gatwick Zoo and Bird Garden   Map 4 TQ24

Nearly ten acres of landscaped grounds are laid out to form natural habitats for the zoo's hundreds of birds and mammals, nearly all of whom breed each year. One particularly popular feature is the large monkey island, which contains both Spider and Squirrel Monkeys. In the Tropical Gardens, exotic butterflies flutter around you as you wander through the fascinating jungle setting.

☎Crawley (0293) 862312.

Open: Easter–Oct daily 10.30–6 (or dusk).
Admission: Zoo & Aviaries £2 (children 3–14 £1, senior citizens £1.50).
Butterfly & Tropical Gardens £1.50 (children 80p, senior citizens £1).
Combined ticket £3 (children £1.50, senior citizens £2.25)
P. ⊟ 🍴 ♿ shop ✸

CHARTWELL, KENT   Map 5 TQ45

Sir Winston Churchill lived here from 1924 and much of the house can still be seen as it was in his lifetime. Personal mementoes, pictures, maps and documents give visitors an insight into the life and interests of this great statesman. His many gifts and uniforms are housed in a small museum and outside black swans swim on the lake alongside the terraced garden. A fine artist, many of Sir Winston's paintings are on view in his garden studio.

☎Edenbridge (0732) 866368
Located: 2 miles south-east of Westerham.

Open: Mar & Nov, Wed, Sat & Sun 11–4; Apr–Oct, Tue–Thu 12–5, Sat, Sun & Bank Hol Mon 11–5. Gardens & Studio Apr–Oct same times. Closed Good Fri.
Admission: House & garden £2.70 (children £1.40). Studio: 40p. Gardens only £1.10 (children 60p).
Entrance is by numbered ticket in summer, waiting time can be spent in the gardens.
P. ⊟ (licensed but open May–Nov only)
National Trust

CHERTSEY, SURREY   Thorpe Park   Map 4 TQ06

There is fun for all the family in Thorpe Park's 500 acres, one of Europe's leading leisure parks, where the admission charge covers over fifty attractions (watersport, roller skate hire and coin-operated amusements being the only exceptions). You will be transported round the site by landtrain or waterbus to destinations as diverse as Treasure Island, Space Station Zero, Thorpe Farm or Cinema 180! If the family roller-coaster or Phantom Fantasia ghost rides do not appeal to you, test your skill at Crazy Golf, follow a nature trail or enjoy the family show in the new 700 seat theatre – there really is something for everyone here. Additional attractions are arranged throughout the year, and a leaflet listing these is available from the park.

☎(0932) 562633
Located: 1¾ miles north of Chertsey on A320. Off M25 Junction 11 or 13.

Open: Easter–Sep from 10am. Please check opening times before you visit as only open weekends early & late season.
Admission: £7 (children under 14 £6.50, senior citizens £6, children under 4 free).
P. ⊟ (licensed) 🍴 shop ✸ (except guide dogs).

CHESSINGTON, GT LONDON   Chessington World of Adventures   Map 4 TQ16

Children may fail to appreciate the 65 acres of lovely Surrey countryside in which the World of Adventures is set, for their imaginations will be fired by the prospect of such rides as the Runaway Mine Train in Calamity Canyon, the Dragon River Flume in the Mystic East, or the Safari Skyway Monorail with its new perspective over the zoo. The Fifth Dimension plus Circusworld incorporates a circus academy and children's clowntown guaranteed to enthral the youngsters still further.

☎Epsom (03727) 27227
Located: On A243. Off M25 Junction 9.

Open: Apr–Oct daily 10–5 (all attractions); Nov–Mar daily (except 25 Dec) 10–4 (Zoological Gardens only).
Admission: ✳£5.50 (children 4–14 and senior citizens £4.50).
P. ⊟ (licenced) ♿ (most parts) shop ✸

CHILHAM, KENT   Chilham Castle   Map 5 TR05

Hexagonal in shape, this impressive Jacobean manor house and castle keep (not open) occupies a fine site overlooking the River Stour. The gardens, with terraced flower borders, some fine topiary and an evergreen oak tree planted when the house was first built, are surrounded by a park offering attractive woodland and lakeside walks, whilst a visit to Petland is always popular with the children. Everyone will love the colour and pageantry of the medieval era, brought to life here in jousting displays on Sundays throughout the season. Special events include the Chiltern Horse Trials (15 May 1988).

☎(0227) 730319

Open: late Mar–mid Oct daily 11–6 (last entry 5).
Admission: ✱Weekdays (except Mon & Fri) £2 (children £1); Mon & Fri £1.80 (children 90p); Sun (with jousting) £2.50 (children £1.50); Bank Hol Sun & Mon £3.50 (children £1).
P. ⌂ (licensed) & (gardens only) shop

CHISLEHURST, KENT   Chislehurst Caves   Map 5 TQ46

A forty-five minute tour of these mysterious caverns, hewn out over eight thousand years and known as the Enigma of Kent, will lead you through the history and legend of the area. Younger children will also appreciate the Cave's Witch and the Dr. Who Cave. During World War II, fifteen thousand people lived in the caves, and there will be a reunion of these 'shelterers' in May.

☎01-467 3264

Open: Easter-end Sep daily 11–5; end Sep-Easter, Sat & Sun only (daily in school holidays) 11–5.
Admission: 45 minute tour, £1.50 (children 70p); 1½ hour tour, (Sun & Bank Hols) £2 (children £1).
P. ⌂ ⅞ & (except long tour on Sun) shop

COLCHESTER, ESSEX   Colchester Zoo   Map 5 TL92

Set in a 40-acre park, which also contains a 14th to 17th-century church and the historic Stanway Hall, this lovely zoo includes a large collection of mammals, together with reptile house, aquarium and birdland. Falconry displays and sea-lion training sessions are regular features, and this year there will also be a parrot show. The grounds are served in part by the 'Safari Express", a miniature lakeside railway which runs past bird, wolf and rhino enclosures.

☎(0206) 330253
Located: 3m west of town off B1022.

Open: Daily except Xmas Day 9.30–5.30 (one hour before dusk out of season).
Admission: ✱£2.40 (children 3–14 £1, senior citizens £1.90).
P. ⌂ ⅞ & (restricted) shop ✸

DIDCOT, OXFORDSHIRE   Didcot Railway Centre   Map 4 SU58

The golden age of the Great Western Railway is recalled here, an original engine shed housing twenty steam locomotives and a fine collection of passenger and freight rolling stock. The original track has been relaid, a typical GWR station recreated, and on Steamdays you can both see the trains in operation and take a ride on one.

☎(0235) 817200
Located: Access through main entrance of Didcot Parkway Station.

Open: mid Mar–mid Dec Sat, Sun & Bank Hol; Jul–Oct Mon–Fri 11–5.
Steam days first and last Sun of each month Mar–Nov, also Bank Hols, Sun & Wed in Aug, and daily over Spring Bank Hol week.
Admission: ✱£1.30–£3 depending on event (children & senior citizens half price). Special rates for family parties.
P. (at adjacent BR station) ⌂ ⅞ & (advance notice recommended) shop ✸

DORKING, SURREY   Box Hill   Map 4 TQ15

This 800-acre area of wood and chalk downland rises 400ft from the River Mole and is designated a Country Park with nature walks. A walk to the summit is rewarded by magnificent views across the South Downs. Watch out for the box tree which grows wild here. Also at the top is an exhibition centre, a National Trust shop and an 1890's fort.

Located: 1 mile north of Dorking, 2½ miles south of Leatherhead, off A24.

Open: *shop, information room & exhibition Apr–mid Dec, Wed–Sun & Bank Hol Mon (closed Fri, Nov–mid Dec)
P. ⌂ & shop
National Trust

ESHER, SURREY   Claremont Landscape Gardens   Map 4 TQ17

Many of the great landscape gardeners of our time, including Sir John Vanburgh and 'Capability' Brown, have had a hand in forming this magnificent garden, the earliest surviving example of a landscape garden in England. Of special interest is the grotto, the lake, the island with pavillion and the turf amphitheatre. There are many fine walks with excellent viewpoints.

☎(0372) 67841

Open: All year; daily. Apr–Oct 9–7 (or sunset); Nov–Mar 9–4. Closed Xmas Day & 1 Jan.
Admission: Sun £1, (children 50p); Mon–Sat 80p, (children 40p).
P. shop
National Trust

FARNHAM, SURREY   Birdworld and Underwaterworld   Map 4 SU84

Eighteen acres of garden and parkland contain enclosures of birds ranging from the tiny tanager to the great ostrich. A fascinating and imaginatively created Sea Shore Walk shows sea birds in their natural surroundings, complete with waves, whilst the aquarium houses tropical, freshwater and marine fish. Special events are planned for July, which is Zoo Month.

☎Bentley (0420) 22140
Located: 3½ miles south-west of Farnham on A325 beyond Wrecclesham.

Open: daily excluding Xmas Day from 9.30.
Admission: *£1.75 (children 3–14 years £1, senior citizens – except Sun & Bank Hol – £1.50).
P. ⌂ ⊼ & shop 🍴

FISHBOURNE, WEST SUSSEX   Roman Palace   Map 4 SU80

Bring history lessons to life at Fishbourne Roman Palace – the largest Roman residence excavated in Britain. The massive areas of intricate mosaic indicated that this was probably the palace of the local king, Cogidubrus. Even the formal gardens can still be seen – beautifully restored to the original 1st century AD plan. Archaeological finds are on display in the museum.

☎Chichester (0243) 785859 (West Sussex Archaeological Society)
Located: In Salthill Rd.

Open: Mar & Apr, daily 10–5; May–Sep 10–6, Oct 10–5, Dec–Feb, Sun only 10–4
Admission: £1.50 (children 80p).
P. ⌂ & shop 🍴

FRENSHAM, SURREY   Frensham Common   Map 4 SU84

Frensham Common is now part of a vast country park, 1000 acres of which belongs to the National Trust. It is a haven for wildlife and a place where families can still enjoy a peaceful day out, particularly in the area around Frensham Little Pond. The Great Pond is very popular – activities to be enjoyed here include sailing, fishing, walking and horse-riding.

Located: Astride the A287, 4 miles south of Farnham

P. ⊼
Part National Trust

GOSPORT, HAMPSHIRE   Royal Navy Submarine Museum   Map 4 SZ69

The Submarine Alliance, built for World War II and now fully restored to seagoing condition, can be explored by visitors here. It offers an interesting contrast to turn-of-the-century Holland 1, the first underwater craft to be introduced by the navy, and also on show. The museum not only traces the history of the submarine but also shows its development up to the present nuclear age.

☎(0705) 529217

Open: Apr–Oct 10–4.30; Nov–Mar 10–3.30. Closed 24 Dec–2 Jan.
Admission: £2 (children & senior citizens £1.20).
P. ⌷ (licensed) ⟂ shop ⚒

GUILDFORD, SURREY   Loseley Park   Map 4 SU94

Loseley Park, with its elegant Elizabethan mansion, is the perfect setting for a family day out. The house itself boasts many fine works of art and furniture and has historical associations with Henry VIII, Elizabeth I, James I and Queen Mary. An attractive garden terrace is open to visitors. The Park comprises 1,400 acres of farms and woodland and a herd of 700 Jersey cows provide milk and cream for the famous Loseley dairy products. Guided tours and trailer rides introduce the visitor to the farm which also includes rare breeds of sheep and pigs.

☎(0483) 571881
Located: 2½ miles south-west of Guildford

Open: House: end May–Sep, Wed–Sat 2–5. Also Spring and Aug Bank Hol, (Restaurant & Farm Shop 11.30–5). Farm Tours: Apr–Oct Mon–Sat, by appointment only.
Admission: House: £2.20 (children £1.40) Trailer Rides: £1.40 (children £1.20) Farm Walks: £1.20.
P. ⌷ (licensed) ⟂ ♿ (ground floor & gardens only) farm shop ⚒

HALLAND, EAST SUSSEX   Bentley Wildfowl and Motor Museum   Map 5 TQ51

There should certainly be something for all the family here! The attractions include wildfowl from all over the world – black swans, Ne-Ne geese and many others – together with peacocks, flamingoes and cranes. There is also a fascinating collection of vehicles from the golden age of motoring, with veteran, Edwardian and vintage models. Bentley House contains splendid antique furniture and some fine wildfowl paintings. The 4th Annual Vintage Transport Rally will take place here on 31 July 1988.

☎(082584) 573

Open: Apr–Oct daily at 10.30; Nov–Mar weekends (reserve & museum only).
Admission: ✳£2.20 (children £1, senior citizens £1.50).
Family ticket £5.85 (2 adults plus up to 4 children).
P. ⌷ ⟂ ♿ shop ⚒

HAMPTON COURT, GREATER LONDON   Map 4 TQ17

You can enjoy a splendid day out at Hampton Court where there is so much to see. No description will prepare the first-time visitor for the magnificence and size of Hampton Court Palace which contains over a thousand rooms! Begun in Tudor times, it was extended and given a new façade but remains unaltered since about 1700, with much of the original part still evident. An extensive park surrounds the palace, nestling in an elbow of the Thames, and includes the famous maze, formal gardens, Henry VIII's tennis court, a Tudor tilt yard, where jousting tournaments were held, and water features.

☎01-977 8441
Located: On Hampton Court Road (A308) between Kingston-upon-Thames and East Molesey.

Open: State Apartments all year (except Xmas & 1 Jan); Apr–Sep Mon–Sat 9.30–6, Sun 11–6; Oct–Mar Mon–Sat 9.30–5, Sun 2–5.
Admission: fee payable.
P. ⌷ ♿
Dept of Environment

HASCOMBE, SURREY   Winkworth Arboretum   Map 4 SU94

Seasonal walking trail leaflets guide you through this 100-acre hillside arboretum, introducing you to the rare trees and shrubs. Best displays are in May and the end of October, but every season has its charm. Azaleas and bluebells provide a spectacular show in spring. There are two lakes and the hillside offers a fine view across the North Downs.

☏Guildford (0483) 893032
Located: 1 mile north-west on B2130.

Open: daily (except Mon & Fri)
Admission: £1.
🚗 (Apr–mid Nov 2–6, also fine weekends & days in Mar)
National Trust

HAWKINGE, KENT   Kent Battle of Britain Museum   Map 5 TR24

Here, in the actual buildings of the famous Battle of Britain RAF station, you can see a comprehensive collection of the remains of both British and German aircraft involved in the battle. Also on display are full-sized replicas of the Hurricane, Spitfire and Me109 fighters used in the Battle of Britain films, and examples of British and German uniforms and equipment from the 1940 period.

☏(030389) 3140

Open: Easter–Oct Sun & Bank Hols 11–5.30; also Mon–Sat 1–5 July–Oct, (Jun 2–5 Mon–Sat).
Admission: *£1 (children 50p)
P. ♿ (but no purpose-built toilets) shop ✗

HENFIELD, WEST SUSSEX   Woods Mill   Map 4 TQ21

Housed in an 18th-century water mill, the wildlife and countryside exhibition includes live animals, an accurate model of an oak tree and an audio-visual presentation of the work of the Sussex Trust for Nature Conservation. In the grounds, children of all ages will delight in using the nets provided to collect and identify specimens from the dipping pond, and a superb nature trail will lead you through 15 acres of woodland, meadow and marshland beside stream and lake. Special events are scheduled for the first weekend of every month.

☏(0273) 492630
Located: 1 mile south of Henfield on A2037 at junction with Horn Lane.

Open: Good Fri–late Sep, Tue–Thur & Sat 2–6, Sun & Bank Hols 11–6.
Admission: Tue–Thu, £1 (children 50p). Weekend & Bank Hol, £1.20 (children 60p).
P. 🚗 (event weekends) ♿ (ground floor only) shop ✗

HERNE COMMON, KENT   Brambles Wildlife Park   Map 5 TR16

Why not explore the Frog and Toad Farm and a walk-in Chicken range, or pet and feed the inhabitants of Rabbit World and the Children's Farm? This 20-acre wildlife park, set in the old Weald of Kent, offers all these attractions, plus nature trails through beautiful woodland to enclosures of deer, foxes and owls. Older children can let off steam in the adventure playground, whilst younger ones are safe in a special under-5's area.

☏Canterbury (0227) 712379
Located: On A291 halfway between Herne Bay and Canterbury.

Open: Easter–Nov 10–5 daily.
Admission: £1.50 (children 75p).
P. 🚗 ⛽ ♿ (ground floor & grounds only – no purpose built toilets) shop ✗

HERSTMONCEUX, EAST SUSSEX   Royal Greenwich Observatory   Map 5 TQ61

Visit the home of Greenwich Mean Time, and get a new perspective on life through the Observatory's telescopes! In the castle itself are exhibitions of historical interest and modern astronomy, though the rest of the building is not normally open; its grounds include formal gardens, woods and parkland.

☏(0323) 833171 ext 3320
Located: Entry off Wartling Road.

Open: Easter–Sep daily 10.30–5.30 (last admission 4.30).
Admission: *£1.80 (children & senior citizens £1.30).
P. 🚗 ♿ (ground floor & grounds only) shop

HERSTMONCEUX, EAST SUSSEX   Sussex Farm Heritage Centre   Map 5 TQ61

Take a trip to the Heritage Centre to see some of the finest award-winning Shire horses in the South-East. You can admire them at close quarters along with some of the machinery they need to pull, such as a plough or a brewery dray. Farm machinery is in regular use and there is a collection of livestock including several rare breeds. There are craft classes and demonstrations as well as regular wagon rides around the farm.

☏(0323) 832182
Located: In Tilley Lane, Windmill Hill.

Open: ✳ all year 10–5 (or dusk).
Admission: fee payable.
P. ⌂ 👬 ⅊ & shop

HEVER, KENT   Hever Castle and Gardens   Map 5 TQ44

Hever Castle is a history lesson come to life. King Henry VIII courted Anne Boleyn at Hever, her family home, an event well-documented by a fascinating exhibition, complete with wax models, which is housed in the long gallery. The beautiful grounds feature several formal gardens including a spectacular Italian Garden. Children will love the maze and the adventure playground.

☏Edenbridge (0732) 865224
Located: 3 miles south-east of Edenbridge off B2026.

Open: end Mar–early Nov daily (closed 16 June 88). Castle 12–5 (last admission). Gardens from 11am.
Admission: ✳Castle & gardens £3.20 (children 5–16 £1.60, senior citizens £3). Gardens only £2 (children £1.20, senior citizens £1.80).
P. ⌂ (licensed) & (ground floor & gardens only) shop & garden centre ✗ (in Castle)

HUNGERFORD, BERKSHIRE   Littlecote Park   Map 4 SU36

When you visit this award-winning park you can ride the riverside railway, explore a 17th-century village or enjoy displays of jousting and falconry. The magnificent Tudor mansion, visited by nearly every British monarch since Henry VII, is also open to the public. Special events planned for 1988 include a veteran car rally on Saturday 28 May, steam rally on 14–15 June, family pageant and celebration of three hundred years of Anglo-Dutch friendship on 23–24 July.

☏(0488) 84000

Open: ✳Apr–Oct daily 10–6.
Admission: ✳£3.50 (children 4–14 £2.50, senior citizens £3).
P. ⌂ (licensed) 👬 & (ground floor & gardens only) shop & garden centre.

IPSDEN, OXFORDSHIRE   Wellplace Bird Farm   Map 4 SU68

There is a delightful collection here of all those birds and animals which children love most – lambs, monkeys, donkeys, otters, ponies and racoons among them. The aviaries contain more than a hundred varieties of birds.

☏Checkendon (0491) 680473

Open: ✳Apr–Sep daily 10–5.30 (6pm Sun).
Admission: fee payable.
P. ⌂ 👬 & shop garden centre ✗

for ISLE OF WIGHT see page 46

KEW, GREATER LONDON   Kew Gardens   Map 4 TQ17

This 300-acre Royal Botanic Gardens boasts over 50,000 different types of plants and flowers. A dazzling array of orchids, ferns, cacti and many rare specimens are to be found in the elegant greenhouses and museums. The Exotic Pagoda was the work of Sir William Chambers in 1761 whereas the Princess of Wales Tropical Conservatory was a new addition in 1987. Promenade Concerts are held here in August and in September there is an exciting Clog and Apron Race.

☏01-940 1171 ext 4622

Open: daily at 9.30 but closed on Xmas Day & New Years Day. Closing times vary from 4pm to 6.30pm on weekdays & 4pm to 8pm on Sun & Public Hols depending on time of sunset.
Admission: ✳50p (children under 10 free).
P. ⌂ & (ground floor & gardens only) shop ✗ (ex guide dogs)

KNEBWORTH, HERTFORDSHIRE   Knebworth House   Map 4 TL22

This magnificent stately home with spectacular High Gothic style of decoration, is notable for its State Drawing Room and Banqueting Hall and has been the family home of the Lyttons since 1490. A fascinating British Raj exhibition relates the story of Lord Lyttons vice-royalty. The 250 acre grounds include formal gardens with a herb enclosure designed by Gertrude Jekyll. Children will be impressed by the wide range of equipment in the adventure playground, especially the recently built 'Fort Knebworth'. Other features include the deer park, narrow gauge steam railway and museum, and nature trails.

☎Stevenage (0438) 812661
Located: Direct access from A1(M) at Junction 7 (Stevenage south).

Open: Weekends, Bank Hol & School Hols late Mar–late May; late May–early Sep Tue–Sun; rest of Sep weekends only. House & Gardens 12–5, Park 11–5.30.
Admission: ✳House, Gardens, Park & Playground £3 (children & senior citizens £2.50). Park & Playground only £1.50.
P. ☕ (licensed) ⊼ & (ground floor & gardens) shop

LAMBERHURST, EAST SUSSEX & KENT   Bewl Bridge Reservoir   Map 5 TQ63

The southeast's largest reservoir, Bewl Bridge boasts 15 miles of shoreline and holds 6,900 million gallons of water. If you are an energetic family prepare to spend eight hours walking right around it. For the less hardy there are marked trails and special paths where you might enjoy a shorter walk. There is also an adventure playground. You can learn all about the reservoir and the surrounding High Weald from the visitor centre. Passenger cruises are available throughout the summer and on winter weekends.

Located: 2 miles south off A21

P. ☕ (Apr–early autumn) ⊼ &

LEIGHTON BUZZARD, BEDFORDSHIRE   Narrow Gauge Railway   Map 4 SP92

All aboard for a ride to the Stonehenge Works, on one of the twenty-two diesel, steam and petrol locomotives. The railway is run by volunteers, and special events are planned for the summer months but please check in advance.

☎(0525) 373888
Located: At Pages Park Station, Billington Road.

Open: Sun Apr–Sep, Bank Hol Mon & Easter weekend. Also some Sats & Weds in Jul & Aug. Please check for specific dates.
Admission/Fare: £2.20 (children & senior citizens £1.10, under 5 free)
P. ☕ & shop

LEITH HILL, SURREY   Map 4 TQ14

Every season has something to offer the visitor to Leith Hill, from the carpets of bluebells in springtime to the rich autumn hues, and in winter the stark leafless trees only accentuate the vast rolling beauty of a landscape that spans 13 counties. The best viewpoint is from the top of the 64ft tower built on the summit by Richard Hull, owner of Leith Hill Place, in 1766.

Located: 4½ miles south-west of Dorking: bounded by A25, A24, A29 and B2126.

Open: all year.
Admission: fee payable to Leith Hill Tower.
P.
National Trust

for LEPE see page 48

The Isle of Wight has been described as a landscape in miniature and it certainly has everything offered by the mainland. But the island also has a unique charm as a result of its separateness and of its size – just 23 miles across and 13 miles from north to south. Excellent ferry services from Lymington, Southampton, Portsmouth and Southsea put the Isle of Wight within easy reach of day-trippers from the mainland as well as longer-term holidaymakers, and children in particular will find the crossing an exciting start to the journey. The Victorians were the first to 'discover' the island as a holiday resort – indeed, Queen Victoria and Prince Albert built here what was to become their favourite holiday retreat – Osborne House (see Star Attractions). Since those times tourism has become the main industry, and some fine resorts have developed around its shores – helped not inconsiderably by the favourable climate. Isle of Wight resorts frequently top the sunshine tables issued by the Met Office, notably Sandown, Shanklin and Ventnor on the sheltered south-east coast. Wide expanses of sandy beach, gently shelving into the sea for safe bathing, and a complete range of holiday amusements and entertainment make these places a popular choice for family holidays. There are a number of quieter seaside places too, such as the villages of Seaview and Bembridge, which also have good sandy beaches.

Cowes is, of course, the yachting capital of Britain and home of the sports governing body – the Royal Yacht Squadron. Cowes Week is the islands foremost event, when the international yachting fraternity descends on the port to take part in the races, or simply to see and be seen. Two other major sailing events which start and finish at Cowes are the Round-the-Island Race and the Fastnet Race, but whenever you visit the waters here will always be busy with craft of all sizes.

Ryde is the other major ferry port from the mainland – the place which had the world's first scheduled hovercraft service – but it is also a resort with five miles of sandy beach backed by elegant Victorian buildings and a wide, tree-lined esplanade.

Apart from its resorts, the Isle of Wight's coastline has a number of interesting features. The Needles are probably the most famous landmark – a line of chalk pinnacles which extend into the sea on the western tip of the island. They lie at the end of Alum Bay, itself something of a curiosity for the many-hued sandstone of its cliffs. Up to twenty different shades can be identified, from pink to dark brown, and, although visitors are no longer permitted to scramble over the cliffs to collect samples, there is no shortage of souvenir items available. Chines are another famous feature here – deep clefts in the chalk cliffs of the southern coast, notably at Shanklin, where delightful gardens line the winding ravine, and at Blackgang, where a theme park has been developed (see Star Attractions).

The entire coastline of the Isle of Wight is easily accessible with a good main road encircling the island, but visitors should not entirely disregard the interior. Parkhurst Forest is well worth a visit, with lots of marked walks through varied woodland, but probably best known as one of the last refuges in Britain of the red squirrel. There are rolling chalk downs, largely owned by the National Trust, which preserve many unusual species of wild flowers as well as providing some spectacular views. And there are pretty villages with thatched cottages and tempting tea shops, such as Calbourne, Godshill, Shorwell and Brightstone.

One thing is for certain – a day out on the Isle of Wight just won't be long enough.

☆ STAR ATTRACTIONS

Blackgang Chine Fantasy Theme Park

The Isle of Wight's answer to Disneyland! But Blackgang Chine is not new – it was opened in 1843 as a scenic garden. The gardens are still here, but Blackgang's younger visitors come to explore such delights as the Wild West Cowboy Town, Nurseryland, Jungleland or the Smugglers' Cave. A dinosaur park has giant models and there is lots more to see and do. Adults, meanwhile, can visit the maritime exhibition and the whole family will be impressed by the specatcular coastal views from the Look Out.

☎(0983) 730330
Located: At Blackgang.

Open: Apr–Oct daily from 10am; closes at 10pm late May–Sep, otherwise 5pm.
Admission: ✳£1.65 (children £1).
P. ⌂ (licensed) ⛾ & (ground floor & gardens only) shop

Isle of Wight Steam Railway

Steam trains operate through nearly two miles of beautiful wooded country, with passengers transported in restored carriages some 60 or 70 years old. The locomotives in use are particularly interesting, with Isle of Wight names – Calbourne (1891) and Freshwater (1876) – and have been fully restored by volunteer enthusiasts to their Southern Railway liveries.

☎(0983) 882204
Located: At Haven Street Station.

Open: Trains run on Suns & BH Mons & certain other days throughout the summer, 10.45–4.45.
Admission: Details of rates on application.
P. ⌂ ⛾ (with assistance) shop

Robin Hill Adventure and Zoological Park

There are lots of exciting and unusual attractions for children here, particularly in 'Freeriderland', where they can try their skill with BMX bikes, grass sledges, paddle boats and archery. There is also an Assault Course, a nature trail and water gardens. The zoo part of the park has over a hundred species of mammals, birds, reptiles and insects, including a large tropical Jungle House and a ten-acre walk-through enclosure. The park covers over eighty acres of downs and woodland.

☎(0983) 527352
Located: At Robin Hill, Arreton.

Open: Mar–Oct daily 10–6.
Admission: £2.50 (children £1.80).
P. ⌂ (licensed) ⛾ & (with assistance) shop

Osborne House

This magnificent Italianate villa overlooking the Solent was built for Queen Victoria and Prince Albert and it became their favourite holiday retreat. Edward VII donated it to the nation, since when visitors have been able to view the State Apartments which remain in their original form. The terraced gardens are delightful, but perhaps the most fascinating thing here is the Swiss Cottage in the gardens. It was built as a play house for the royal children and here, under the direction of the Prince, they learned such skills as cooking, gardening, carpentry and needlework.

Located: 1 mile south-east of East Cowes.

Open: late Mar–Oct, Mon–Sat 10–5, Sun 11–5.
Admission: ✳£2.20 (children £1.10).
P. ⌂ & (ground floor & gardens only).
English Heritage

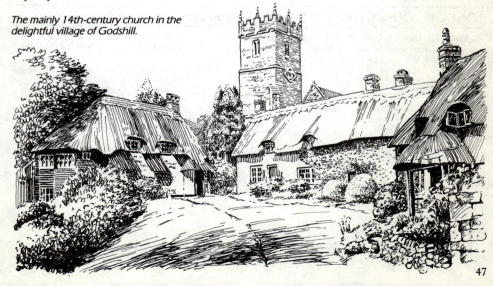

The mainly 14th-century church in the delightful village of Godshill.

LEPE, HAMPSHIRE Lepe Country Park Map 4 SZ49/SU40

A country park with a difference, Lepe has the added bonus of its own stretch of sandy beach and a busy and interesting seascape across the Solent to the Isle of Wight. You can spend the day by the water, fishing, swimming or enjoying some water sports, or alternatively just relax on the grassy parkland while the children have fun in the children's playground. Why not stay all day and have a barbeque at the pre-bookable site.

☎(0703) 899108/(0962) 64221
Located: 3 miles south of Fawley on unclassified road.

Open: all year.
P. ⌂ ⊼

LIGHTWATER, SURREY Lightwater Country Park Map 4 SU96

Lightwater is 125 acres of woodland and heath situated close to the boundaries of Surrey, Hampshire and Berkshire. There is much here of interest to the nature lover and a nature trail leading from the car park offers instant access to the rich and varied habitats. Fishing and horse riding are popular pastimes.

☎Bagshot (0276) 72662
Located: Off A322.

Open: all year.
P. ⊼

LIPHOOK, HAMPSHIRE Hollycombe Steam Collection Map 4 SU83

Here, historic woodland gardens with attractive walks house a collection of steam-driven equipment ranging from a 2'-gauge railway, which climbs to give spectacular views of the South Downs, to a 7¼" miniature railway. The Hollycombe tramway runs between the steam farm and the saw mill, whilst steam roundabout, fairground organ and bioscope recall the entertainment of a bygone era. The huge engine rescued from an ex-LMS Railway paddle steamer, Caledonia, can be seen working, and there are demonstrations of harvesting and steam rolling as well as traction engine rides. A Festival of Steam is scheduled for the Spring Bank Holiday.

☎(0428) 724988
Located: 1½ miles south-east of Liphook on unclass Midhurst Rd.

Open: Apr–mid Oct, Bank Hol & Sun, also during second half of Aug; 1–6 (rides 2–6).
Admission: £2 (children & senior citizens £1.50).
P. ⌂ ⊼ shop ⊁

for LONDON – see Colour feature beginning on page 65, and pages 73–80.

LONDON COLNEY, HERTFORDSHIRE Mosquito Aircraft Museum Map 4 TL20

Eighteen De Havilland aircraft are on show here – all with intriguing names such as Venom, Vampire and Horsa. There are also three World War Two Moquitos.

☎Bowmansgreen (0727) 22051
Located: 5 miles south of St Albans on A6.

Open: *Easter–Oct, Sun & Bank Hol Mons 10.30–5.30. Also Thu 2–5.30 Jul–Sep.
Admission: *75p (children 25p).
P. & shop

Symbols
☎ telephone number
P. parking on the premises
⌂ refreshments available
⊼ picnic area
& accessible to wheelchair-bound visitors
⊁ no dogs
* indicates 1987 details

LONG MELFORD, SUFFOLK   Kentwell Hall   Map 5 TL84

Much of Kentwell Hall remains as it was in Tudor times – a mellow redbrick manor surrounded by a broad moat, and built to an E-plan with an inner courtyard. Once again a thriving family home, the present owners are striving to restore and maintain this delightful house so that visitors might appreciate the uniqueness of Kentwell. An exhibition of Tudor style costumes gives a flavour of the period and, outside, a fascinating mosaic maze will entertain the children. There is also a rare breeds farm and various events are planned throughout the year.

☏Sudbury (0787) 310207

Open: Easter, then early Apr–mid Jun Wed & Sun 2–6 (closed mid Jun–mid Jul for historic recreation of Tudor domestic life – special rates apply); mid Jul–Sep Wed–Sun 2–6. Also open Bank Hol weekends 11–6.
Admission: £2.20 (children 5–16 £1.20; senior citizens £1.90).
P. ⌨ ⅏ (ground floor & gardens only) shop ⅋

LYMPNE, KENT   Port Lympne Zoo   Map 5 TR13

This large zoo enjoys an enviable location on a wooded estate alongside an elegant mansion and gardens. Specialising in rare breeds, you'll see rhinos, elephants, wolves, Siberian tigers and many more. An interesting way to view is by the special safari trailer which may be booked in advance in high season.

☏Hythe (0303) 64646

Open: *daily 10–5, 4pm in winter (closed Xmas day).
Admission: fee payable.
P. ⌨ ⅀ ⅏ (ground floor only) shop ⅋

MAIDENHEAD, BERKSHIRE   Courage Shire Horse Centre   Map 4 SU88

Many of the gentle giants you see here are actually stars in their own right, having faced an audience of millions on the television and having appeared at many major shows. You can see them being groomed at the working stable, watch the farrier at work, or marvel at the gleaming array of horse brasses. Also on display are some of the hundreds of rosettes and trophies awarded to these magnificent animals. There is a free guided tour and an enthralling audio visual presentation. Youngsters will also appreciate the children's playground and the section on birds and smaller animals.

☏Littlewick Green (062882) 4848
Located: In Cherry Garden Lane at Maidenhead Thicket, off A4.

Open: Mar–Oct, daily 11–5.
Admission: £1.75 (children 4–15 & senior citizens £1.25).
P. ⌨ (licensed) ⅀ ⅏ shop

MARWELL, HAMPSHIRE   Marwell Zoological Park   Map 4 SU52

Conservation of endangered species is the priority of this world-famous British wild animal collection, where groups of rare beasts thrive and breed in one hundred acres of spacious enclosures. Such traditional favourites as giraffe, monkeys, rhinos, zebras and camels are not forgotten, however, and the zoo has one of the largest collections of big cats in the country. You can see more than a thousand animals from over a hundred species, and new exhibits are constantly being added, but don't worry about long walks around the zoo – cars can be driven into the zoo. Numerous special events are arranged throughout the year.

☏Owslebury (096274) 406

Open: All year daily, except Xmas Day. Summer 10–6 (last admission 4.30); Winter last admission one hour before dusk.
Admission: *£3 (children 3–14 £1.80, senior citizens £2.50).
P. ⌨ (licensed) ⅀ ⅏ shop ⅋

MIDDLE WALLOP, HAMPSHIRE   Museum of Army Flying   Map 4 SU23

This award-winning museum, overlooking a military airfield and offering weekend helicopter flights throughout the season, tells the story of army flying from the 19th century to the present day. Displays include vintage aircraft, kites and balloons, and details of the story are filled in by photographic records and dioramas. A special commemorative exhibition traces the involvement of the American 'Colonel' S.F. Cody with the first British airship, Nulli Secundus, and with British Army Aeroplane No 1 which achieved the first sustained powered flight in this country.

for NEW FOREST see opposite page.

☎Andover (0264) 62121 ext 421

Open: daily (except Xmas) 10–4.30.
Admission: £2 (children, students & senior citizens £1).
P. ▱ ⊼ & shop ✗

NEWHAVEN, EAST SUSSEX   Newhaven Fort   Map 5 TQ40

This restored Victorian fort was built in 1860 to protect the area against invasion. There is a military museum as well as a fascinating maze of underground tunnels. Especially for the children, there is an assault course and an amusements section. The site is at present undergoing redevelopment.

☎(0273) 517622

Open: daily 10–6 May–Oct.
Admission: small fee payable.
P. ▱ ⊼ shop

NEW MILTON, HAMPSHIRE   Sammy Miller Museum   Map 4 SZ29

Described as the world's motorcycle heritage, this museum is a must for all bikers. It houses one of the largest collections of fully-restored motorcycles in Europe, including some extremely rare machines and many which are still fully competitive. The collection is constantly changing, with special events throughout the year.

☎(0425) 619696

Open: Apr–Sep daily 10.30–4.30; Oct–Mar Sat & Sun only 10.30–4.
Admission: £1.50 (children & senior citizens 75p).
P. ▱ & (but no purpose-built toilets) shop ✗

NEWPORT, ESSEX   Mole Hall Wildlife Park   Map 5 TL53

Attractively set in the grounds of a part-Elizabethan hall (not open), the park contains a large collection of animals and birds in enclosures and pools. During the warmer months the family can also visit the butterfly and insect house.

☎Saffron Walden (0799) 40400
Located: at Widdington

Open: daily (except Xmas) 10.30–6 (or dusk). Butterfly House open mid Mar–mid Nov.
Admission: £2.50 (children & senior citizens £1.50). Winter rates half price.
P. ▱ ⊼ shop ✗ (except in car park)

NEW ROMNEY, KENT   Romney, Hythe and Dymchurch Railway   Map 5 TR02

The world's smallest public railway runs across Romney Marsh from Hythe to Dungeness Lighthouse via New Romney and Dymchurch on thirteen-and-a-half miles of 15″ gauge track. Though locomotives are only one-third normal size, they haul up to two hundred passengers at twenty-five miles an hour! If you break your journey at New Romney, you can visit a large indoor railway exhibition. Special events during the year include a Grand Open Day and Steam Up on 15 May 1988.

for OLD WARDEN see page 52

☎(0679) 62353

Open: Easter–Sep daily; Mar & Oct weekends only. Apply for times and fares.
P. (at Hythe, New Romney & Dungeness) ▱ (at New Romney & Dungeness) shop (at Hythe & New Romney)

Planted by order of William the Conqueror in 1078 for his favourite sport – deer hunting – the New Forest once stretched from the River Avon to Southampton Water and from the borders of Wiltshire as far as the English Channel. William the Conqueror's successor William Rufus was equally fond of deer hunting and the Rufus Stone at Stoney Cross now marks the spot, and tells the tale of how an arrow, intended for a deer, glanced off a tree, mortally wounding the king instead. Today, only 144 square miles remain of what is called a forest, but is in fact a delightful combination of forest and open moorland with streams and rivers, areas of grassland where wild New Forest ponies graze and pretty villages with picturesque cottages and ancient churches. The woods provide a glorious area for walking and riding at any time of the year, each season having its own special attractions, and wild ponies and deer are often to be seen wandering freely in these woods as well as on the moorland. The Rhinefield and Bolderwood Ornamental Drives have been laid out along an unclassified road which links Brockenhurst to the A31. Several walks have been waymarked from the drives, too, so that drivers can also get a good look at the woodland. Other delightful walks can be found at Oberwater and on Wilverley Plain. The area is rich in many other types of wildlife too including otters, badgers, bats, different varieties of birds and even butterflies. Lyndhurst is the administrative centre of the Forest and is where the ancient Court of Verderers have their headquarters. According to ancient, as well as modern, law members of this court administer the laws of the Forest protecting the well-being of the people and animals that live there. Agisters, or forest officers, dressed in traditional green, patrol the Forest keeping a watchful eye on the land and enforcing the laws where necessary. This includes cutting the tails of the New Forest ponies to show that their owners have paid their dues – failure to do so results in ponies being impounded and their owners fined. Apart from Lyndhurst there are many other attractive towns and villages within this area worthy of exploration including Brockenhurst and the pretty market town of Ringwood on the edge of the Forest which is a particularly attractive touring centre.

For places to visit in the area check the location atlas at the end of the book.

There are no cars to interrupt the grazing New Forest ponies at Buckler's Hard.

OLD WARDEN, BEDFORDSHIRE   Shuttleworth Collection   Map 4 TL14

Visitors here will be enthralled by these specimens of early aviation, housed six hangars on this classic grass aerodrome. All flyable, these aircraft span the history of powered flight from the 1909 Blériot to the 1941 Spitfire. In the garage you'll see roadworthy motor vehicles dating from the era of the 1898 Panhard Levassor. There is also a coachroom containing carriages of earlier years.

☎**Northill (076727) 288**
Located: 2 miles west from roundabout on A1, Biggleswade bypass.

Open: ✻daily 10.30–5.30, last admission 4.30. Closed 1 week at Xmas.
Admission: fee payable.
P. ▱ (licensed) ⅋ shop ⼎ (in hangars)

OWER, HAMPSHIRE   Paultons Park   Map 4 SU31

Beautiful parkland covering some 140 acres is home to over two hundred kinds of animals and birds at Paultons Park. There is plenty here for children, including the 'Magic Forest', 'Kids Kingdom', an adventure playground and train. Take one of the many woodland walks, or enjoy a stroll by the huge 10 acre lake but be sure to visit both the Village Life and Romany museums.

For OXFORD see opposite page.

☎**Southampton (0703) 814442**

Open: mid Mar–Oct daily 10–7 (last admission 5pm). Earlier closing time during early & late season.
Admission: ✻£2.50 (children £1.60, senior citizens & disabled £1.90).
P. ▱ ⛱ ⅋ shop & garden centre ⼎

PENSHURST, KENT   Penshurst Place   Map 5 TQ54

Already centuries old when Sir Philip Sidney was born here in 1554, this magnificent manor house contains the world-famous chestnut-beamed Great Hall – the oldest and finest in England. State rooms are splendidly furnished, and the Toy Museum delights adults and children alike. The extensive Tudor gardens lead on to a leisure area with venture playground, countryside exhibition and nature trail.

☎**(0892) 870307**
Located: On B2176.

Open: Apr–Sep Tue–Sun & Bank Hol Mon. Grounds 12.30–6, House 1–5.30.
Admission: House & Grounds £2.75 (children £1.50, senior citizens £2).
Grounds & venture playground £2 (children £1, senior citizens £1.50).
P. ▱ (licensed) ⛱ ⅋ (ground floor & grounds only) shop ⼎

PETWORTH, WEST SUSSEX   Petworth House   Map 4 SU92

Petworth is a beautiful 17th to 19th-century mansion with a lake and a garden landscaped by 'Capability' Brown. Captured in paintings by William Turner, this striking piece of architecture is complemented by an equally impressive 700-acre deer park. Inside is a notable picture gallery, a 14th-century chapel and some fine Grinling Gibbons carvings.

for PORTSMOUTH see page 54

☎**(0798) 42207**

Open: Apr–Oct Tue (except following Bank Hol Mons), Wed, Thu, Sat, Sun & Bank Hol Mons, 1.30–5. Deer Park open daily 9–sunset.
Admission: £2.50. Connoisseurs Day on Tue (extra rooms shown) £3 (children £1.50)
▱ ⼎ (in house)
National Trust

PULBOROUGH, WEST SUSSEX   Parham House and Gardens   Map 4 TQ01

This beautiful mansion built in Elizabethan times, contains a fine collection of rare needlework, Elizabethan, Jacobean and Georgian portraits and furniture. A walk in the grounds reveals an enchanting walled garden with herbaceous borders, a herb garden and an orchard. Interesting statuary is set amidst seven acres of tree studded parkland, and there is a children's play area and picnic enclosure.

for QUAINTON see page 55

☎**Storrington (09066) 2021**
Located: 3 miles south-east, off A283.

Open: Easter Sun–1st Sun Oct, Wed, Thu, Sun & Bank Hols. Gardens & picnic area 1–6, House 2–6, (last admission 5.30pm).
Admission: House & gardens £2.50 (children £1.50, under 5 free, senior citizens £2). Gardens only £1 (children 75p).
P. ▱ ⛱ ⅋ (ground floor & gardens only) shop & garden centre ⼎ (in house)

Oxford's beautiful skyline of pinnacles, spires, turrets and towers has earned it the name 'the city of dreaming spires'. This city (together with Cambridge) is Britain's most famous seat of learning and of the many historic colleges that make up the university most of their exquisite chapels, libraries, galleries, quadrangles and gardens are open to the public, posting opening times at their respective main gates. Student life is apparent everywhere in Oxford during term time – the streets teem with undergraduates on bicycles while in the summer they are also to be seen punting or rowing on Oxford's two rivers – the Isis and Cherwell. Oxford is a major shopping centre with all the main departmental stores, and there are exciting and unusual shops too as well as the colourful covered market. With such a vast student population to keep amused it is not surprising that Oxford has superb facilities for spectator and participant sports – including one of the country's top ice skating rinks. And when it comes to the arts, visitors usually have a difficult choice to make between theatre, concert, opera, dance or the cinema.

☆STAR ATTRACTIONS

Christchurch College

This fine college founded by Cardinal Wolsey has one of the loveliest sites in Oxford with beautiful gardens that lead down to water meadows by the River Cherwell. High above the main gateway is Christopher Wren's Tom Tower where Great Town, an old bell taken from Osney Abbey, still rings out 101 times each evening to summon students back to college, a reminder of the time when there were only 101 students in this college. The chapel of Christchruch – famed for its wonderful choristers – is in fact Oxford's cathedral.

Magdalen College

Magdalen College stands beside the River Cherwell and is one of the richest of Oxford's colleges. Its beautiful quadrangle surrounded by cloisters gives it an almost monastic air, while within the grounds there is a deer park where open-air plays are performed in the summer. Magdalen also plays an important part in the May Day celebrations. For, after an evening of May balls, students, many of them aboard punts, cluster around Magdalen Bridge to listen to the choristers singing from Magdalen Tower.

Details about visiting these and other University colleges are available from the Oxford Information Centre, St Aldgate's.

Carfax Tower

This tower is all that remains of St Martin's Church, but visitors may climb to the top from where there are stunning views across this beautiful city.

Located: St Aldate's.

Open: late Mar–late Oct, 10–6, Sun 2–6; late Oct–late Nov 10–4, Sun 1–4.
Admission: ✻40p (children 10p).
☎(0865) 278000

Ashmolean Museum

The Ashmolean Museum, founded in 1683, is one of the oldest and also one of the finest museums and art galleries to be found in the country. It possesses a remarkable collection of Roman, Egyptian and Greek archaeological discoveries – in particular St Arthur Evans' finds from the Palace of Knossos on Crete, as well as fine European paintings belonging to the University, bronzes, silverware, musical instruments and oriental art.

Located: Beaumont Street.

Open: all year (except Easter, during St Giles' Fair in early Sep, Xmas and 1 Jan) Tue–Sat 10–4, Sun 2–4.
Admission: free.
& Shop ✻

PORTSMOUTH Hampshire Map 4 SZ69

The flagship of maritime England, Portsmouth is known to have had a harbour since Roman times and important naval connections as far back as the 14th century. So, it is not so surprising that many of the attractions to be found in this city – the buildings, the superb museums and art galleries, the world's most famous wooden warships and even the cathedral should have a strongly maritime flavour to them. Portsmouth also has many links with literature: Sir Arthur Conan Doyle practised here as a doctor, H. G. Wells worked here and Charles Dickens was born and lived here for a short time. His house, furnished in 1800s style, displays some of his possessions for the public to see. This is a city with something for everyone – there are fine beaches that offer safe bathing, fishing and boating, beautiful gardens and parks – many of which have amusements for children, guided walks around the city, sporting facilites to satisfy all tastes, excellent shops and eating establishments. Portsmouth also has an exciting and entertaining nightlife as well as being one of the country's principle centres for the arts attracting top musical and theatrical artists and leading internatinal orchestras.

☆STAR ATTRACTIONS

HMS Victory

Nelson's flagship, HMS Victory, displayed in Portsmouth's historic dockyard must rate as one of the most outstanding examples of ship restoration in the world. The ship, restored to the appearance she had before the Battle of Trafalgar, is still in commission and is staffed by officers and men from the Navy and Marines.

☎(0705) 819604
Located: HM Naval Base.

Open: daily (except 25 Dec) Mon–Sat 10.30–5.30, Sun 1–5.30 (closes 4.30 Nov–Feb).
Admission: High season £1.80 (children £1), family ticket £4.60; Low season £1.50 (children 90p) family ticket £3.90.
Shop ✗

Royal Naval Museum

The Royal Naval Museum is the only one of its kind in the country, devoted exclusively to the history of the Navy. This museum has splendid collections of uniforms, medals, figure-heads and models of ships as well as many relics of Nelson and his men, including a panorama of the Battle of Trafalgar complete with realistic sound effects.

☎(0705) 733060
Located: HM Naval Base.

Open: daily (except 25 Dec) 10.30–5 (some seasonal variation).
Admission: 75p (children 50p), family ticket £2.
☕ ♿ (ground floor only) shop ✗

The Mary Rose

The nation held its breath when Henry VIII's favourite ship, the 15th-century Mary Rose, was raised from the Solent in 1982. Today visitors can watch the restoration work on this ship's hull in progress from special viewing galleries and visit the nearby boathouse where many of the everyday objects she carried into battle are displayed. This exhibition is supported by recreations of scenes of what life on board the Mary Rose must have been like.

☎(0705) 750521/839766
Located: College Road, HM Naval Base.

Open: daily (except 25 Dec) 10.30–5.30 (5pm Nov–Feb).
Admission: High season £2.80 (children £1.80) family ticket £7.50; Low season £2.50 (children £1.50) family ticket £6.50.
☕ ♿ (exhibition and one gallery of Ship Hall only) shop ✗

Cumberland House Natural Science Museum and Butterfly House

This facinating museum looks at the natural history and geology of the area around Portsmouth and includes displays of local woodland, chalk downs and marshland. There are also freshwater and marine aquaria for visitors to look at, a butterly house in which British butterflies fly free between May and October and even a full-sized replica of a dinosaur called an Iguanodon – a great favourite with children.

☎(0705) 827261
Located: Eastern Parade.

Open: daily (except 24–26 Dec) 10.30–5.30.
Admission: *60p (children 30p).
P. Shop ✗ (except guide dogs).

QUAINTON, BUCKINGHAMSHIRE   Buckinghamshire Railway Centre

Map 4 SP71

Ride on a vintage steam train, from the large collection of standard-gauge locomotives and rolling stock on display here or follow the 'Site Ramble' which takes you around the twenty-acre centre, starting at the station and terminating near the miniature railway. Look out for the unusual 'Underground' train, somewhat larger than the 'tube' trains, the Exhibition Hall and the Railway Shop.

☎(029675) 450
Located: At Quainton Station off A41.

Open: Sat & Sun late Mar–Oct, also Wed Jun–Aug, 10–5.30.
Admission: £2.20 (children & senior citizens £1.10). Family ticket £5.50.
P. ⌷ 𝓕 & shop

QUEEN ELIZABETH COUNTRY PARK, HAMPSHIRE   Map 4 SU71

Hang gliding, grass skiing, walking or pony trekking – these are just some of the activites on offer at this magnificent country park on the South Downs. Butser Hill is the highest point in the park and here you can enjoy exploring a reconstructed, working Iron Age farmstead. The Park Centre offers information, displays, craft demonstrations, a film theatre and a bookshop.

☎Horndean 595040
Located: On the A3 south of Petersfield

Open: *Park open all year.
Centre: daily Mar–Oct 10–6: Sun only Nov–Feb 10–5.
P. (fee payable) ⌷ 𝓕 & shop

RISELEY, BERKSHIRE   Wellington Country Park   Map 4 SU78

The lake – with its facilities for fishing, boating and windsurfing – will be a focus of attention for those members of the family who are keen on watersports. No one should feel left out, however, for the park's woodland and meadows also contain five nature trails, the Thames Valley time trail, a miniature steam railway, the National Dairy Museum and a collection of small domestic animals.

☎Heckfield (0734) 326444

Open: Mar–Oct daily, Nov–Feb Sat & Sun only, 10–5.30.
Admission: £1.70 (children 5–15 90p).
P. ⌷ 𝓕 & shop

ROMSEY, HAMPSHIRE   Broadlands   Map 4 SU32

Formerly the residence of Earl Mountbatten of Burma, this elegant 18th-century mansion is now the home of Lord and Lady Romsey. The richly decorated interior boasts many fine works of art and the magnificent grounds alongside the River Test are a tribute to the landscaping genius of 'Capability' Brown. The Mountbatten Exhibition and an audio visual show trace the eventful lives of Lord and Lady Mountbatten while the Imperial Collection of Crown Jewels of the World shows, in perfect facsimile, crowns, tiaras etc from twelve countries.

☎(0794) 516878
Located: Main entrance on A31 Romsey By-pass.

Open: Apr–Sep 10–5. Closed Mon except Aug, Sep & Bank Hols.
Admission: £3.40 (children 12–16 £1.80; children under 12 free; senior citizens £2.40).
P. ⌷ 𝓕 & (ground floor only) shop ⵜ

SANDLING, KENT   Museum of Kent Rural Life   Map 5 TQ75

The story of life in the Kent countryside unfolds as you walk around this 27 acre site. Exhibits of agricultural equipment, crops and livestock show traditional farming methods, and a number of displays can be found in the Oast House and Hoppers Huts. Probably best to visit on a dry day!

☎Maidstone (0622) 63936
Located: In Lock Lane.

Open: late Mar–mid Oct, Mon, Tue, Thu & Fri 10–5, Sat 12–5, Sun 12–6.
Admission: 80p (children, senior citizens & disabled 40p).
P. ⌷ 𝓕 & (ground floor only) shop garden centre ⵜ

SEDLESCOMBE, EAST SUSSEX   Nortons Farm Museum   Map 5 TQ71

The carthorse era lives on here in a fine display of carts, ploughs and hand tools, and with a farm trail around fruit fields and arable land, where the heavy horse is still used. 'Pick Your Own' facilities are available.

☎(042487) 471
Located: 4½ miles north-west of Hastings on A21.

Open: Apr–Sep daily 9–5.
Admission: Free.
P. ☕ (summer only) 🍴 🍽

SELBORNE, HAMPSHIRE   Map 4 SU73

The quaint little village of Selborne nestles at the foot of a 700ft chalk hill clad with beech trees. The renowned Zig-Zag path leads to the hill top, where splendid views make the rather arduous climb well worth the effort. Another path, known as the Bostal, is somewhat easier to negotiate, and also affords good views. But take care the paths can become extremely slippery in wet weather. Gibert White, the famous naturalist was born in Selborne, and lived here all his life. Much of his work can still be seen, for it was he who created the Zig-Zag path and the gardens at The Wakes which now houses a museum. Galleries here illustrate the stories of White and of the explorers Captain Oakes (of Antarctic fame) and Frank Oakes, explorer of Southern Africa.

☎(042050) 275 (Museum)

Open: Museum: Tue–Sun & Bank Hols 12–5.30 (last admission 5).
Admission: Museum: £1 (children 50p & senior citizens 75p).
P. ♿ (ground floor & garden only) shop 🍽 (except guide dogs).

SHEFFIELD PARK GARDEN, EAST SUSSEX   Map 5 TQ42

This magnificent 150-acre garden was laid out by 'Capability' Brown in the 18th-century. It is a beautiful park with no less than five lakes and a notable collection of rhododendrons and azaleas. There is charm in every season; watch out for the waterlilies, bluebells, daffodils and gentians.

☎Danehill (0825) 790655
Located: 5 miles east of Haywards Heath, off A275.

Open: Apr–early Nov, Tue–Sat 11–6, Sun & Bank Hols 2–6 or sunset. Sun in Oct & Nov, 1pm–sunset. Last admission 1hr before closing. Closed Good Fri & Tue after Bank Hol.
Admission: Apr & Jun–Sep £2.20 (children £1.10; May, Oct & Nov £2.80 (children £1.40).
P. ☕ shop 🍽
National Trust

SHEFFIELD PARK STATION, EAST SUSSEX   Bluebell Railway   Map 5 TQ41

From Sheffield Park Station trains steam along five miles of standard-gauge track through the Sussex countryside to Horsted Keynes – the Bluebell Railway boasting the South of England's largest collection of locomotives and carriages. It is possible to book dinner on the train on certain Saturdays between April and October, and 'Santa Specials' run in December. Both stations have been authentically restored, and a museum situated on platform two at Sheffield Park includes interesting signs, models, tickets and other memorabilia.

☎Newick (082572) 3777 (2370 for train information).
Located: 4½ miles east of Haywards Heath, off A275.

Open: Trains run Jan & Feb Sun; Mar, Apr, Nov & Dec Sat & Sun; May & Oct Wed, Sat & Sun; Jun–Sep & Easter week daily.
Admission: To platform, museum and loco sheds only ✳60p (children 30p)
Train fares – 3rd class return ✳£2.60 (children 3–13 £1.30). Family saver (2 adults & 2 children) £6.80.
P. ☕ (licensed) 🍴 ♿ (most parts) shop

SINGLETON, W. SUSSEX Weald and Downland Open Air Museum Map 4 SU81

Historic buildings from all over south-east England have been rescued and painstakingly reconstructed here, complemented by displays of rural crafts and industries. A medieval farmhouse, working watermill, market hall, 16th-century treadwheel and village school are just some of the exhibits you can enjoy, and the workshops of carpenter, blacksmith and plumber are particularly fascinating. The buildings are set in pleasant surroundings, so you can picnic by the millpond or take a walk through attractive woodland.

☎(024363) 348

Open: Apr–Oct daily 11–6; Nov–Mar, Sun & Wed only 11–5.
Admission: *£2 (children £1.10, senior citizens £1.50).
P. ⌷ ⊼ ⅖ (ground floor & gardens only) shop

SOUTHAMPTON, HAMPSHIRE Maritime Museum Map 4 SU41

Southampton has a long and proud maritime history which includes the Pilgrim Fathers, the activities of the Allied forces in World War II and, of course, the era of the transatlantic luxury liners. This interesting museum tells the complete story, and is housed in a 600-year-old building, once a wool warehouse, with buttressed stone walls and old roof timbers.

☎(0703) 223941 & 224216
Located: at The Wool House, Town Quay.

Open: *Tue–Fri 10–1 & 2–5, Sat 10–1 & 2–4, Sun 2–5. Closed Xmas & New Year's Eve.
Admission: *free.
⅖ (ground floor only) shop ⅟

ORDNANCE SURVEY
LEISURE GUIDE
ISLE OF WIGHT

Escape across the water to an island of contrasts and a slower pace of life. Walks, a round-the-island drive, places to stay PLUS detailed, large-scale Ordnance Survey maps. High chalk cliffs, sandy bays, bird-haunted mudflats and windswept coast – the Island, never remote but always apart, has drawn those who seek what Karl Marx called 'a little paradise'. Today's 'overners' from the mainland will find pretty villages, seaside resorts, manor houses, Victorian churches, lighthouses and even vineyards, all set in a varied landscape. All these are described and illustrated in a colourful gazetteer and in features written by local experts. Walks, a motor tour, a directory of practical information packed with useful addresses, and detailed Ordnance Survey maps complete this guide to a unique part of England.

Available at most AA Centres and good bookshops. £7.95 softback £9.95 hardback

SOUTHAMPTON, HAMPSHIRE   Southampton Hall of Aviation   Map 4 SU41

Discover the history of the Solent aircraft industry, including that of the legendary Spitfire, and see one of the last ever models to be produced. Visitors can actually board a four-engined Sandringham Flying Boat, and take a guided tour around its flight deck. Many other aircraft, models and engines are on show – a must for all prospective pilots!

☎(0703) 635830
Located: In Albert Road South.

Open: Tue–Sat 10–5 & Sun 12–5. Also open Bank Hol Mon & Mon during School Hols. Closed Xmas.
Admission: £1.40 (children 70p & senior citizens £1).
P. ⌨ ♿ (ground floor only) shop ✻

SOUTHEND-ON-SEA, ESSEX   Never Never Land   Map 5 TQ88

At Never, Never Land you'll enter a fantasy land peopled by cartoon-type animals and fairytale characters. You'll see your favourite television characters such as He-man and the Masters of the Universe, and Sindy's here, complete with stunning wardrobe. Entering through a cave, the whole two-acre complex is made up of tableaux magically illuminated by means of the latest technology and with stunning sound effects. Truly an 'out-of-this-world' experience.

☎(0703) 881352
Located: In the Shrubbery on the Esplanade.

Open: Apr–mid Nov daily from 10am, closing times varies according to season.
Admission: £1.50 children and senior citizens 50p. Family ticket £2.
⌨ ♿

TILFORD, SURREY   Old Kiln Agricultural Museum   Map 4 SU84

An insight into days gone by on the farm can be enjoyed here at the Old Kiln. As well as the farm implements and machinery there are examples of crafts and trades allied to farming. The attractive garden and woodland surroundings contain the larger exhibits, and old farm buildings house the Smithy and the wheelwright's shop.

☎Frensham (025125) 2300

Open: Apr–Sep, Wed–Sun & Bank Hols 11–6.
Admission: fee payable.
P. ⊼ ♿ shop

TITCHFIELD, HAMPSHIRE   Carron Row Farm Museum   Map 4 SU50

Once part of the grounds of nearby Titchfield Abbey this museum and grounds offer the family an enjoyable day out. Outside there is a small flock of St Kilda sheep, a narrow-gauge railway, fish ponds and a pets corner. On Sundays you can watch a parade of Shire horses and Shetland ponies. The museum and barn house a wide range of exhibits such as agricultural implements, carts, ploughs and rural craft tools. There is also a replica of a farm kitchen and a blacksmith's shop.

☎(0329) 43169 or 45102
Located: In Segensworth Rd.

Open: ✱Easter–Oct 10.30–5.30, (closed Mon & Tue in Apr, May & Oct except Bank Hols).
Admission: ✱£1.25 (children & senior citizens 75p).
P. ⌨ ⊼ shop

TWICKENHAM, GREATER LONDON   Rugby Football Union Tour   Map 4 TQ17

The very word 'Twickenham' evokes many a boyhood dream and the magical atmosphere of the big Rugby Football match days. A guided tour of the ground takes you behind the scenes to see changing and medical rooms, the famous double baths, kit displays and the collection of trophies in the Committee Rooms. A 15-minute film shows the build-up to a big match and some of Twickenham's greatest moments, whilst the museum traces the development of the RFU.

☎01-892 8161

Open: All year Mon–Fri. Tours 10.30 & 2.15. Closed week before internationals.
Admission: £1 (children & senior citizens 50p).
P. ♿ (ground floor only) shop

UPPER HAMBLE COUNTRY PARK, HAMPSHIRE   Map 4 SU41

This Country Park enjoys a peaceful location around the banks of the River Hamble. There are magnificent ancient woodlands and spectacular views of the river. Within the park is the Hampshire Farm Museum and the Queen Elizabeth II Jubilee Activities Centre for the Handicapped.

Located: ½ mile east of M27 Junction 8, & 1½ miles south-east Hedge End.

Open: all year.
P. (charge Apr–Sep) ⌶ ⼐ ⅋ shop

WADDESDON, BUCKINGHAMSHIRE   Waddesdon Manor   Map 4 SP71

A little bit of France in England – this Rennaissance-style château was built in 1874–89 for Baron Ferdinand de Rothschild. Inside, there is a wealth of French royal decorative art and some fine English 18th-century portraits. Children will enjoy the grounds complete with deer and aviary, as well as a play area.

☏Aylesbury (0296) 651282
Located: 6 miles north-west of Aylesbury off A41.

Open: late Mar–Oct. House: Wed–Sun 1–6 (closes 5pm weekdays in Mar, Apr & Oct). Grounds: Wed–Sat from 1pm (11.30am Sun). Good Fri & Bank Hol Mons, House & Grounds 11–6 (closed Wed after Bank Hol). Children under 10 not admitted to House.
Admission: House & grounds: £3 (children 10–17 £1.50): additional rooms extra £1 (children 10–17 50p). Grounds only: £1.50 (children 5–17 75p). Children under 5 admitted free.
P. ⌶ shop & produce stall
National Trust

WEMBLEY, GREATER LONDON   Wembley Stadium Tour   Map 4 TQ18

Aspiring World Cup players will thrill to the sights and sounds of Britain's number one stadium, home of the England football team, in a special fifteen-minute audio visual presentation. It will all seem possible too, as you walk up Players' Tunnel to the roar of the crowd, explore the dressing rooms, visit the Royal Box and gaze into the famous Wembley Trophy Cabinet, with its cups and medals dating back fifty years.

☏01-903 4864

Open: All year, daily (except Xmas Day, Boxing Day, New Year's Day & the day of an event). Tours on the hour 10–3, (4 in summer).
Admission: £2.50 (children under 5 free, chidren over 5 & senior citizens £1.50).
P. ⌶ ⅋ (by prior booking, limited access) shop ⅋

WEST WYCOMBE, BUCKINGHAMSHIRE   West Wycombe Caves   Map 4 SU89

Reputedly ancient in origin, the caves were extended in the 1750's and are said to have housed some of the meetings of the famous Hell-Fire Club. From a large flint forecourt half-way up West Wycombe Hill, a long winding passage leads past various small chambers – some transformed into colourful scenes by artificial stalagmites and stalactites, others containing life-size models of famous men associated with the area.

☏High Wycombe (0494) 24411

Open: Mar–Oct daily 11–6.
Admission: £2 (children & senior citizens £1).
P. ⌶ shop & garden centre ⅋

WEYHILL, HAMPSHIRE   Hawk Conservancy   Map 4 SU34

This specialist collection of birds of prey maintains a 'breed and release' programme for British species and also cares for and rehabilitates hundreds of injured birds each year. Hawks, eagles and falcons, trained by traditional methods, are flown daily (weather permitting), and the collection includes owls, vultures and kites.

☏(026477) 2252

Open: Mar–last Sun Oct daily; 10.30–4 Spring & Autumn; 10.30–5 Summer.
Admission: *£2 (children 3–15 £1, senior citizens £1.50).
P. ⌶ ⅋ (no special toilets) shop ⅋

WHIPSNADE, BEDFORDSHIRE　Whipsnade Zoo Park　Map 4 TL01

Over two hundred birds and animals are displayed in near natural surroundings in this famous 500-acre open-air zoo on the edge of the Chilterns. Attractions include the Children's Zoo, dolphin displays and a Discovery Centre, whilst birds of prey can be seen in flight during the summer months. Various special events will mark July, which is National Zoo Month. You can use your car inside the zoo, too (for an extra charge), or you might like to take a twenty-minute trip on the Roadtrain; there is also a steam railway running through the 'Asian Plains' during April and October.

☎(0582) 872171

Open: Mon–Sat 10–6, Sun & Bank Hol 10–7 or sunset. Birds of Prey displays May-Sep daily (except Fri).
Admission: *£3.20 (children under 5 free, 5–15 & senior citizens £1.60).
P. ⌂ ⊼ ㅅ (most areas) shop ✗

for WINCHESTER see opposite page　For WINDSOR see page 62

WINDSOR GREAT PARK, BERKSHIRE　Map 4 SU97

This lovely area of parkland and forest is a remnant from what was once a vast royal hunting preserve, but today its many varieties of deer have a more peaceful existence. Ancient oaks, among the oldest in the country, can be seen here. To the south is Virginia Water, a lovely lake with waterfowl and also within its boundaries are two delightful gardens. Savill Garden, near Egham, is a famous woodland garden, particularly lovely in the spring; Valley Gardens, near Virginia Water, cover 300 acres and are noted for rhododendrons, magnolias, camellias and other woodland trees and shrubs.

Location: extends south from Windsor to A329 at Virginia Water. The A332 Windsor – Bagshot road passes through park and has several parking places.

Open: Park always open; Savill Garden – daily (except 25–28 Dec) 10–6 (or sunset if earlier); Valley Gardens – daily 8–7.
Admission: Park free; Savill Garden £1.80, children under 16 free, senior citizens £1.60; Valley Gardens free, but charge for parking £1.50 (£2 Apr–May)

WISLEY, SURREY　Wisley Garden　Map 4 TQ05

This splendid garden of the Royal Horticultural Society shows every aspect of gardening at its best. Budding young gardeners and past masters will all learn a thing or two here, and there is an advisory service for specialist advice. But even if your only pleasure in a garden is looking at it – you won't be disappointed. The wooded slopes are massed with rhododendrons and azaleas, there are heathers of every hue and wild daffodils grow in an alpine meadow. There are also fruit and vegetable gardens and greenhouses.

☎Guildford (0483) 224163

Open: *all year, Mon–Sat 10–7 or dusk (4.30pm Jan, Nov & Dec), Sun 2–7 or dusk. Sun am members only. Closed 25 Dec. Glasshouses close at 4.15 or sunset Mon–Fri, 4.45 at weekends & Bank Hols.
Admission: fee payable.
P. ⌂ (licensed) ⊼ ㅅ shop & garden centre ✗

WITNEY, OXFORDSHIRE　Cogges Farm Museum　Map 4 SP31

This intriguing museum portrays the farming and country life of the Edwardian period. The Manor House has been restored to how it must have been some eighty years ago, complete with two working kitchens and a dairy, whilst flowers, fruit and vegetables of the period are grown in the enchanting walled garden. Within the surrounding farmyard and buildings demonstrations of farm machinery and tools, give the visitor a clear picture of farm life as it was in the early 20th century. Pigs, sheep, cattle and horses roam the fields nearby.

☎(0993) 72602
Located: At Cogges, ½ mile south-east of Witney off A4022.

Open: end Mar–early Nov, Tue–Sun 10.30-5.30, (4.30 Oct & Nov). Also open Bank Hol Mon.
Admission: *£1.50 (children, senior citizens & students 80p).
P. ⌂ ⊼ ㅅ shop

for WOBURN see page 64

The beautiful and ancient city of Winchester was once the administrative and religious capital of England, and although this particular honour was passed onto London many centuries ago, the city's historical importance is captured in its fine old buildings and many museums. At the very heart of Winchester is its majestic cathedral, while the medieval Castle Hall, Winchester College, and the old High Street dominated at one end by the medieval Westgate and at the other end by the mighty statue of King Alfred, also help set the city's historic tone. Today the High Street has been carefully transfomed into a delightful traffic-free shopping area in which large stores and small boutiques, eating houses and inns blend harmoniously. Winchester has many other attractions – there are lovely walks to be enjoyed in parks and gardens as well as alongside the River Itchen. There are two theatres which feature the best of professional and amateur dramatics and concerts are frequently held in the Guildhall, Cathedral, Great Hall and College.

☆ STAR ATTRACTIONS

Great Hall of Winchester Castle

The Great Hall is all that remains of Winchester Castle and is one of the finest medieval halls in the country. This was once the political, administrative and social centre of the castle where early parliaments were held and justice was administered. Dominating the hall is the legendary Round Table believed to be 700 years old. On the east wall of the hall is a 'family tree' of the knights of the shire between 1283 and 1868 while an imposing bronze statue of Queen Victoria, presides over the scene. Through a discreet doorway is the delightful Queen Eleanor's garden, opened in 1986 by HM the Queen Mother who described it as 'this fairy tale garden'.

☎ (0962) 841841
Located: Castle Avenue (off High Street).

Open: daily (except Good Fri & 25 & 26 Dec) 10–5 (4 Nov–Feb weekends).
Admission: free but contributions appreciated.
&. shop ✻

Winchester College

Winchester College offers visitors the chance to see round one of the oldest, most famous and still one of the best public schools in the country. The college was founded in 1382 by William of Wykeham (Bishop of Winchester from 1367 to 1404) who also founded New College, Oxford. Many of the college buildings date back to the 14th century and the chapel, chantry and cloisters are particularly lovely.

☎ (0962) 64242
Located: College Street.

Open: daily except Sun mornings. Guided tours during summer.
Admission: ✲£1 (children 75p).
&. (ground floor & grounds only) ✻

Farley Mount Country Park

Within this lovely country park are more than 1,000 acres of glassy slopes and woodland, overlooking the Test and Itchen Valleys, which provide superb walks and lovely picnic areas. The park has an interesting pyramid-shaped monument built in the late 18th century by a grateful rider who escaped unhurt after his horse had fallen into a 25ft deep chalk pit during a fox hunt. Farley Mount has a covered barbecue which can be booked for family or party entertainment and the park also offers an exciting programme of activities for children.

☎ (0962) 64221
Located: 3 miles west of Winchester on unclassified Sarum Road.

Open: daily.
P. ⊼

Symbols

☎	telephone number
P.	parking on the premises
⊐	refreshments available
⊼	picnic area
&.	accessible to wheelchair-bound visitors
✻	no dogs
✲	indicates 1987 details

Nine Centuries a Royal Home

Generations of kings and queens have spent much of their time at Windsor, ever since William the Conqueror chose this chalk ridge by the Thames, guarding the approach to London, as the site for a major castle. Subsequent monarchs have added to his work, and today Windsor boasts the biggest inhabited castle in the world. Around it has grown an attractive and busy little town which now attracts some three million visitors each year.

Accustomed to tourism on this scale, Windsor offers every assistance to sightseers. Guided tours are readily available on foot or by river, in an open-topped bus or – expensive but stylish – in a horse-drawn carriage. The 'sights' include not only the castle (where one could easily spend a full day) but also the Guildhall, completed in 1689 by Sir Christopher Wren, or the house in Church Street where Nell Gwynne lived. A stroll down from the Castle and across the Thames by Windsor Bridge brings you to Eton, home of the 500-year-old public school – and, today, of numerous antique shops.

☆ STAR ATTRACTIONS

Madame Tussaud's Royalty and Empire Exhibition
The latest audio-visual technology helps recapture the grander side of Queen Victoria's reign at this colourful exhibition in the original 19th-century station buildings. A full-size replica of the royal train and many waxwork figures are used in a reconstruction of the Diamond Jubilee celebrations. Other famous Victorian personalities are depicted in a special film show.

☎(0753) 857837
Located: Windsor and Eton Central Station, Thames Street.

Open: daily, winter 9.30–4.30, summer 9.30–5.30. Closed Xmas Day.
Admission: ✶£2.65 (children £1.85).
⌨ & (ground floor only) shop ✸

Windsor Castle
Perhaps the most popular visitor attraction is the State Apartments, a series of magnificent rooms, sumptuously furnished and hung with fine works of art. The rooms are still regularly used on royal occasions. A favourite with adults and children alike is Queen Mary's Dolls' House designed by Sir Edwin Lutyens as a gift to Queen Mary in 1924, the model measures 8ft by 5ft and is enchanting in its detail, which extends to monogrammed linen, leather-bound books in the library and working model cars in the garage. St George's Chapel is an architectural masterpiece; beneath its exquisite fan-vaulting lie buried ten monarchs including Henry VIII and Charles I, whose body was brought here secretly by his friends for burial. The changing of the guard ceremony takes place outside the castle at about 11am daily except Sundays.

☎(0753) 868286

Open: ✶*Castle Precincts* Open daily (except morning of 21 Apr and 16 June) from 10am. Closes 7.15 summer, 5.15 spring & autumn, 4.15 winter.
St George's Chapel Open weekdays 10.45–3.45, Sun 2–3.45. Closed 2–24 Jan, 20, 21 & 27 Apr, 13–17 Jun & Xmas. Can close other times at short notice.
State Apartments Open early Jan–early Mar; mid May–1 Jun; late Jun–early Dec from 10am. Closes 5 in summer, 3 in winter. Can close other times at short notice.
Queen Mary's Dolls House Open all year (except Xmas, New Year & Good Fri) Mon–Sat 10.30–5 (closes at 3 in winter). Also open Sun afternoons in summer.
Curfew Tower Tue–Sat 11–1 & 2–4.
All parts of the castle are always subject to closure, sometimes at very short notice.
Admission: Castle Precinct free. Admission charge for State Apartments, Queen Mary's Doll's House, Exhibition of Drawings, St George's Chapel & Curfew Tower.
& (Castle Precincts and St George's Chapel, and by prior arrangement in State Apartments, Queen Mary's Doll's House and Exhibition of Drawings) shop ✸

Windsor Safari Park and Seaworld
Many kinds of wild animal can be seen at close quarters at this 140-acre park. Visitors may drive through reserves where the larger animals roam; walk through woodland inhabited by deer and wallabies; or sit and watch performing dolphins, sealions and killer whales. There are also amusements, an adventure playground and a boating lake.

☎(0753) 869841
Located: South-west off town on B3022.

Open: daily from 10am. Closing times vary with season. Closed Xmas Day.
Admission: £5 (children £4).
P. ⌨ (licensed) 🍴 & Shop ✸ (free kennels provided)

Opening doors to the World of books

Book Tokens can be bought and exchanged at most bookshops

WOBURN, BEDFORDSHIRE   Woburn Abbey and Deer Park   Map 4 SP93

A splendid, palatial mansion, Woburn Abbey is one of the most famous stately homes in Britain. Its magnificent state apartments are filled with an abundance of fine furnishings and paintings. Browse around the Antiques Centre in the South Stable block, which houses forty individual shops each with its own authentic façade, and experience the atmosphere of a city street many years ago. Extensive grounds surround the Abbey, and it can be fun to try and recognise the various species of deer in the park. Visit the Chinese dairy which overlooks a pond with Chinese ducks, and watch the potter at work in the Pottery. Young visitors will enjoy the children's playground and pets' corner.

☎(0525) 290666

Open: **Abbey**, New Year's Day; Sat & Sun only Jan–Mar 11–4.45; daily Apr–Oct 11–5.45 (6.15pm Sun). Last admission 45 mins before closing time.
Deer Park, New Year's Day; Sat & Sun only Jan–Mar 10.30–3.45; daily Apr–Oct 10–4.45 (5.45 Sun).
Admission: ✳Abbey & Deer Park £3.50 (children £1.50 senior citizens £2.75). Family ticket £9–£11.
Deer Park only: car & passengers £2, motor cycles & passengers £1.
P. ☐ (licensed) & (park and gardens only) shop garden centre ✶ (in house except guide dogs)

WOBURN, BEDFORDSHIRE   Woburn Wild Animal Kingdom   Map 4 SP93

The Wild Animal Kingdom lies a short ride from Woburn Abbey, where visitors can go on safari and spot the lions, tigers, monkeys and numerous other species. Amusements galore are to be enjoyed at the Leisure Complex, especially the Elephant Display, Rainbow Ride, Pets Corner, Boating Lakes and Cabin Lifts.

☎(052525) 407

Open: mid Mar–Oct 10–5
Admission: ✳£4.50 (children £3 & senior citizens £3.50).
P. ☐ (licensed) & shop ✶

WOODSTOCK, OXFORDSHIRE   Blenheim Palace   Map 4 SP41

This palace is perhaps best known as the birthplace of Sir Winston Churchill, now buried in the village churchyard of Bladon on the southern edge of a park. The grounds were originally landscaped by Henry Wise and 'Capability' Brown. The palatial baroque mansion, started in 1705 by Vanbrugh for the first Duke of Marlborough, contains fine furniture, china and pictures; terraced water gardens are an attractive feature, and the grounds also contain a Butterfly House, plant centre and adventure playground.

☎(0993) 811325

Open: Palace & gardens mid Mar–Oct daily 10.30–6 (last admission 5).
Park all year 9–5.
Admission: ✳£3.90 (children 16 & 17 & senior citizens £2.90, children 5–15 £1.70, under 5 free).
P. ☐ & shops & garden centre.

WYCH CROSS, EAST SUSSEX   Ashdown Forest Farm   Map 5 TQ43

Rare and endangered breeds of farm animal are kept in a traditional setting in the heart of Ashdown Forest, showing visitors how farming used to be. There is also a collection of old farm machinery and implements.

☎Nutley (082571) 2040

Open: ✳ daily 11–6 or dusk (closed 25 Dec).
Admission: fee payable.
P. ☐ ⊼ & shop ✶

CHILDREN'S LONDON

'London is the most interesting, beautiful and wonderful city in the world to me' said the writer H G Wells in 1911. For any child, the excitement of exploring this great city for the first time must be one of the experiences of a lifetime. It is a huge city with a tremendous amount to offer, from pageantry to panoramas, from museums to markets, from palaces to parks. To make sure your family get the best out of it, you need to plan your expeditions carefully and in the pages that follow we have suggested a few of the most interesting areas for a day trip. But first, we remind you of the marvellous ceremonial events and sights which can offer a very special day out in London.

Details of opening times and charges for the places in our colour feature can be found on page 73. Other places to visit in London can be found on page 76.

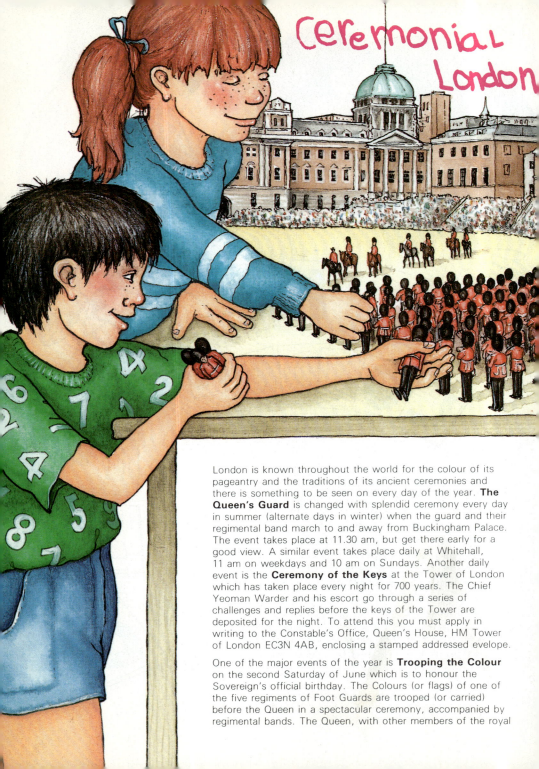

Ceremonial London

London is known throughout the world for the colour of its pageantry and the traditions of its ancient ceremonies and there is something to be seen on every day of the year. **The Queen's Guard** is changed with splendid ceremony every day in summer (alternate days in winter) when the guard and their regimental band march to and away from Buckingham Palace. The event takes place at 11.30 am, but get there early for a good view. A similar event takes place daily at Whitehall, 11 am on weekdays and 10 am on Sundays. Another daily event is the **Ceremony of the Keys** at the Tower of London which has taken place every night for 700 years. The Chief Yeoman Warder and his escort go through a series of challenges and replies before the keys of the Tower are deposited for the night. To attend this you must apply in writing to the Constable's Office, Queen's House, HM Tower of London EC3N 4AB, enclosing a stamped addressed evelope.

One of the major events of the year is **Trooping the Colour** on the second Saturday of June which is to honour the Sovereign's official birthday. The Colours (or flags) of one of the five regiments of Foot Guards are trooped (or carried) before the Queen in a spectacular ceremony, accompanied by regimental bands. The Queen, with other members of the royal family then returns to Buckingham Palace ahead of her marching Guards. A good place to see this with children is on the St James's Park side of the Mall. Tickets for seats on Horse Guards Parade are drawn by lot — write before 1st March to The Brigade Major (Trooping the Colour), Headquarters of the Household Division, Horse Guards, London SW1 2AX. Only two tickets can be obtained for each application, but if you will settle for a seat at a rehearsal on one of the two previous Saturdays you should state that in your letter.

The State Opening of Parliament in mid November is quite spectacular, when a royal procession travels from Buckingham Palace to the Palace of Westminster and back.

In late May and early June you might attend a performance of **Beating the Retreat** (with drums) or **Sounding the Retreat** (with bugles) on Horse Guards Parade — a reminder of the days when British garrisons abroad would call those outside the gates to return to the safety of the garrison at the end of the day. Tickets are available from the end of February from Premier Box Office, 1B Bridge Street, London SW1 (01-839 6815).

One more great pageant is the **Lord Mayor's Show** on the second Saturday in November. The Lord Mayor has ridden by coach to be 'shown' to the people since the 14th century and today he or she is accompanied by a terrific procession of floats and military bands. There is often a display of fireworks in the evening too.

Getting Around

Part of the fun of London is just travelling around and this is undoubtedly best done by public transport (telephone 01-222 1234 for information on London Regional Transport and special day tickets). If your time is limited, there are a number of non-stop panoramic bus tours which will take in most of the famous sights. There is also a regular daily Culture Bus which allows you to get off at any of twenty well chosen places, to continue your journey by a later bus using the same ticket (telephone 01-629 4999 for information). One of the new London sights is the developing Docklands area and this can now be seen from the Docklands Light Railway which, suspended above the ground for much of its route, gives you a splendid view. One of the most exciting ways of seeing London is from the River Thames and trips start and return to Westminster Bridge, Charing Cross Pier, Festival Pier, Tower Pier and Greenwich from about 10 in the morning every half hour until late afternoon. In the summer there are evening cruises too (telephone 01-730 4812 for information). If you like to explore on foot you might like to see the sights from the Silver Jubilee Walkway which stretches from Lambeth Bridge to the Tower of London and back along the other side of the river — a long way, but it can be tackled in short stretches. The route is marked by discs set into the pavement, or you can get an illustrated guide from tourist information outlets.

A Day out around the Tower

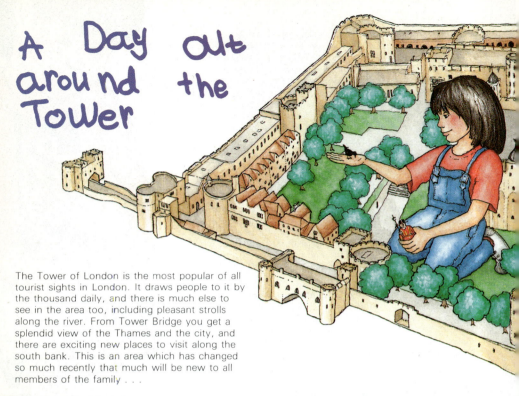

The Tower of London is the most popular of all tourist sights in London. It draws people to it by the thousand daily, and there is much else to see in the area too, including pleasant strolls along the river. From Tower Bridge you get a splendid view of the Thames and the city, and there are exciting new places to visit along the south bank. This is an area which has changed so much recently that much will be new to all members of the family . . .

The Tower of London

The Tower is one of the most important and best preserved castles in England. It was begun by William the Conqueror in 1078 to control the rebellious Londoners. Since then it has served as a royal palace, a mint, an arsenal, a menagerie, a public records office and a notorious state prison for those aristocrats who incurred the displeasure of the monarch. It now contains the Royal Armouries, including Henry VIII's huge suits of armour, and the Crown Jewels, displayed in the security of the new Jewel House. The world-famed 'beefeaters', or Yeoman Warders, in their splendid uniforms unchanged since Henry VIII's reign, guide one around the Tower, giving a very special flavour to the experience.

Tower Bridge

Five times a week Tower Bridge opens to let ships through; seven days a week it is open to the public. Inside you can learn about the bridge and its history, see the Victorian steam pumping engines which once opened the bridge and admire the terrific panorama from the glazed-in overhead walkways.

HMS Belfast

The last survivor of the Royal Navy's big gunships, the cruiser HMS Belfast is now a floating museum, moored in the Thames. You can explore the ship on a clearly explained route taking in the bridge, mess-rooms, engine rooms, galley and punishment cells and you can see special displays on D-Day (in which HMS Belfast led the naval bombardment) and other naval topics.

Schooner Kathleen and May

You can explore the last surviving three-masted topsail schooner which traded around the coast of Britain and learn about that trade and the history of this beautiful ship.

The London Dungeon

This is a blood-chilling exhibition of authentic medieval history and torture with life-size scenes of legends and kings, commoners and thieves, the tortures of the Tower and the Plague, with eerie sound and dramatic lighting effects. Not advised for the tender-hearted!

A Day out in Whitehall and St. James's

The area around Whitehall has been the centre of government for centuries: the Houses of Parliament, Westminster Abbey, where kings and queens are crowned and buried, government offices and, most importantly, the palace of the reigning monarch. The green expanse of St James's Park, with its lake with many waterfowl including the famous pelicans, makes a lovely place to walk, relax and picnic between visits. In summer there may be a band playing too.

Buckingham Palace

You cannot actually go into the palace, of course, but once you have watched the Changing of the Guard you could go around to the side and visit the Royal Mews. Here you will see the Queen's horses and the state coaches in which the royal family travel on great occasions. The Queen's Gallery in part of the palace is also open and here you can view selected paintings from the Royal Collection.

The Guards Museum

One of London's newest museums displays the history of the Queen's Regiments of Foot Guards, who you may have seen at their ceremonial duties during your day out.

Cabinet War Rooms

You can visit the underground accommodation designed to protect the Cabinet and Chiefs of Staff of the armed forces against air attacks in the Second World War. You see 19 rooms including the Cabinet Room, the Transatlantic Telephone Room, the Map Room, where information about operations on all fronts was collected, and the Prime Minister's Room — all of which remain much as they were then, even down to the 'utility' pencils and magazines of the day.

Westminster Abbey

In the architectural magnificence of this 13th — 16th-century building you can see the pageant of British history. There are the tombs of kings and queens and countless memorials to the great and famous. Henry VII, Queen Elizabeth I and Queen Mary I are all buried here. The Coronation Chair made for Edward I and used by all monarchs since is here. The poet Chaucer was buried in the Abbey and there are memorials in Poet's Corner to many well-loved authors, including Lewis Carroll of Alice in Wonderland fame. In the Cloisters are illuminated panels showing the stages in the construction of the Abbey and you can make your own brass rubbing here too. The Chapter House was used by England's parliament for three centuries.

Houses of Parliament

To visit the Palace of Westminster and Westminster Hall you have to make arrangements with your MP or a Peer. However, you can listen to a debate from the Strangers' Galleries either by joining the queue at St Stephen's entrance (sometimes the queue is very long, at other times surprisingly short) or by applying to your MP, a Peer or through your Embassy or High Commission.

A Day Out in Kensington

Exhibition Road in Kensington is just what it says: in it or very near to it are no less than four great national exhibitions or museums. Not so far away is Kensington Gardens, a splendid place to play and picnic, to visit the State Apartments in Kensington Palace or perhaps to go for a row on the Serpentine. All that may be more than enough for one day, but there is much else to do, so why not come again?

The Natural History Museum

Whether you want to see the vast Blue Whale, a tiny hummingbird or a gigantic dinosaur, this is the place — and there is much more besides. There are exhibitions about human biology, the origin of the species, British natural history and discovering mammals. A wide range of activity sheets will help you during your visit.

The Science Museum

Someone once calculated that, if you looked carefully at each exhibit, it would take you two years to get around the Science Museum! You can see a life-size model of the first landing on the moon, famous locomotives, cars and aircraft and new exhibitions in 'Launch Pad' — the hands-on technology experience with many exciting opportunities for exploring how and why things work. Another new exhibition is 'Exploration of Space' showing the development of space flight from the earliest Chinese gunpowder rockets to the age of the manned space satellite.

The Geological Museum

The national museum of earth science has age-old fossils, magnificent gem-stones, and even a piece of the Moon. The Story of Earth exhibition has some amazing displays and everyone will enjoy the simulated earthquake and erupting volcano.

The Victoria and Albert Museum

Among the varied exhibits concerned with the decorative arts, the renowned Costume Hall and the Oriental and European armour are likely to especially interest children. Seek out the enormous 16th-century Great Bed of Ware, and John Constable's paintings of the English landscape.

Kensington Palace

Set within Kensington Gardens, right by the Round Pond (with its water fowl and model sailing ships) is this Palace where the young Victoria was told she had become Queen. There is an exhibition of clothes worn at court, royal toys and pictures and furniture from the Royal Collection. You can wander through the rooms where royalty once lived — indeed, some members of the present royal family still have apartments here, and you may see one of them take off in their helicopter while you are there.

The Commonwealth Institute

You can see the whole world here! Each country in the Commonwealth has its own exhibition in this exciting modern building. There are also special exhibitions, music and story-telling sessions. This is a very special place for children, always throbbing with activity, and quiz sheets are available.

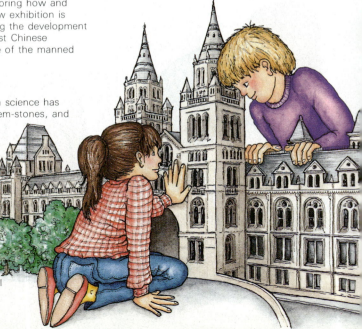

A Day out in Bloomsbury and Covent Garden

The British Museum is the greatest treasure house of the nation and, because it is free, you can plan to make several visits to enjoy its displays to the full. It is not far from Bloomsbury to the bustle and excitement of Covent Garden with its shops, cafes, market, street entertainment and museums.

The British Museum

Here you can find out about daily life in ancient Egypt, Greece, Rome and Roman Britain. You can see the stunning Elgin Marbles (the great stone relief carvings from the Parthenon in Athens), the treasures of the Sutton Hoo burial ship, two original copies of Magna Carta, splendid illuminated medieval manuscripts and the original Alice in Wonderland . . . the list seems almost endless. One visit can only give you a taste for more. A children's trail is available.

Pollock's Toy Museum

A small wonderland of Victorian toy theatres, peep-shows and optical toys. There are old dolls and dolls' houses too, and teddy bears, folk toys and board games, Cut-out theatres, miniatures and old-fashioned toys are on sale.

Unicorn Theatre for Children

The theatre has a varied programme of plays and shows for children from about 4 to 12 years old. There are school performances on week-end afternoons.

Covent Garden

There is so much to see and do in Covent Garden that you could spend a whole day just there. The old flower, fruit and vegetable market which made it famous have moved south of the Thames. New shops, cafes and activities have flooded in to fill the space. The streets around are full of interesting shops and craft and art galleries too. There are entertainers outside St Paul's Church and also at the other end of the market buildings. There is a craft market at weekends, antiques on Mondays and at Christmas time all the fun of the fair comes to Covent Garden with old fairground rides.

London Transport Museum

In the former Flower Market you can see exhibits of London's public transport from 1829 to the present day. There are horse-drawn omnibuses, trams, railway engines and rolling stock, exhibits on the new Dockland Light Railway and, of course, London's red buses. You can 'drive' a tram, a tube train and a bus and work points and signals in a full-size tube tunnel section. There are children's acitvity sheets.

Theatre Museum

One of London's newest museums, in which the story of the theatre, ballet and circus is told through stage models, costumes, puppets and in many other ways.

A Day out at the Centre of London

To many people the statue of Eros in Piccadilly Circus stands right at the centre of London. Not far away is another central point in Trafalgar Square, from where all distances from London are measured. This whole area is a busy and exciting place to spend a day, yet St James's Park is nearby for relaxation and a picnic.

The London Experience

Multi-screen audio-visuals with the latest sound and light technology bring you the story of London from earliest times to the present in this extraordinary show.

Light Fantastic World Centre of Holography

This is the largest exhibition of holography in the world, displaying those fascinating multi-dimensional pictures made by lasers — including the biggest hologram of all.

Guiness World of Records

Divided into six 'Worlds', this exhibition brings the world's records to life in a three-dimensional display of superlatives. Compare your weight with that of the world's heaviest man; see the greatest animal leaps; watch the exploration of space; match the world's tallest structures against London's skyline; select your own favourite sports records; hear the top-of-the pops of the past and see much else that is the biggest, the smallest, the fastest or the best.

Museum of Mankind

Devoted to the life and cultures of people around the world, the Museum of Mankind has marvellous exhibitions which are changed from time to time, so check to see what is on.

Recent exhibitions have included Bolivian Worlds, Madagascar, and The Living Arctic: Hunters of the Canadian North. Film shows are held on Tuesdays and Fridays and worksheets are available.

Trafalgar Square

Lord Nelson towers 185 feet above you on his column in the centre of the square, guarded by four huge lions. Other national worthies stand around the square. At Christmas time the tree given to Britain by the Norwegians is surrounded by carol singers each evening. You can feed the famous pigeons or have your own picnic in the square — which the pigeons will want to share!

The National Gallery

The national collection of masterpieces of European paintings from 1200 to 1900, many of them familiar to us all. Guided tours are available and there are special holiday events.

National Portrait Gallery

The portraits and photographs of the famous and infamous people of British history are beautifully displayed in this gallery. What did Henry VIII and his six wives look like? What did your favourite author look like? Here you will be able to find out. Sometimes a charge is made for special exhibitions.

Details of Places Featured in Children's London

HMS Belfast
☎01–407 6434
Located: Morgan's Lane, Tooley Street, SE1.
Underground: Tower Hill; Monument; London Bridge.
Open: All year daily (except Good Fri, May Day, Xmas & 1 Jan) 11–5.50 (closes 4.30 Nov–late Mar).
Admission: £3 (children £1.50).
Shop ⚹

British Museum
☎01–636 1555
Located: Great Russell Street WC1.
Underground: Tottenham Court Road; Goodge Street; Russell Square; Holborn
Open: All year daily (except Good Fri, May Day, Xmas & 1 Jan) 10–5, Sun 2.30–6.
Admission: Free, but occasional charge for special exhibitions.
⌨ (licensed) 占 shop ⚹ (except guide dogs)

Buckingham Palace
Queen's Gallery
☎01–930 4832 ext 321
Underground: Victoria; St James's Park.
Open: All year (except short periods between exhibitions) Tue–Sat & Bank Hol Mons 10.30–5, Sun 2–5.
Admission: £1.20 (children 50p).
占 (ground floor only) shop ⚹
Royal Mews
☎01–930 4832 ext 634
Underground: Victoria; St James's Park.
Open: Wed & Thu 2–4 (except Royal Ascot Week) and at other times when published.
Admission: 40p (children 20p).
占 (ground floor only) shop ⚹ (except guide dogs)

Cabinet War Rooms
☎01–930 6961
Located: Clive Steps, King Charles Street, SW1.
Underground: Victoria, St James's Park.
Open: Daily (except Mon in winter, Good Fri, May Day, Xmas & 1 Jan) 10.30–5.15.
Admission: £2.80 (children £1.50).
占 shop ⚹ (except guide dogs)

Commonwealth Institute
☎01–603 4535
Located: Kensington High Street, W8.
Underground: High Street Kensington.
Open: Daily (except Good Fri, May Day, Xmas & 1 Jan) Mon–Sat 10–5.30, Sun 2–5.

Admission: Free
P. ⌨ (licensed) 占 shop ⚹ (except guide dogs)

Geological Museum
☎01–589 3444 (due to change during currency of this guide).
Located: Exhibition Road, SW7.
Underground: South Kensington.
Open: All year (except Good Fri, May Day, Xmas & 1 Jan), Mon–Sat 10–6, Sun 1–6.
Admission: £1 (children 50p).
⌨ 占 (except mezzanine floor) shop ⚹ (except guide dogs)

Guards Museum
☎01–930 4466
Located: Wellington Barracks, SW1.
Underground: St James's Park.
Open: Due to open in February 1988. Details of times and admission charges not available at time of going to press.

Guinness World of Records
☎01–439 7331
Located: The Trocadero Centre, Piccadilly Circus, W1.
Underground: Piccadilly Circus.
Open: Daily 10am–11pm (closes at 10.30pm on Sun).
Admission: £3.35 (children £2).
占 shop ⚹ (except guide dogs)

Houses of Parliament
☎01–219 3090 & 3100
Underground: Westminster.
Open: For Strangers' Galleries join queue at St Stephens entrance House of Commons: from approx 4.30pm Mon–Thu, 9.30 Fri; House of Lords: from approx 2.30pm Tue, Wed & some Mons, 3pm Thu, 11am Fri or by arrangement with MP for House of Commons or Peer for House of Lords.
Admission: Free, although guides require payment if employed.
占 (by arrangement) ⚹ (except guide dogs)

Kensington Palace
☎01–937 9561
Located: The Broad Walk, Kensington Gardens, W8.
Underground: Queensway; Bayswater; High Street Kensington.
Open: All year daily (except Good Fri, Xmas & 1 Jan) Mon–Sat 9–5, Sun 1–5. →

Admission: ✱£2.50 (children £1.50).
♿ (ground floor only) shop ✹

Light Fantastic World Centre for Holography
☎01–734 4516
Located: The Trocadero Centre, Coventry Street, W1.
Underground: Piccadilly Circus; Leicester Square.
Open: Daily Mon–Wed 10–6, Thu & Fri 10–8, Sat 10–7, Sun 11–6.
Admission: £1 (children 50p).

London Dungeon
☎01–403 0606
Located: 28–34 Tooley Street, SE1.
Underground: Tower Hill; Monument; London Bridge.
Open: All year daily (except Xmas) 10–5.30 (closes 4.30 Oct–Mar).
Admission: £3.50 (children £2) (due for revision in June).
🍴 ♿ shop ✹

London Experience
☎01–439 4938 or 01–734 0555
Located: The Trocadero Centre, Coventry Street, W1.
Underground: Piccadilly Circus; Leicester Square.
Open: Daily 10.20–8.20 with continuous 40 minute performances.
Admission: £2.50 (children £2).

London Transport Museum
☎01–379 6344
Located: The Piazza, Covent Garden WC2.
Underground: Covent Garden; Leicester Square; Charing Cross.
Open: Daily (except Xmas) 10–6.
Admission: ✱£2.40 (children £1.10). Family ticket £5.50.
🍴 ♿ shop ✹ (except guide dogs)

Museum of Mankind
☎01–437 2224 ext 43
Located: 6 Burlington Gardens, W1.
Underground: Piccadilly; Green Park.
Open: All year daily (except Good Fri, May Day, Xmas & 1 Jan) Mon–Sat 10–5, Sun 2.30–6.
Admission: Free.
♿ shop ✹ (except guide dogs)

National Gallery
☎01–839 3321 (01–839 3526 for recorded information)
Located: Trafalgar Square, WC2.
Underground: Charing Cross; Embankment; Leicester Square.
Open: All year daily (except Good Fri, May Day, Xmas & 1 Jan) Mon–Sat 10–6, Sun 2–6.
Admission: Free.
🍴 (licensed) ♿ shop ✹

National Portrait Gallery
☎01–930 1552
Located: 2 St Martin's Place, WC2
Underground: Charing Cross; Embankment; Leicester Square.
Open: All year daily (except Good Fri, May Day, Xmas & 1 Jan) Mon–Fri 10–5, Sat 10–6, Sun 2–6.
Admission: Free, but charge made for special exhibitions.

Natural History Museum
☎01–589 6323 ext 595 (due to change during the currency of this guide).
Located: Cromwell Road, SW7.
Underground: South Kensington.
Open: All year daily (except Good Fri, May Day, Xmas & 1 Jan) Mon–Sat 10–6, Sun 2.30–6.
Admission: £2 (children £1).
🍴 ♿ (most parts) shop ✹ (except guide dogs)

Pollock's Toy Museum
☎01–636 3452
Located: 1 Scala Street, W1.
Underground: Goodge Street; Tottenham Court Road.
Open: Mon–Sat 10–5 (closed Xmas).
Admission: ✱60p (children 30p).
shop ✹

Schooner Kathleen & May
☎01–403 3965
Located: St Mary Overy Dock, Cathedral Street, SE1.
Underground: Tower Hill; Monument; London Bridge.
Open: Daily (except Xmas & New Year) 10–5 (11–4 Nov–Mar and all weekends).
Admission: £1 (children 50p). Family ticket £2.50.
shop ✹

Science Museum
☎01–589 3456 ext 632
Located: Exhibition Road, SW7.
Underground: South Kensington.
Open: All year daily (except Good Fri, May Day, Xmas, & 1 Jan) Mon–Sat 10–6, Sun 2.30–6.
Admission: Free.
🍴 ♿ shop ✹

Theatre Museum
☎01–836 7891
Located: Russell Street, Covent Garden, WC2.

Underground: Covent Garden; Leicester Square; Charing Cross.
Open: Tue–Sun 11–7 (closed Good Fri, Xmas & 1 Jan).
Admission: £2.25 (children £1.25).

Tower Bridge
☎01–407 0922
Underground: Tower Hill; London Bridge.
Open: All year daily (except Good Fri, Xmas & 1 Jan) 10–5.45 (closes at 4pm Nov–Mar).
Admission: £2 (children £1).
& shop ✱

HM Tower of London
☎01–709 0765
Located: Tower Hill, EC3
Underground: Tower Hill; London Bridge SE1.
Open: All year (except Good Fri, Xmas & 1 Jan; Jewel House closed in Feb) Mon–Sat 9.30–5 (4 Nov–Feb), Sun 2–5 (Mar–Oct only).
Admission: ✱£4 (children £2).

Unicorn Theatre for Children
☎01–836 3334
Located: 6 Great Newport Street, WC2.

Underground: Leicester Square.
Open: Public performances Sat & Sun 2.30.
Admission: Prices on application.

Victoria and Albert Museum
☎01–589 6371 ext 372 (01–581 4894 for recorded information)
Located: Cromwell Road, SW7.
Underground: South Kensington.
Open: All year daily (except Good Fri, May Day, Xmas & 1 Jan) 10–5.50, Sun 2.30–5.50.
Admission: By donation – suggested £2, (children under 12 50p).
🍴 (licensed) & shop ✱

Westminster Abbey
☎01–222 5152
Located: Broad Sanctuary, SW1.
Underground: St James's Park.
Open: Nave & Cloisters daily 9–4 (7.45 Wed) Royal Chapels, Poet's Corner, Choir & Statesmen's Aisle Mon–Fri 9–4, Sat 9–2 & 3.45–5.
Admission: Nave & Cloisters free; Royal Chapels, Poet's Corner, Choir & Statesmen's Aisle £1.60 (children 40p).

GUIDE TO
NATIONAL TRUST
PROPERTIES IN BRITAIN

Hundreds of castles and historic houses; breathtaking gardens and parks; spectacular tracts of unspoilt countryside and coastline. The fascinating stories of all these places are told in this guide and there are nearly 200 specially commissioned photographs. Detailed maps show the locations of every property.

FURTHER PLACES TO VISIT IN LONDON

The highlights of London for children have been featured in the colour pages beginning on page 65. Here we list a further selection of places to visit within the capital which are ideal for a family day out. A London Underground Map to help you plan your travel around the city can be found on page 80.

Bethnal Green Museum of Childhood

If your children have ever wondered what there was to play with before 'Masters of the Universe' and 'Transformers' were invented, then take them along to this delightful museum. A branch of the Victoria and Albert Museum, it contains an important collection of old toys, dolls, puppets, model soliders, games etc. There is also a children's costume section and a display of Wedding Dresses and Spitalfields Silk.

☎01-980 2415
Located: Cambridge Heath Road, E2.

Underground: Bethnal Green, Whitchapel.
Open: Mon–Thu & Sat 10–6, Sun 2.30–6 (Closed May Day, Spring Bank Hol, Xmas and 1 Jan).
Admission: free.
P. & (by prior arrangement) shop ✗ (except guide dogs)

Greenwich Maritime Exhibits

The National Maritime Museum, in a magnificent setting, has boats and barges, paintings, models, uniforms and much else to do with the sea, including displays of naval battles, voyages of discovery and special film shows. The museum includes the Old Royal Observatory where you can stand astride the original Greenwich Meridian and see the largest refractive telescope in the UK. Nearby, on the river is the Cutty Sark Clipper Ship which was launched in 1869 and was built for speed. She was, indeed, a world beater and you can walk around her and see in her holds the displays on her history, together with a fine collection of old ships' figureheads. Another historic craft at Greenwich is the tiny Gipsy Moth IV, in which Sir Francis Chichester made history in 1966 by sailing around the world single handed.

☎01-858 4422 ext 221 (Maritime Museum), 01-858 3445 (Cutty Sark and Gipsy Moth IV)
Located: Greenwich Pier/Romney Road, SE10

Getting there: Train to Maze Hill; by boat from Westminster, Charing Cross, Festival or Tower Piers; by Docklands Light Railway to Island Gardens, then through Greenwich Foot Tunnel.
Open: all year daily (except Good Fri, May Day, Xmas & 1 Jan) Mon–Sat 10–6, Sun 2–6 (closes 5 in winter) Gipsy Moth and Cutty Sark open 12 on Sun.
Admission: National Maritime Museum & Observatory £2.20 (children £1.10); Cutty Sark £1.20 (children 60p); Gipsy Moth IV 20p (children 10p).
🖵 (at Maritime Museum) ✗ (guide dogs allowed at Maritime Museum & Observatory)

Imperial War Museum

Founded in 1917 and established by act of Parliament in 1920, this museum illustrates and records all aspects of the two World Wars and other military operations involving Britain and the Commonwealth since 1914. An extremely varied collection of exhibits is on display, ranging from tanks and aeroplanes to weapons and uniforms, as well as paintings by official war artists.

☎01-735 8922
Located: Lambeth Road, SE1.

Underground: Lambeth North.
Open: all year daily (except Good Fri, May Day, Xmas & 1 Jan) Mon–Sat 10–5.50, Sun 2–5.50.
Admission: free.
& shop ✗ (except guide dogs)

London Planetarium

Part of the same complex as Madame Tussaud's is the exciting armchair space spectacular in which representations of the heavens are projected onto a giant copper dome with an accompanying commentary. Special sound and light effects highlight the work of great scientists with three-dimensional displays in the Astonomers Gallery. In the evenings the dome becomes the Laserium and there are rock concerts with pulsating accompanying laser images in Europe's only laser concert.

☎01-486 1121 (Laserium 01-486 2242)
Located: Marylebone Road, NW1.

Underground: Baker Street.
Open: all year daily (except Xmas Day) 11–4.30
Admission: Planetarium £2.50 (children £1.60) (no children under 5); Laserium £3.75 (children £2.75).
🗗 shop ✳

London Toy and Model Museum

This lively museum is always buzzing with the excited chatter of children, while their parents and grandparents unashamedly indulge in nostalgia for the toys of the past. The collections here are huge: thousands of model soldiers lined up in their regiments; hundreds of trains, cars and boats; dolls houses furnished and fitted out with miniature antiques; games, teddy bears and much more. Outside there is a large garden where youngsters can let off steam in the full-size playbus or on the garden railway while their adult companions can take refreshment on the patio.

☎01-262 9450/7905
Located: 21–23 Craven Hill, W2

Underground: Queensway, Bayswater, Lancaster Gate.
Open: all year daily (except Xmas Day, 1 Jan & Mon, but open Bank Hol Mon) Tue–Sat 10–5.30, Sun & Bank Hol Mon 11–5.30.
Admission: £2.20 (children 80p). Family ticket (2 + 2) £5.
🗗 ♿ (ground floor & gardens only) shop ✳

London Zoo

More than 8,000 animals live in the zoo. They range from boas to bush-babies, pandas to penguins, and from the entertaining apes and monkeys to the huge elephants and tall, elegant giraffes. In summer there are camel, pony and donkey rides, or trips in a pony- or llama-drawn cart. You can attend the elephant's bath, meet the animals at their afternoon show and watch flying demonstrations of the bird of prey. Feeding times are 3.30 – 4.15 in summer, an hour earlier in winter, and there is a special feed for snakes, alligators and lizards in the Reptile House on Fridays.

☎01-722 3333
Located: in Regents Park, NW1.

Underground: Camden Town.
Open: Mon–Sat 9–6 (10–dusk in winter), Sun in summer 9–7 (closed Xmas Day)
Admission: £3.90 (children £2).
🗗 (licensed) ⴷ ♿ (ground floor & gardens only) shop ✳

Madame Tussaud's

Mingle with the Royal Family, your favourite pop or football star, the Prime Minister or famous historical figures in this world-famous waxwork exhibition. Visit the gruesome Chamber of Horrors if you have the nerve! Madame Tussard's is very popular, so you may have to queue to get in.

☎01-935 6861
Located: Marylebone Road, NW1.

Underground: Baker Street.
Open: all year (except Xmas Day) 10–5.30.
Admission: £4.30 (children £2.80).
🗗 shop ✳

Symbols
☎   telephone number
P.   parking on the premises
🗗   refreshments available
ⴷ   picnic area
♿   accessible to wheelchair-bound visitors
✳   no dogs
✱   indicates 1987 details

The Monument

Splendid views over the City can be obtained from the top of this famous landmark. It was designed by Sir Christopher Wren and Robert Hooke to commemorate the Great Fire of London which devastated the City in 1666 and was erected between 1671 and 1677. Its height of 202ft is said to equal the distance from its base to the place in Pudding Lane where the fire started, destroying nearly 90 churches and 13,000 houses. A climb of 311 steps will take you to the railed-in summit.

☎01-626 2717
Located: Monument Street, EC3.

Underground: Monument.
Open: all year, Apr–Sep Mon–Fri 9–6, Sat & Sun 2–6; Oct–Mar Mon–Sat 9–2 & 3–4.
Admission: fee payable.
⚥

Museum of London

Here you can learn about the history of London from prehistoric times right up to the present day. There are displays showing the various periods: Roman London, Medieval London, London of the Tudors and Stuarts, with a model of the Great Fire, Georgian London and an 18th-century prison cell, Victorian and 20th-century London. The Lord Mayor's coach is there and there are also special changing exhibitions. Children's quizzes are available and there are extra activities in the school holidays.

☎01-600 3699 ext 240
Located: London Wall, EC2.

Underground: St Paul's; Moorgate; Barbican (closed Sun).
Open: all year (except Bank Hols) Tue–Sat 10–6, Sun 2–6.
Admission: free.
⌑ (licensed) & shop ⚥ (except guide dogs)

National Army Museum

Exhibits here are displayed in chronological order from 1485 onwards, relating the history of the British Indian and Colonial forces. There are uniforms, weapons, prints, photographs, letters, glass and silver and mementoes of British soldiers. There is a special display of the orders and decorations of the Duke of Windsor and also those of five great Field Marshals – Lord Roberts, Gough, Kitchener and Wolseley and Sir George White VC. The picture gallery includes portraits by Beechy, Romney and Lawrence and battle scenes.

☎01-730 0717
Located: Royal Hospital Road, SW3.

Underground: Sloane Square.
Open: all year daily (except Good Fri, May Day, Xmas & 1 Jan) 10–5.30, Sun 2–5.30).
Admission: free.
⌑ & shop ⚥

Royal Air Force Museum

All aspects of RAF history are covered here in twelve galleries, but it is, of course, the planes which attract most attention. There are examples of aircraft from the early pioneering days of the Bleriot XI to the impressive 'Lightning'; the adjacent Battle of Britain Museum has British, German and Italian aircraft which took part in the great air battle of 1940; the vast new Bomber Command Museum contains such famous aircraft as the Lancaster, Wellington and Vulcan bombers.

☎01-205 2266 ext 38
Located: at Hendon Airfield NW9. Entrance via M1, A41 (Aerodrome Road, off Watford Way) or A5 (Colindale Avenue, off Edgware Road).

Underground: Colindale.
Open: All year (except Good Fri, May Day, Xmas & 1 Jan) Mon–Sat 10–6, Sun 2–6.
Admission: ✳RAF Museum free; Battle of Britain Museum £1 (children 50p); Bomber Command Museum £1 (children 50p).
P. ⌑ (licensed) ⟊ & shop ⚥

St Paul's Cathedral

St Paul's is the third largest Christian church in the world. The Great Fire of London destroyed the old cathedral in 1666 and Sir Christopher Wren's masterpiece arose from the ashes between 1675 and 1710. In the magnificent Dome is the Whispering Gallery where, if you whisper against one wall, your message can be heard at the other side of the gallery. There is a fantastic view from the Dome. In the Crypt are the tombs of the cathedral's architect, Wren, and the great admiral, Lord Nelson.

☎**01-248 2705**

Underground: St Paul's.
Open: all year 8–6, except Sun which is open for worship only. Tourist office, Mon–Fri 10.45–6, Sat 11–4.15.
Admission: donation.

Thames Barrier and Visitor Centre

The Thames Barrier is one of London's newest landmarks, not only an imposing sight but also a remarkable feat of engineering. It was contructed to avert a very real danger of flooding in the captial and has ten massive steel gates mounted between nine concrete piers. The gates are tested every month. The visitor centre, just 300 metres downstrem, employs equally modern technology to explain what the barrier does and why it was built.

☎**01-854 1373**
Located: Visitor Centre, Unity Way SE18.

Train: to Charlton.
Open: daily (except Xmas & 1 Jan) 10.30–5 (5.30 weekends).
Admission: price on application.
P. (charge) ⌑ ☍ & (except riverside) shop
⚡ (except guide dogs)

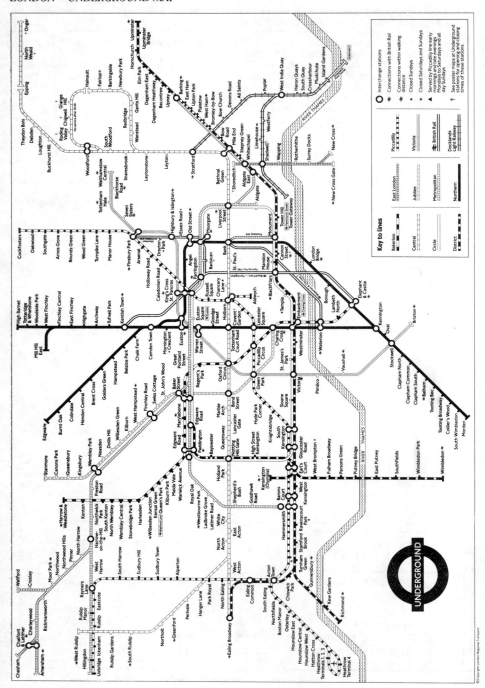

Central England and East Anglia

Stretching from the wide, flat lands bordering the North Sea, through the rolling shires and the industrial heart of England, and west to the wild Welsh Marches, this is an area of enormous diversity.

East Anglia, Lincoln and the Fenlands still retain a sense of rural timelessness. Their landmarks are the spacious 'wool' churches of Suffolk, the amazing man-made waterways of the Norfolk Broads and the splendours of the university town of Cambridge. In spring the bulb fields of Lincoln challenge those of Holland.

From these remoter lands we move to the heart of England: the rolling country of the shires and to Shakespeare country and his birthplace at Stratford-upon-Avon. Industry dominates the Midlands and Birmingham but not far away is the marvellous strong, wild country of the Peak District of Derbyshire and the moorlands of Staffordshire. In much of this area the natural beauty of the countryside is dotted with splendid examples of our industrial heritage which we have now come to value and admire.

Then we come again to an area which is steeped in the past, the lovely black-and-white town of Ludlow and the hillside town of Shrewsbury and the land rising to the Welsh borders.

ACTON SCOTT, SHROPSHIRE   Acton Scott Working Farm Museum   Map 7 SQ48

This unusual working farm still employs methods used at the turn of the century. Work is carried out by horse or by hand and you'll see some rare breeds of farm animal too. You're more than welcome to 'muck-in' with some farm work, while the less enthusiastic might be content to watch the cider making or craft demonstrations.

☎**Marshbrook (06946) 306/7**
Located: At Wenlock Lodge, 3 miles south of Church Stretton, off A49.

Open: Apr–Oct, Mon–Sat 10–5, Sun & Bank Hols 10–6.
Admission: ✱Apr–May & Sep–Oct £1.20 (children & senior citizens 60p); Jun–Aug & Bank Hols £1.50 (children & senior citizens 75p).
P. ⌷ 🛆 ᕳ (ground floor only) shop ✻

ALTON, STAFFORDSHIRE   Alton Towers   Map 7 SK04

Alton Towers celebrates its Diamond Jubilee in 1988, and the occasion is to be marked by a succession of special events throughout the year. The leading European leisure park, it boasts over a hundred attractions – among which are some of the world's most exciting rides and shows. Visitors can also enjoy the magnificence of what was once the estate of the Earls of Shrewsbury, exploring the famous ruins and wandering through gardens which are reputed to be among the best in Europe, with their magnificent Pagoda Fountain, Chinese Temple and Rock Gardens.

☎**Oakamoor (0538) 702200**

Open: late Mar–early Nov. Attractions 10–5, 6 or 7pm. Park closes 1 hour after attractions close.
Admission: ✱£5.99 (children under 4 free, senior citizens £1.99).
P. ⌷ 🛆 ᕳ shops

BANHAM, NORFOLK   Banham Zoo and Monkey Sanctuary   Map 5 TM08

Conservation is the keyword here. Set amid 20 acres of parkland and gardens Banham Zoo specializes in rare and endangered species and has a notable collection of monkeys and apes. Other animals and birds to be seen here include snow leopards, black panthers, otters, maned wolves, camels, macaws and flamingoes. July of each year is National Zoo Month when many extra activities are planned.

☎**Quidenham (095387) 476**
Located: In the Grove.

Open: all year; 10–6.30 (or dusk if earlier).
Admission: £2.50 (£1.50 Sat), children £1.50 (£1 Sat). Senior citizens £2 (£1.50 Sat), children under 4 free.
P. ⌷ (licensed) 🛆 ᕳ shop & garden centre ✻

BELTON, LINCOLNSHIRE   Belton House, Park and Gardens   Map 8 SK93

This splendid mansion, built between 1684 and 1688, houses a fine collection of paintings, furniture, oriental porcelain and tapestries. Speaker Cust's silver and the Brownlow family's silver gilt collection are on display, as are unique mementoes of the Duke of Windsor. The house is set in 1,000 acres of rolling parkland which includes Belmount Tower and has 19th-century formal gardens with an orangery. An extensive adventure playground and attrative riverside picnic area are provided for visitors, and boat trips and miniature railway rides are available in the summer.

☎**Grantham (0476) 66116**
Located: On A607, close to A1.

Open: Apr–Oct Wed–Sun & Bank Hol Mon (closed Good Fri). House 1–5.30 (last admission 5). Grounds 11–5.30.
Admission: £2.60 (children £1.30).
⌷ shop
National Trust

Symbols	
☎	telephone number
P.	parking on the premises
⌷	refreshments available
🛆	picnic area
ᕳ	accessible to wheelchair-bound visitors
✻	no dogs
✱	indicates 1987 details

BELVOIR, LEICESTERSHIRE   Belvoir Castle   Map 8 SK83

Belvoir Castle, home of the Duke and Duchess of Rutland, is
a building of fairy-tale proportions, with towers, turrets and
battlements. Housing many notable art treasures, it stands in
lovely grounds overlooking the picturesque Vale of Belvoir.
Apart from these obvious attractions there are many special
events throughout the year to interest the family, from
Medieval Jousting to a Teddy Bears' Picnic.

☎Grantham (0476) 870262
Located: Between A52 & A607

Open: mid Mar–beginning Oct Tue–Thu &
Sat 12–6, Sun 12–7, Bank Hol Mon only 11–
7; Oct, Sun only 12–6. Last admission ¾ hr
before closing time.
Admission: £2.50 (children £1.40).
P. ⌂ ⴲ ⅋ (no disabled toilet) shop & garden
centre ✻ (except guide dogs)

BEWDLEY, HEREFORD AND WORCESTER, Severn Valley Railway – See BRIDGNORTH

BEWDLEY, HEREFORD AND WORCESTER
West Midland Safari and Leisure Park   Map 7 SO77

This 200-acre park contains over forty species of wildlife,
whilst an exciting amusement area offers a multitude of
attractions. These range from Pets Corner and the Sea Lion
Show to fantastic rides such as the Cobra and Big Apple
Rollercoasters, the Rio Grande Railway, the Mississippi
Paddle Cruiser, or the Pirate Ship – all designed to keep the
family enthralled all day.

☎(0299) 402114 or 402631
**Located: At Spring Grove, on A456
between Bewdley and Kidderminster**

Open: Apr–Oct daily 10–5.
Admission: ✱£5.50 (children 4–16 & senior
citizens £4.50, children under 4 free).
P. ⌂ (licensed) ⴲ ⅋ shop & garden centre
✻ (in reserves – kennels provided)

BIRMINGHAM, WEST MIDLANDS   Birmingham Nature Centre   Map 7 SP08

Here a series of indoor and outdoor enclosures house a range
of British and European animals in conditions which simulate,
as near as possible, their natural habitat, and which also attract
wild birds and butterflies to the area.

☎021-472 7775
**Located: In Pershore Road, Edgbaston,
at south-west entrance to Cannon Hill
Park, opposite Pebble Mill Road.**

Open: mid Mar–Oct daily 10–5.
Admission: free.
P. ⴲ ⅋ shop ✻ (except guide dogs)

BIRMINGHAM, WEST MIDLANDS   Birmingham Railway Museum   Map 7 SP08

This working railway museum now has twelve steam locomotives and a workshop fully equipped to deal with their
problems and to keep its thirty-six carriages, wagons and other
vehicles – many of which are of historic interest – in a good
state of repair. Steam-hauled rides are available on certain
days.

☎021-707 4696
Located: 670 Warwick Road, Tyseley

Open: ✱daily (except Xmas & New Year) 10–
5. Steam events first sun in month & Bank
Hol Mon. Apr–Dec.
Admission: fee payable.
P. ⌂ ⅋ (grounds & ground floor only) shop ✻

BIRMINGHAM, WEST MIDLANDS   Museum of Science and Industry   Map 7 SP08

Exhibits here trace the growth of industry and science from
the Industrial Revolution to the present day. The Engineering
Hall, once a Victorian plating works, displays machine tools,
electrical equipment and working engines powered by steam,
gas and hot air, whilst the James Watt Building contains the
oldest working steam engine in the world, dated 1779. The
aircraft section includes a World War II Spitfire and Hurricane, together with a collection of aircraft engines. There are
also transport and science sections and a Music Room and Pen
Room.

☎021-236 1022
**Located: In Newhall St, close to the Post
Office Tower.**

Open: all year except Xmas & New Year's
Day; Mon–Sat 9.30–5 & Sun 2–5.
Admission: free.
⅋ shop ✻ (except guide dogs)

BRADGATE PARK & SWITHLAND WOOD ESTATE, LEICESTERSHIRE Map 8 SK51

Herds of red and fallow deer wander through Bradgate Park's 850 acres of natural parkland, with its rocky hills, woods, heath, bracken and moorland offering many pleasant walks and picnics. The Park also contains the ruins of Bradgate House, home of Lady Grey, and the Old John Tower, built in 1786. Swithland Wood covers some 140 acres of ancient woodland – mainly oaks, birches and limes, which once contained a prosperous slate quarrying industry.

☏Leicester (0533) 871313 ext 492 (The Ranger)
Located: 6½ miles north-east of Leicester, off B5327.

Open: Park daily to pedestrians during daylight hours. Ruins Apr–Oct Wed, Thu & Sat 2.30–5, Sun 10–12.30. Registered disabled or permit holders issued by Bradgate Park Trust may drive through the park Apr–Oct Thu 2.30–7.30 & Sun 9–11am.
Admission: Free. Car parks 20p.
P. (3 car parks adjoining Bradgate Park, 2 adjoining Swithland Wood) ⛼ ♿ (except grass paths) shop

BRESSINGHAM, NORFOLK Bressingham Live Steam Museum Map 5 TM07

A footplate ride on a standard gauge locomotive could make a dream come true! So take a steam-hauled ride on a 9½-inch, 15-inch or 2-ft gauge train through the wooded Waveney Valley or around Europe's largest hardy plant nursery. There's an exhibition hall here too, steam roundabout, forty road and rail engines, plus six acres of informal gardens to discover.

☏(037988) 386
Located: On A1066 near Diss

Open: Museum only, Easter Sun & Mon plus Suns in Apr. Museum & gardens Bank Hol Mon & Sun from May–late Sep; Thu from Jun–early Sep; also Weds in Aug.
Admission: *£1.50 (children 80p, senior citizens £1.20).
P. ☕ ⛼ ♿ shop & garden centre

BRIDGNORTH, SHROPSHIRE Midland Motor Museum Map 7 SO79

An exciting collection of over ninety sports and racing cars, and racing motor cycles, illustrate vividly the development of these vehicles from the 1920's to the present day, are housed in the converted stable here at Stanmore Hall. You can also follow a nature trail through the beautiful grounds of the Hall, which also has its own camping park. A National Jaguar Owners Club meeting will take place here on 12 June 1988.

☏(0746) 761761
Located: At Stanmore Hall, 1½ miles from Bridgnorth on A458 Stourbridge Rd.

Open: daily, except Xmas Day, 10–5.
Admission: £2.50 (children 5–14 £1.20, senior citizens £1.95). Family ticket (2 adults, up to 5 children) £7.
P. ☕ (licensed) ⛼ ♿ shop 🐕̸ (except car park)

BRIDGNORTH, SHROPSHIRE Severn Valley Railway Map 7 SO79

Services to Bridgnorth on this standard gauge steam railway – probably the best example of its kind in the country, with an extensive collection of locomotives and rolling stock – travel through 16 miles of picturesque scenery beside the River Severn. You could even feed the family on one of the special Sunday Luncheon trains or treat yourself to dinner one Saturday evening. Details of Steam Galas and a Vintage Vehicle Weekend can be obtained from the railway office, and Santa Specials run during the month before Christmas.

☏Bewdley (0299) 403816

Open: *late Mar–Oct weekends & Bank Hols, then daily mid May–mid Sep. Santa Steam Specials end Nov–mid Dec weekends only.
Admission: Fares depend upon length of journey. Phone for details.
P. ☕ ⛼ ♿ shop

BROADWAY, HEREFORD & WORCESTER   Broadway Tower Country Park
Map 4 SP03

The sixth Earl of Coventry built the tower here in 1799 from which the park derives its name. Today it has exhibitions on three floors and an observation room where a telescope gives magnificent views over some twelve counties. There are nature walks to follow, rare and interesting animals to see, and an adventure playground and barbeque to enjoy.

☎(0386) 852390

Open: Apr to first weekend in Oct, daily 10–6.
Admission: £1.75 (children & senior citizens £1). Family rate (2 adults & 4 children) £5.
P. ⌗ 🍴 ᶑ (ground floor & gardens) shop

BROMSGROVE, HEREFORD & WORCESTER   Avoncroft Museum of Buildings
Map 7 SO97

Among the buildings of architectural and historic interest which have been re-erected on this lovely 15-acre site are a working windmill, a blacksmith's shop and a cockpit theatre, whilst houses range from an old merchant's house to a 1946 prefab, and there are such glimpses of the life of other generations as a Georgian ice house, an 18th-century dovecot and an earth closet!

☎(0527) 31886
Located: In Redditch Road, Stoke Heath

Open: Jun, Jul & Aug daily 11–5.30; Apr, May, Sep & Oct daily (except Mon) 11–5.30; Mar–Nov daily (except Mon & Fri) 11–4.30. Open Bank Hols.
Admission: £1.90 (children 95p, senior citizens £1.10). Family ticket (2 adults & 2 children) £4.95.
P. ⌗ 🍴 ᶑ (ground floor & gardens) shop

BUNGAY, SUFFOLK   The Otter Trust   Map 5 TM38

Though the Trust's specific conern is to prevent the extinction of the British otter by breeding young in captivity and then releasing them into the wild, it is also involved in world-wide conservation. This, the world's largest collection of otters, is housed in semi-natural enclosures, each with a stream flowing through it, and set amongst the beautiful surroundings of the Waveney Valley. The grounds also include three lakes, with a large collection of waterfowl, and offer attractive riverside walks and picnic areas.

☎(0986) 3470
Located: At Earsham, 1½ miles from Bungay on the Harleston Road.

Open: Apr–Oct daily 10.30–6.
Admission: ✳£2. (children £1, senior citizens £1.50).
P. ⌗ 🍴 ᶑ shop ✼

CAISTER-ON-SEA, NORFOLK   Caister Castle and Motor Museum   Map 9 TG51

The Motor Museum contains vehicles spanning the period from 1893 to the present day. It is in the grounds of a substantial remains of a moated castle, together with a 98ft tower and the 1951 Festival of Britain Tree Walk, brought here from Battersea Park.

☎Wymondham (057284) 251

Open: mid May–Sep, Sun–Fri 10.30–5.
Admission: Fee payable.
P. ⌗ ᶑ shop

CAMBRIDGE   Cambridgeshire   Map 5 TL45

Historic University of the Fen Country

This graceful city's tradition as a centre of learning dates back more than 700 years. Long before then, it was a Roman camp by a ford on the River Granta. Its Norman castle led the campaign against Hereward the Wake, and several of the city's surviving churches were already here by the 12th century. After the founding of the first University college, Peterhouse, in 1284, Cambridge quickly became a respected intellectual centre.

Today the University has 31 colleges. Parts of them are open to the public most days, with some restrictions in term time, especially during examinations in May and early June. The dozen or so colleges founded in medieval times are the most visited – especially those overlooking the Backs, where punts glide in summer on the River Cam and there are pleasant towpath walks. One of the most famous sights from here is 15th-century King's College Chapel, a magnificent, pinnacled building whose beauty is matched by the music of its renowned choir, who sing Evensong here most days during term time, as well as the celebrated Service of Nine Lessons and Carols, broadcast every Christmas Eve.

Next to King's is Queen's College. Beside it, the river is spanned by the wooden Mathematical Bridge – so called because it was originally built on geometrical pinciples, without any nails or bolts. Further down the river, beyond Clare Bridge (the city's oldest) is the 'Bridge of Sighs', supposed to resemble its Venetian namesake but actually quite unlike it. It is part of St John's College, which also has a fine Tudor gateway.

There is always plenty to do in Cambridge. Student events include Rag Week in February, and May Week (actually in June) when there are dazzling May balls in the colleges, boat races – 'the Bumps' – on the river, and the Footlights Revue at the Arts Theatre. Other year-round attractions include several museums such as the Folk Museum and the Whipple Science Museum.

☆STAR ATTRACTIONS

Fitzwilliam Museum

Art and archaeology form the basis of the displays at Cambridge's largest museum, founded in 1816. The paintings range from early Italian panels to the work of the French Impressionists. Coins, manuscripts, porcelain, armour and textiles make up other permanent displays, and there are frequent temporary exhibitions.

☎(0223) 332900
Located: Trumpington Street.

Open: all year (except Good Fri, May Day & Xmas) Tue–Sat 10–5, Sun 2.15–5. Also open Easter Mon, Spring & Summer Bank Hols.
Admission: free.
🖙 (licensed) & shop 🐕 (except guide dogs)

Scott Polar Research Institute

Established as a memorial to Captain Scott and his companions, the Institute incorporates an interesting museum. Photographs, diaries and souvenirs of Scott's expeditions are among the exhibits, and there are also displays related to Polar research today, including sections on Antarctic geography and geology.

☎(0223) 336540
Located: Lensfield Road.

Open: Mon–Sat 2.30–4. Closed some public & university hols.
Admission: free.
shop 🐕

University Botanic Garden

These beautifully kept gardens, established in 1762, cover some 40 acres south of the city centre. A scented garden and a lovely rockery are among many attractive features which complement the collection of botanical specimens. The glasshouses are also open to visitors.

☎(0223) 336265
Located: Cory Lodge, Bateman Street.

Open: Mon–Sat 8–6 (or dusk if earlier); May–Sep also open Sun 2.30–6.30. Glasshouses 11–12.30 & 2–4.
Admission: free.
🗻 & 🐕 (except guide dogs)

CASTLETON, DERBYSHIRE   Blue-John Cavern and Mine   Map 7 SK18

These water-worn caves are about half a mile long and have chambers as high as 200 feet. They are among the finest examples of such caverns in the area and there are no less than 14 veins of the famed Blue John stone.

☎Hope Valley (0433) 20638 or 20642

Open: daily 9.30–6 or dusk (telephone for winter opening). Closed 25 & 26 Dec and 1 Jan.
Admission: ✳ £2 (children £1).
P. shop

CASTLETON, DERBYSHIRE   Peak Cavern   Map 7 SK18

In the Grand Entrance Hall of these caves, ropes have been made for over five centuries and there are still traces of a row of workers' cottages. The limestone caves are among the most spectacular in the district. There is an illuminated underground walk about half a mile long.

☎Hope Valley (0433) 20285

Open: Apr–mid Sep daily 10–5.
Admission: £1.60 (children 80p).
P. shop

CASTLETON, DERBYSHIRE   Speedwell Cavern   Map 7 SK18

This old Derbyshire lead mine is approached by an exciting mile long guided journey by boat along an illuminated subterranean waterway, 840 feet below the ground. Speedwell Cavern also boasts a 'bottomless pit'.

☎Hope Valley (0433) 20512
Located: Winnats Pass.

Open: daily 9.30–5.30 (closed 25 & 26 Dec and 1 Jan.).
Admission: £3 (children under 14 £2).
P. shop

CHATSWORTH, DERBYSHIRE   Map 8 SK27

The palatial 17th-century home of the Duke and Duchess of Devonshire contains one of the richest collections of fine and decorative art in private hands. Children will enjoy the Farmyard and Adventure Playground. There is a Farming and Forestry Exhibition and numerous events throughout the year including an Angling Fair, Country Fair and Horse Trials.

☎Baslow (024688) 2204
Located: 3½ miles east of Bakewell

Open: daily end Mar–Oct 11.30–4.30 (garden 5pm). Farmyard and Adventure Playground 10.30–4.30.
Admission: House & garden £3.50 (children £1.75, senior citizens £2.75), family ticket £9. Garden £1.70 (children 85p), family ticket £4. Farmyard & Adventure Playground £1.50 (children £1) family ticket £5.
P. ⌂ (licensed) & (garden only) shop & garden centre.

COCKLEY CLEY, NORFOLK   Iceni Village and Museums   Map 5 TF70

Two thousand years ago the Iceni tribe had an encampment on this very site, and a full-scale reconstruction shows how they lived. There is also a historical museum housed in a cottage built in 1450 containing exhibitions and models which trace local life from prehistoric to modern time. There are also agricultural, vintage engine and carriage museums to discover. An early Saxon church dating from about 620 is of interest, and there is also a nature trail to follow.

☎Swaffham (0760) 21339

Open: Good Fri–end Oct daily 2–5.30pm (from 11am, mid Jul–mid Sep).
Admission: £1.95 (children 6–16 80p, students & senior citizens £1.10, children under 6 free)
P. ⍭ & (ground floor & grounds only) shop

COSFORD RAF, WEST MIDLANDS   Aerospace Museum   Map 7 SJ70

The York, the Hastings, Victor and Vulcan bombers, the Belfast freighter and the last airworthy Britannia – all these classic planes are represented here, in one of the biggest aviation collections in the UK. A Research and Development display includes the famous TSR2, Fairey Delta 2, Bristol 188 and many other important aircraft, and there is also a British Airways exhibition hall and a comprehensive missile display.

☎Albrighton (090722) 4872/4112

Open: Mar–Nov daily; Dec–Feb weekdays only; 10–4 (last admission).
Admission: £2.50 (children & senior citizens £1).
P. ⌨ 🍴 ⅋ (ground floor only) shop ✻ (in hangars)

COVENTRY, WEST MIDLANDS   Coventry Cathedral   Map 4 SP37

The old cathedral was destroyed in the bombing of the city during the last war, and the present building, designed by Sir Basil Spence, was consecrated in 1962. It contains outstanding examples of modern art – notably the West Screen (a wall of glass engraved with angels and saints by John Hutton), some unsurpassed stained glass and the Sutherland tapestry. The bells have been restored, and there is a viewing chamber in the tower, whilst the new Visitors' Centre offers the chance to enjoy the skills of modern technology.

☎(0203) 27597
Located: At 7 Priory Row.

Open: Easter–end Sep 9.30–7.30; Oct–Easter 9.30–5.30 (except for services). Visitors Centre 9.30–5.
Admission: Cathedral tours, £1 (children & senior citizens 50p). Visitors Centre, £1.25 (children 6–16, students & senior citizens 75p, children under 6 free).
⌨ (licensed) ⅋ shop ✻

COVENTRY, WEST MIDLANDS   Coventry Toy Museum   Map 4 SP37

See for yourself what toys your grandparents might have played with! The traditional pastimes of childhood are all here – trains, dolls, dolls' houses and games, feature prominently in this interesting collection. The earliest examples date from the middle of the 18th-century century and provide an intriguing contrast to the museums more up-to-date exhibits which date to 1951.

☎(0203) 27560
Located: In Much Park Street.

Open: daily 2–5pm.
Admission: 60p (children & senior citizens 40p).
P. shop ✻

COVENTRY, WEST MIDLANDS   Museum of British Road Transport   Map 4 SP37

Here you can admire the sleek lines of "Thrust 2", the holder of the world land speed record – but you can also come to understand something of the part that Coventry and the West Midlands area in general have played in the development of transport throughout the world. There are over 400 exhibits, including cars, commercial vehicles, motor cycles and bicycles, together with relevant materials associated with the industry. Special events include the Coventry Shakespeare Veteran Car Run and Nostalgia Weekends.

☎(0203) 832425
Located: In St Agnes Lane, Hales Street.

Open: Apr–Sep Mon–Fri 10–4, Sat & Sun 10–5.30; Oct–Mar Fri 9.30–4, Sat & Sun 10–5.
Admission: *£1 (children & senior citizens 50p). Family rate (2 adults & 2 children) £2.50.
⅋ shop ✻

CRICH, DERBYSHIRE   National Tramway Museum   Map 8 SK35

A unique experience for youngsters – vintage tramcars and unlimited rides along a one-mile stretch of tramway with views over the Derwent Valley, and a chance for older family members to relive some youthful memories. Also see the period street project with the reconstructed Georgian Assembly Rooms façade from Derby.

☎Ambergate (077385) 2565
Located: in Matlock Road (off B5035)

Open: Apr–Oct Sat, Sun & Bank Hols; May–Sep also Mon–Thu; also Fri late Jul–early Sep, plus pre-Xmas weekends; 10–5.30 (6.30 weekends).
Admission: £2.40 (children £1.20, senior citizens £2).
P. ⌨ 🍴 ⅋ shop

DRAYTON, STAFFORDSHIRE   Drayton Manor Park and Zoo   Map 4 SK10

There is fun unlimited for all the family within Drayton's 160 acres of parkland and lakes. When you have explored the open-plan zoo, you still have the promise of thrills on the thirty-five rides offered by the amusement park – why not try the Looping Roller Coaster, for example, the Paratower, Log Flume, Cable Cars or Jungle Course? If you prefer, you can take a more sedate ride along the lakeside on a miniature railway where passenger carriages are hauled by a scale model of a 19th-century North American locomotive, or follow a marked nature trail and walks through forty acres of woodland.

☎Tamworth (0827) 287979
Located: On A4091, 1 mile south of junction with A5, 1½ miles south of Tamworth.

Open: Easter–Oct daily 10.30–6.
Admission: *£1.20 (children 60p). Car park 30p.
P. ☕ (licensed) ♿ shop & garden centre ⸸ (except park)

DUDLEY, WEST MIDLANDS   Black Country Museum   Map 7 SO99

You will take a step back in time as you walk round this regional open-air museum, where original buildings have been re-erected to illustrate the area's old way of life. Explore the chainmaker's house (complete with brewhouse), cottages, chemist's shop, chapel, pub, and the canal boat dock with its narrow boats; find out about coal-mining, and watch demonstrations of chainmaking and glass-cutting in traditional workshops. Trips into the famous Dudley Tunnel are also available daily from the site.

☎021–557 9643
Located: In Tipton Rd (opposite Dudley Guest Hospital).

Open: daily except Xmas Day, 10–5 (reduced hours in winter).
Admission: £3 (children £2, senior citizens £2.50).
P. ☕ (licensed) ⊼ ♿ (ground floor only) shop

DUDLEY, WEST MIDLANDS   Dudley Zoological Gardens and Castle   Map 7 SO99

The impressive ruins of a 13th-century castle look down over the 1,000 animals which now inhabit its forty acres of wooded grounds; visitors can reach this vantage point by chairlift from the main entrance 200ft below. Dudley Zoo is famous for its breeding of such rare specimens as the ring-tailed lemur and the silvery marmoset, but it also includes such traditional favourites as lions, tigers, bears, monkeys and reptiles, clever use being made of the pits left after mineral excavations to house some of the larger animals. The children's farm features a collection of small animals and forms an interesting contrast to the life-size models in the *Land of the Dinosaurs* exhibition. Other attractions include a fair, a miniature railway and a ski slope.

☎(0384) 52401

Open: all year (except Xmas Day) Mon–Sat 9–5, Sun 10–5. Last admission 3.30.
Admission: £2.50 (children £1.25, under 3 free).
P. ☕ (licensed) ⊼ ♿ shop ⸸

DUXFORD, CAMBRIDGESHIRE   Imperial War Museum   Map 5 TL44

If you go along to Duxford on a summer weekend you'll be able to try a pleasure flight or, for the faint-hearted, there is always the flight simulator. But there's no need to experience flying, as this section of the Imperial War Museum has plenty for those who just want to look and learn. There are collections of military aircraft, armoured fighting vehicles and other large exhibits in hangars that date from the First World War. On the airfield there are over 90 historic aircraft alongside Duxford Aviation Society's civil aircraft collection, including *Concorde 01*.

☎Cambridge (0223) 833963
Located: Off M11 junction 10, at Duxford Airfield on A505.

Open: daily (except Good Fri, May Day Bank Hol, Dec 24–26 & Jan 1), 10.30–5.30, (closes 3.45 winter months). Limited viewing Nov–Mar, phone for full details.
Admission: Mar–Oct £3.50 (children 5–16 & senior citizens £1.80). Winter season £1 (children 5–16 & senior citizens 50p).
P. ☕ (licensed) ⊼ ♿ (except aircraft) shop ⸸

EASTON, SUFFOLK   Easton Farm Park   Map 5 TM25

You'll get a real taste of farming at Easton. You can visit the Victorian Dairy, or, in contrast, watch real cows being milked in a modern unit. Forty species of farm animal can be seen here including many rare breeds. There are working Suffolk horses and collections of early farm machinery and rural bygones. For children there is a pets paddock and an adventure playpit.

🕾**Wickham Market (0728) 746475**
Located: Outside Wickham Market on B1116.

Open: Easter–Oct daily 10.30–6, (last admission 4.30).
Admission: *£2 (children £1, senior citizens £1.50).
P. ⌑ 🕂 ₺ (ground floor only) shop

ELVASTON, DERBYSHIRE   Elvaston Castle Country Park   Map 8 SK43

The attractive 200-acre country park, landscaped in the early 18th-century, contains formal gardens, a walled Old English Garden, extensive topiary gardens, parkland and woodland. The working Estate Museum recreates the lifestyle of a country house estate at the turn of the century and illustrates the craft skills involved in its running. A programme of events is planned for 1988 and includes antiques fairs in April, May and August, craft fairs (during April and October, a radio rally in June and a steam rally in July. There is also a caravan and camping site in the park.

🕾**Derby (0332) 71342**
Located: Borrawash Road

Open: Country Park, daily 9am until dusk. Estate Museum, Easter–Oct Wed–Sat 1–5pm, Sun & Bank Hol Mon 10–6. Park Information Centre & Shop, Easter–Oct daily 12 noon to 4.30. Closed some Mons in Spring & Autumn (but not Bank Hols), rest of year Sun only.
Admission: Museum, 60p (children & senior citizens 30p). Country Park, no charge. Car Park, Weekends & Bank Hol 50p.
P. ⌑ (in season) 🕂 ₺ (ground floor only in museum) shop

FILBY, NORFOLK   Thrigby Hall Wildlife Gardens   Map 9 TG41

The beautiful landscaped gardens of Thrigby Hall are the setting for a selection of Asian mammals, birds and reptiles. The gardens also feature a yew walk, a 250-year-old summer house, a tropical house, bird house and an ornamental waterfowl lake. There is also a slide theatre.

🕾**Fleggburgh (049377) 477**
Located: On unclassified road, off A1064.

Open: daily 10–5.
Admission: £2 (children 4–14 £1, senior citizens £1.50).
P. ⌑ (Apr–Sep) 🕂 ₺ shop ✻ (except guide dogs)

FROGHALL, STAFFORDSHIRE   Froghall Wharf Passenger Service   Map 7 SK04

Forget the hustle and bustle of modern life as you take a trip on "Birdswood", the only horse-drawn boat operating on the Caldon Canal today. The cruise follows one of the most attractive sections of canal in the country, passing through the Churnel Valley, where peace and tranquillity characterise a setting almost unchanged in a hundred years. On your return to the Wharf you can enjoy a meal in the Eating House or Restaurant.

🕾**Ipstones (053871) 486**
Located: At Canal Basin, Foxt Road (¼ miles north on A52).

Open: Public Service Easter–Sep, Thu & Sun at 2pm. Also in summer months every first and third Sat there are evening meal trips. Telephone for further details and information, including private charter. Restaurant all year Tue–Sat (evenings only). Eating House Spring Bank Hol–Sep, Tue–Sun 11–6; Oct–Spring Bank Hol, Thu–Sun 11–5.
Admission: Trip £3.25 (children £2.25). Evening trip including meal £10.25 (children £9.25).
P. ⌑ (licensed) 🕂 ₺ (no disabled toilet) ✻ (in restaurant)

90

GREAT WITCHINGHAM, NORFOLK   Norfolk Wildlife Park   Map 9 TG01

Meet the stars of the film *Santa Claus – The Movie!* This unique team of trained reindeer pull a wheeled sledge round the Park most afternoons, and you can see them being harnessed and worked. The forty acres of beautiful countryside also house a large collection of British and European wildlife, whilst pets corner and the exciting play areas – their modern equipment includes an overhead cable way – provide additional attractions for children.

for GREAT YARMOUTH see page 92

☎Norwich (0603) 872274
Located: 12 miles north-west of Norwich, on A1067.

Open: all year, daily 10.30–6 or sunset if earlier.
Admission: ✳£2 (children under 16 £1, senior citizens £1.80).
P. ⌂ (licensed) ⊞ & (no disabled toilet) shop ✻

GUILSBOROUGH, NORTHAMPTONSHIRE   Guilsborough Grange Wildlife Park   Map 4 SP67

Thirty acres of magnificent parkland offer fine views over the surrounding countryside, and here you can meet at close quarters a wide variety of birds and animals. These range from such native species as deer, badgers, owls and bats to the more exotic big cats, monkeys and parrots. Birds of prey are featured too, and falconry displays take place daily, weather permitting.

☎Northampton (0604) 740278
Located: 6 miles from M1 junction 18 on the West Haddon Road.

Open: daily 10–6 or dusk.
Admission: £2 (children & senior citizens £1).
P. ⌂ ⊞ & shop.

HOUGHTON, NORFOLK   Houghton Hall   Map 9 TF72

Built for Sir Robert Walpole in the 18th-century, to the design of Colen Campbell and Thomas Ripley, the Hall is one of the best examples of Palladian architecture in the country. The state rooms, decorated and furnished by William Kent, contain fine paintings and china. Children will be fascinated by a large collection of model soldiers and will enjoy a visit to the stables to see the heavy horses, Shetland ponies, harness room and coach house. The house is surrounded by beautiful parkland, and there is a children's playground too.

☎East Rudham (048522) 569
Located: 1¼ miles off A148, between Kings Lynn & Fakenham.

Open: Easter Sun–last Sun in Sep, Thu, Sun & Bank Hols 12.30–5pm (house open at 1pm).
Admission: £2.50 (children 50p, under 5 free, senior citizens £1.80).
P. ⊞ & shop

ILKESTON, DERBYSHIRE   American Adventure Theme Park   Map 8 SK44

Experience the thrills and spills of the Wild West at this amazing 120-acre theme park. Come rain or shine there's fun here for all the family. To start with, a ride on the Santa Fe Railroad will introduce you to the complex, as will a trip on the lake on one of the traditional river boats. Over seventy amusements include the High Sierra Wagon Train – a big-wheel ride, Thunder Canyon Runaway Train and the Yankee Clipper. Younger children will love the Shining Water Canoe Ride. Live interest is provided by a herd of North American Bison and ponies in the Alamo Pony Corral. Watch out for General Custer and Chief Sitting Bull.

for IRONBRIDGE see page 93

☎Langley Mill (0773) 769931
Located: Between Heanor and Ilkeston, 5 miles from M1 Junction 26.

Open: Easter Week, then weekends only to Spring Bank Hol; daily Spring Bank Hol–end Sep; weekends only, Oct 10–6.
Admission: Adults & children (over 3) £5.95. Special discounts for senior citizens & disabled.
P. ⌂ (licensed) ⊞ & shop ✻

A Seaside Playground Steeped in History

One of Britain's great traditional holiday resorts, Great Yarmouth is a historic town and port with much to interest visitors, in addition to all the fun of the seaside. Centuries of prosperous trading had made it one of England's wealthiest towns long before the first sea-bathers came here in the 18th century. Medieval merchants had built not only the fine town wall, much of which is still there, but also many handsome houses, including the Tolhouse, now one of several museums in the town. A reminder of its days as a courthouse and prison is its dungeon, where four grim cells can still be seen. Other medieval legacies are the quaint, narrow lanes known as the Rows, and the vast parish church of St Nicholas. Later prosperity left fine 18th-century buildings such as the Custom House and St George's Church, now an arts centre.

Many visitors come here for the splendid beaches, stretching for over 15 miles from Winterton on Sea in the north to Hopton on Sea in the south. Some areas are quieter, backed by dunes, as at Caister, or cliffs, as at Hopton and Gorleston. Other stretches, such as Great Yarmouth's own popular beach, offer every facility – beach huts, refreshments, pony rides and Punch and Judy to name a few. For wet days there is the Marina Leisure Centre, which has an indoor beach, a swimming pool with a wave-making machine, and facilities for squash, snooker and table tennis. There are five theatres to choose from, while the Hippodrome is one of Britain's only two permanent, purpose-built circuses.

☆STAR ATTRACTIONS

Maritime Museum for East Anglia

Today, Great Yarmouth's maritime activity lies chiefly in Continental cargo and ferry traffic, as well as supplies to the North Sea oil and gas industry. Not so long ago, however, it was a great fishing port, and had a thriving shipbuilding industry. All aspects of Yarmouth's rich maritime heritage are featured in this museum, which is housed in a Victorian home for shipwrecked sailors. Paintings, models and items of nautical gear all help recapture the area's long and varied history of seafaring.

☎(0493) 842267
Located: Marine Parade.

Open: all year: Jun to Sep, daily except Sat, 10–5.30; Oct, Mon to Fri 10–1 and 2–5.30, Sun 1–5.30; Nov to May, Mon to Fri 10–1 and 2–5.30. Closed Good Fri and Xmas.
Admission: 40p (children 10p) late May–Sep; 20p (children 10p) Oct–late May.
Shop ✗

Merrivale Model Village

An acre of landscaped gardens with waterways and flowering trees and shrubs is the setting for this 1-in-12 scale model. Castles, cottages, farms and bridge are among the 200 pint-size replicas. There is a 2½-inch-gauge model railway and model boats, cars and lorries complete the scene. The village is illuminated after dusk in summer.

☎(0493) 842097
Located: Marine Parade (near Wellington Pier).

Open: late May–Sep daily 9.30 am–10pm.
Admission: ✱£1 (children 50p; under 3 free).
P. ⌷ ⏚ ⏚ Shop

Nelson's Monument

Fine views of land and sea reward those who climb the 217 steps to the top of this 144ft-high column. It was built in 1819 – more than 20 years before its famous London cousin – in honour of Admiral Lord Nelson, a Norfolk man, born in 1758 at Burnham Thorpe. However, it is not his statue that tops the monument, but a figure of Britannia.

☎(0493) 855746
Located: South Beach.

Open: Jul & Aug daily except Sat, 2–6; also 21 October (Trafalgar Day) 10–1 & 2–5.30.
Admission: 30p (children 15p).

IRONBRIDGE, SHROPSHIRE   Ironbridge Gorge Museum   Map 7 SJ60

There's a sense of living history at Ironbridge, the birthplace of the Industrial Revolution and now the site of several museums and items pertaining to this important period in British history. The focal point of the Gorge is the handsome Iron Bridge (1779), the first cast-iron bridge in the world. The Museum Visitor Centre should be visited first, to allow you to plan a route around this six square-mile site. Other museums include the Museum of Iron and the Old Furnace, the Jackfield Tile Museum, Blists Hill Open Air Museum – a recreated Victorian township, and the Coalport China Museum. National winner of *AA Best Museum Award 1987*.

☎(095245) 3522

Open: late Feb–Nov daily, 10–6. Please telephone for details of winter opening.
Admission: ✳Passport to all sites – £4.75 (children £3, senior citizen £4).
P. ☕ (licensed) 🍴 & shop

KELLING, NORFOLK   Kelling Park Aviaries   Map 9 TG04

Bird-lovers will be fascinated by this fine collection of European and tropical birds, including birds of prey, owls, pheasants and cockatoos. Fascinating bird demonstrations are held when weather permits. There is also a children's playground and four acres of beautiful grounds which feature a lovely water garden.

☎Holt (0263) 711071
Located: In Weybourne Rd

Open: daily 10–5.
Admission: £1 (children 50p).
P. ☕ (licensed) 🍴 & shop

KENILWORTH, WARWICKSHIRE   Stoneleigh Abbey   Map 4 SP27

Originally a Cistercian Abbey, Stoneleigh has been described as the grandest, most dramatic Georgian mansion of Warwickshire. Three wings are open for you to judge for yourself, plus the private quarters if booked in advance. The Abbey also offers a children's adventure playground, nature trail, woodland walks, and on Sunday and Bank Holidays, a model railway.

☎(0926) 52116 or 57766

Open: Apr & May Sun & Bank Hols; Jun–Aug daily (except Fri & Sat); Sep Sun only, 1–5.30. Last admission 5. Gardens open 11.30–5.30.
Admission: £2.20 (children & senior citizens £1.50); grounds only £1.50 (children & senior citizens £1). Senior citizen rates Mon & Tue only.
P. ☕ (licensed) 🍴 & shop✖

KILVERSTONE, NORFOLK   Kilverstone Wildlife Park   Map 5 TL98

Children and adults alike will be fascinated by the miniature horses and donkeys to be seen here, and by the range of some six-hundred predominantly Latin American animals and birds which include jaguars, monkeys, maned wolves, tapirs, parrots and cats. You can also visit the deer park, walk by the river or take a ride on a miniature train, and there is even an adventure playground for children.

☎Thetford (0842) 5369 or 66606

Open: daily 10–6.30 (dusk in winter).
Admission: ✳£2.20 (children 4–14 £1.10, senior citizens £1.75).
P. ☕ (mid Mar–Oct, licensed) 🍴 & shop & garden centre ✖

LILFORD PARK, NORTHAMPTONSHIRE   Map 4 TL08

Deer herds roam freely over the 240 acres of parkland here, that surround the 17th-century Jacobean Hall. Although Lilford Hall is not open to the public, the grounds offer a wealth of attractions to its visitors. Aviaries are stocked with hundreds of birds, including the Lilford crane and Little Owl – a native of Europe which was first established in Britain through birds released from Lilford. The park also contains a flamingo pool, a children's farm, an adventure playground and pleasant riverside walks, with picnic spots along the banks of the Nene. In the stable block and old coaching house is a crafts and gifts centre.

☎Clopton (08015) 648 or 665
Located: On A605 between Oundle & Thrapston.

Open: Easter–Oct daily 10–6 (or dusk).
Admission: £1.40 (children 3–16 70p, under 3 free). (Price excludes Bank Hol weekends).
P. ☕ 🍴 & shop ✖

LINCOLN   Lincolnshire   Map 8 SK97

Ancient Hill City amid the Plains

A stupendous three-towered cathedral and a great Norman castle crown the hill from which this historic city commands the flat lands that surround it. Steep, narrow streets which contain some of England's oldest houses link the two parts of the city, known as 'above hill' and 'below hill'.

The former Celtic hillfort of Lindon had, by AD96, become a well-planned Roman town, Lindum Colonia, hub of an important farming area. Remains of the Roman city wall include the remarkable Newport Arch in Bailgate – England's only Roman gateway still used by traffic.

After the Norman Conquest, large areas of 'above hill' were cleared to make way for two vast new buildings – the castle and the cathedral. Later, the medieval wool trade brought prosperity which left the city some fine parish churches and timber-framed houses, which contribute much to the historic atmosphere to be enjoyed in a walk round Lincoln's streets.

☆STAR ATTRACTIONS

Greyfriars City and County Museum

Equally interesting for its displays and for the building that contains them, this was Lincoln's first public museum, opened in 1906 in part of a former Franciscan friary. Dating from about 1230, Greyfriars is probably England's earliest Franciscan church. It has two storeys: a fine vaulted undercroft and an upper floor with a splendid timber barrel roof. Local archaeological finds form the basis of the collection; they include a remarkable prehistoric dugout boat, about 3000 years old, which was found near the River Witham.

☎(0522) 30401
Located: Broadgate.

Open: Mon–Sat 10–5.30, Sun 2.30–5. Closed Good Fri & Xmas.
Admission: 25p (children 10p). Additional charge for special exhibitions.
P. & (ground floor only) Shop ✷ (except guide dogs)

Lincoln Castle

William the Conqueror ordered the building of a castle here in 1068, and although his great stronghold has seen later additions, its basic plan has remained the same. Lincoln is one of only two Norman castles in England with two mounds. On one stands the Lucy Tower, or keep, whilst the other supports the Observatory Tower – so called because a turret was added to its Norman base in the 19th century by a governor who used it to observe the stars. A third tower, Cobb Hall, was the castle dungeon. Some of its cells still have rings where prisoners were tied, and executions took place on its roof until 1859. Another grim reminder of past punishments is the 18th-century former prison, built inside the castle bailey. A more cheering pastime on a visit to the castle is a walk along part of the ramparts, from where there are magnificent views over the city and the countryside beyond.

☎(0522) 511068
Located: Castle Hill.

Open: Summer Mon–Sat 9.30–5.30, Sun 11–5.30; Winter Mon–Sat 9.30–4.
Admission: 50p (children 30p).
P. Shop ✷

Cathedral

One of England's most spectacularly sited cathedrals, this great church was mostly built in the 13th century, after a fire and then an earth tremor had reduced most of the Norman cathedral to ruins. The west front of the earlier building escaped, however, and its lovely carvings of animals and figures, including one depicting Noah's Ark, are still among Lincoln's chief treasures. Inside, at the opposite end, is another masterpiece, the Angel Choir, which has 28 beautifully carved angels on its gallery. It is also the place to hunt for the famous carving of the Lincoln Imp.

Located: Minster Yard.

Open: May–Aug, Mon–Sat 7.15am–8pm, Sun 7.15–6pm; Sep, Mon–Sat 7.15am–7pm, Sun 7.15am–6pm; Oct–Apr, daily 7.15am–6pm.

LINTON, CAMBRIDGESHIRE   Linton Zoological Gardens   Map 5 TL54

The accent is on conservation at this attractive 10-acre zoo, with animals and birds housed in landscaped enclosures resembling, as closely as possible, their natural habitat. Big cats, bears, wallabies, llamas, parrots, birds of prey and insects are just some of the creatures you'll meet. For a real treat why not come along at 3.30 p.m. on Saturday between 28 May–27 August 1988 and be introduced to Blossom and Boris – the Boa Constrictors!

☎Cambridge (0223) 891308
Located: At Mortimer House, Hadstock Rd.

Open: daily 10–7 (last admission 6.15). Closed 25 & 26 Dec.
Admission: *£2 (children £1, senior citizens £1.50).
P. ⊡ (Mar–Oct) ⊼ & shop ✗ (except in car park)

LONG SUTTON, LINCOLNSHIRE   Butterfly Park   Map 8 TF42

Stroll through one of Britain's largest tropical houses where hundreds of butterflies from all over the world fly freely in a beautiful landscaped setting of tropical plants, ponds and waterfalls. Outdoors, visit the Butterfly and Bee Garden, Wildflower Meadows, Wildfowl and Conservation Ponds, Farm Animals and the Adventure Playground.

☎Holbeach (0406) 363833
Located: off A17 near junction with A1101.

Open: Easter–Oct daily 10–6.
Admission: £2 (children £1, senior citizens £1.75).
P. ⊡ (licensed) ⊼ & shop

LOUGHBOROUGH, LEICESTERSHIRE   Great Central Railway   Map 8 SK51

The 'Thomas the Tank Engine Enthusiasts' Weekend' (24–25 Sep 1988) should prove a great success with the kids! This private steam railway operates over five miles from Loughborough Central to Rothley (all trains calling at Quorn and Woodhouse), and there's a museum and locomotive depot at the Loughborough end of the line.

☎(0509) 230726
Located: Great Central Road.

Open: Sat, Sun & Bank Hol Mon & Tue, also summer Wed & Thu in high season (Closed Good Fri & 25 Dec).
Admission: £2 (children & senior citizens £1). Family ticket (2 adults & up to 3 children) £5.50.
P. ⊡ (Loughborough Central & Rothley) & shop

LOWESTOFT, SUFFOLK   East Anglia Transport Museum   Map 5 TM59

In this "action" museum the emphasis is truly on movement – a reconstructed 1930's street scene forms the background for old working vehicles, and where rides can be taken on trams, trolley-bus and a narrow-gauge railway. There are also motor, electric and steam-driven vehicles on display, all contained on this lovely 3-acre woodland site.

☎Norwich (0603) 44999
Located: In Chapel Road, Carlton Colville.

Open: Easter–end Sep Sun & Bank Hols 11–5; also Sats in Jun 2–4pm (static display only); Sats in Jul, Aug & Sep 2–4pm; Mon–Fri in Aug 2–4pm.
Admission: £1.20 (children & senior citizens 60p).
P. ⊡ & (no disabled toilets) shop

Symbols
☎	telephone number
P.	parking on the premises
⊡	refreshments available
⊼	picnic area
&	accessible to wheelchair-bound visitors
✗	no dogs
*	indicates 1987 details

LOWESTOFT, SUFFOLK   Pleasurewood Hills American Theme Park   Map 5 TM59

East Anglia's first theme park offers experiences galore – Astroglide and fantasy canal journey, chair lift and veteran car ride, sky leap and pirate boat trip! Children can roller-skate themselves or watch the roller-skating parrots, show their skill with remote control boats or play robot noughts and crosses, enjoy the Western Show or enter the Wonderful World of Story Books. When they have finally exhausted themselves, you can take advantage of attractive picnic areas and free wood-fired barbecues.

☎(0502) 513626/7
Located: Off A12 between Great Yarmouth & Lowestoft.

Open: Easter to Spring Bank Hol Sat, Sun & Bank Hol Mon; then daily to late Sep; late Sep–early Oct Sat & Sun 10–6 (dates may vary).
Admission: *£4.50 (children over 4 £4, under 3 free, senior citizens £2.50).
P. ⌂ ⟠ & shops ✗

MARKET BOSWORTH, LEICESTERSHIRE   Bosworth Battlefield Visitor Centre
Map 4 SK40

In 1485, Richard III met the future Henry VII on Bosworth Field, and the outcome of their encounter changed the course of English history. An extensive Visitor Centre interprets the Battle through exhibitions, models and films, whilst illustrated Trails are available to guide you round the area where the fighting actually took place. A series of Special Event Days is planned between July and September 1988, details of which are available from the centre.

☎(0455) 290429
Located: At Sutton Cheney, 2½ miles south of Market Bosworth.

Open: Country Park & Trails all year during daylight hours. Visitor Centre Apr–Oct Mon–Sat 2–5.30pm, Sun & Bank Hol Mon 1–6pm.
Admission: Visitor Centre £1.20 (children & senior citizens 80p). Special charges on main Special Events Days.
P. ⌂ (licensed) ⟠ & shop ✗ (in Visitor Centre)

MARKET BOSWORTH, LEICESTERSHIRE   Market Bosworth Light Railway
Map 4 SK40

A regular train service, powered for the most part by steam, runs between Shackerstone and Market Bosworth. The railway museum has an extensive display of small relics, and a good collection of rolling stock is on view.

☎Leicester (0533) 605748 & Tamworth (0827) 880754 (weekends)
Located: At Shackerstone Station 5 miles north-west of Market Bosworth on unclass road.

Open: Easter–Sep Sun & Bank Hols 11–6; Oct–Easter Sun 12 noon to 4.30.
Admission: *40p (children 20p). Return train fare £1.65 (children 90p). Family rate £4.50.
P. ⌂ (licensed on train) & (no disabled toilets) shops

MATLOCK, DERBYSHIRE   Riber Castle Wildlife Park   Map 8 SK36

Set on 853-foot-high Riber Hill, the 19th-century castle is surrounded by twenty acres of wildlife park where the emphasis is on rare animals and endangered species. The park also contains the world's most comprehensive collection of Lynx and there is an adventure playground for children.

☎(0629) 2073

Open: daily except Xmas Day 10–5 (4pm in winter).
Admission: *£2 (children £1, under 5 free).
P. ⌂ (licensed) ⟠ & shop ✗ (except in picnic area & car park)

MATLOCK BATH, DERBYSHIRE   Gulliver's Kingdom and Royal Cave   Map 8 SK25

This Theme Park is designed specifically to appeal to the younger members of the family. Set in 15 acres of wooded hillside, it boasts over 40 attractions – Playworld, Ghost House, Model Village and Railways, computerised Royal Cave, Dinosaur Trail and Safari Terrace, to name but a few!

☎**Matlock (0629) 55970**
Located: A6 from Buxton to Derby, take turning opposite The Pavilion

Open: Easter–mid Sep daily 10.30–5 or later.
Admission: fee payable.
P.

MATLOCK BATH, DERBYSHIRE   Heights of Abraham   Map 8 SK25

It's a spectacular cable car ride across the Derwent Valley to the 35 acres of woodland, Prospect Tower, two show caverns and picnic and play areas that comprise the Heights of Abraham. The lofty Victorian Prospect Tower, on the summit of the Heights, offers a breathtaking vista of Derbyshire and its surrounding counties. The atmosphere and sounds of a local lead mine are recreated at the Great Rutland Cavern and Nestus Mine, but the more intrepid visitor will surely want to explore the underground passages of the Great Masson Cavern whose walls are veined with calcite and fluorspar.

☎**Matlock (0629) 2365**
Located: Access by cable car from Matlock Bath Railway Station car park.

Open: Great Rutland Cavern & Nestus Mine Easter–Oct, 10–5; Great Masson Cavern Easter–Oct, Sun & Bank Hols 10–5, Aug daily. For Autumn & winter openings telephone for details.
Admission: ✱£1.95 (children £1.20). Cable car £2.95 (children £1.95) return ticket.
P. ⌂ (licensed) ⌇ & shop ⴕ (in caverns).

MATLOCK BATH, DERBYSHIRE   Peak District Mining Museum   Map 8 SK25

Static and moving displays are augmented by an audio-visual programme tracing the history of Derbyshire's lead industry, illustrating the geology associated with the discovery of the ore and exploring the metal's mining, quarrying and smelting. The museum also houses an interesting early 19th-century water pressure pumping engine, the only one of its kind in the British Isles.

☎**Matlock (0629) 3834**
Located: The Pavilion.

Open: daily (except Xmas Day) 11–4 (later closing in summer).
Admission: ✱80p (children & senior citizens 50p).
& (ground floor only) shop

For NORFOLK BROADS see page 98

NOTTINGHAM, NOTTINGHAMSHIRE   Brewhouse Yard Museum   Map 8 SK53

Seventeenth-century buildings spread over a two-acre site contain period rooms and thematic displays depicting the city's daily life in the post-medieval era; the inclusion of exhibits that can either be handled or operated by visitors makes the museum particularly exciting for children. Unusual cellars cut into the rock are on show too, their past uses illustrated by appropriate displays, and cottage gardens include some plants peculiar to the area.

☎**(0602) 411881 ext 67 or 48**
Located: Castle Boulevard.

Open: all year except Xmas Day 10–12 & 1–5 (last admissions 11.45 & 4.45).
Admission: free, but donation appreciated.
& (ground floor only) ⴕ (except guide dogs)

NOTTINGHAM, NOTTINGHAMSHIRE   Industrial Museum   Map 8 SK53

Lace and hosiery making, both traditionally associated with Nottingham, are prominent among displays illustrating the city's industrial history; others include printing, engineering and the pharmaceutical and tobacco industries. These exhibits are housed in an 18th-century stable block, whilst new extensions contain a mid 19th-century beam pumping engine and heavy agricultural machinery. Other items of interest, such as a horse gin from a local coalmine and Victorian street furniture, are on view in the yards outside.

☎**(0602) 284602**
Located: Courtyard Buildings, Wollaton Park.

Open: Apr–Sep Mon–Sat 10–6, Sun 2–6; Oct–Mar Thu & Sat 10–4.30, Sun 1.30–4.30. Beam pumping engine in steam last Sun in each month & Bank Hols.
Admission: free Mon–Sat; 20p (children 10p) Sun & Bank Hols.
P. & shop ⴕ

For continuation of NOTTINGHAM entries see page 99

The Broads are large, shallow lakes, more than thirty in number, which were created as a result of peat digging in medieval times and first became flooded in the 14th century. Several rivers link the Broads together: The Bure, the Yare and the Waveney among them, and together they provide some 200 miles of navigable waterways. Certainly the Broads have long been best known for boating holidays and wherever you go you will see motor launches, yachts and rowing boats by the dozen. Day trippers need not miss out on discovering the true character of the Broads from the water – boats can be hired by the day at a number of centres including Potter Heigham, Horning and Wroxham.

Hickling Broad is one of the widest stretches of water in Norfolk and is the site of a particularly good nature reserve. A number of rare species can be seen in the unique environment of the Broads, including the marsh harrier and the beautiful swallowtail butterfly. The Norfolk Naturalists' Trust manage a number of reserves, including Hickling, and their Conservation Centre at Ranworth is well worth a visit.

A feature of this area are the extensive reed beds which provide the raw materials for thatching. Cut by hand and loaded into flat-bottomed boats, the reed is in great demand both locally and further afield and many of the Broads villages have thatched cottages of a very distinctive style.

At the south-eastern extremity of the Broads is Lowestoft, a coastal town known for its fishing and maritime traditions. Inland of its inner harbour is Oulton Broad, flanked by a park with a swimming pool, bowling greens and a children's playground. This Broad is particularly busy with frequent sailing regattas and exciting power-boat races.

Wroxham is a thriving village-cum-holiday centre on its own Broad and nearby is the award-winning Wroxham Barns craft centre where a variety of crafts can be seen in the making, including, not surprisingly, boatbuilding.

There is a great deal to see and do in the Broads – pretty villages to explore, historic houses, old windmills, wildlife parks – even a taxidermist's workshop to visit. But whatever you are doing, you will find the urge to become waterborne almost overwhelming!

For places to visit in the area check the location atlas at the end of the book.

NOTTINGHAM, NOTTINGHAMSHIRE   Museum of Costume and Textiles

Map 8 SK53

A row of Georgian houses make up this museum, which spans the years from 1730 to 1960 and where appropriately furnished rooms provide an effective setting for the changing fashions of the 18th, 19th and 20th-centuries. The Lord Middleton Collection of 17th-century costumes and embroideries is also on show, and there are displays of dolls, accessories, underwear and textiles. The new Lace Room traces the development of the craft from the earliest handmade pieces to machine work.

for PEAK DISTRICT NATIONAL PARK see page 100

☎(0602) 411881
Located: At 43–51 Castlegate.

Open: daily (except Xmas Day) 10–5.
Admission: free.
& (ground floor only) shop ✴

PETERBOROUGH, CAMBRIDGESHIRE   Ferry Meadows Country Park

Map 4 TL19

This lovely riverside park is the focal point of the 2,000-acre Nene Park and includes Roman remains, a steam railway (see entry under Wansford) and lots of activities. You can windsurf, row or sail on the lake, play golf, ride horses or simply enjoy the lakeside and riverside walks. If you enjoy bird-watching there are observation hides around a carefully designed bird sanctuary.

Located: 2½ miles west of Peterborough, signposted from the A605 Oundle road.

Open: all year.
Admission: there is a charge for parking at weekends and Bank Hols from Easter to Oct.
P. ⌂ 🍴 & shop visitor centre

RAMPTON, NOTTINGHAMSHIRE   Sundown Pet's Corner   Map 8 SK77

Created specially for young children, with pets and farm animals and animated nursery rhymes in an attractive garden setting. There's a Western Street with a 'Crazy Critters' show, Smugglers Cove, Tudor Village, Toddler Town, Noah's Ark, large sandpits and much more, including a Fantasy Castle planned for 1988.

☎(077784) 274
Located: In Treswell Rd.

Open: daily 10–6 or dusk. Closed 25–26 Dec.
Admission: ✴£1.20 (under 2 free).
P. ⌂ 🍴 & shop ✴

REEDHAM, NORFOLK   Pettitts Crafts and Gardens   Map 5 TG40

During the high season children can enjoy live entertainment, but there's plenty to amuse them the rest of the year too. They can see miniature horses, have donkey rides, play crazy golf or putting, or let off steam on the adventure playground. Older children will enjoy the craft demonstrations on candlemaking, taxidermy and feather craft, with opportunities to buy the products. The beautiful gardens are home to peacocks, ornamental pheasants, birds of prey and parrots.

☎Great Yarmouth (0493) 700094

Open: Easter Sun–Oct, Mon–Fri 10–6, Sun 1–5.30 (closed Sat).
Admission: £1.90 (children £1.30). Reduction for disabled.
P. ⌂ 🍴 & shop

RIPLEY, DERBYSHIRE   Midland Railway Centre   Map 8 SK35

For all would-be engine drivers and enthusiasts the centre operates a regular steam-train passenger service for three miles from Butterley Station to Ironville. There's an industrial museum here too which depicts the golden days of the Midland Railway, with exhibits ranging from 1866 steam locomotives to diesels of 1961, plus a large selection of rolling stock spanning some 100 years.

for SHERINGHAM see page 101

☎(0773) 570140/47674
Located: At Butterley Station.

Open: For static display in season. Trains run weekends, Bank Hols & Wed Mar–Dec. Daily mid Jul–Sep 10–5.
Admission: ✴£2 (children £1). Family £5.
P. ⌂ 🍴 shop

This was the first of England's National Parks, established in 1951. Its wild moorland and many scenic dales are popular local tourist spots. The southern part of the Park is known as the White Peak – from the pale-coloured limestone rocks that underly it – while the sombre millstone grit and peaty moorland have given to the nothern area the apt label of the Dark Peak.

One of the most beautiful valleys is Dovedale, where the River Dove follows a winding course through a steep, wooded valley. Crowned with limestone crags weathered by the years into strange shapes, with names such as the Twelve Apostles, Tissington Spires and Lion Rock. There are caves, too, notably Dove Holes and Reynard's Cavern.

The Manifold valley nearby, is equally beautiful and less crowded. The river sometimes does a disappearing trick in dry weather, flowing underground between Wetton and Ilam, a picturesque 19th-century estate village. Thor's Cave, near Wetton was once the home of prehistoric man.

Another popular place for family picnics is the Goyt Valley near Buxton, in the Dark Peak. There are riverside walks, two reservoirs and the picturesque ruins of Errwood Hall built by the Grimshawe Family in 1830.

The Peak District is famous for its caves, and four of the most spectacular are grouped round the village of Castleton (see separate gazetteer entry.)

Many Peak District towns and villages make good centres for exploring the Peak District. Chief of these is Matlock (see separate gazetteer entry), with its cable-car ascent of the Heights of Abraham, a steep limestone bluff above the town. At Tissington and several other villages, the wells are dressed with elaborate flower pictures at ceremonies throughout May and June. These are a sight not to be missed. A custom with a more sombre history is the commemoration, at the end of August, of the Great Plague which devasted Eyam in the 17th century. The villagers, led by their courageous rector, William Mompesson, stayed in their village rather than flee into the surrounding countryside and spread the disease, 259 of them died.

The Pennine Way, a 250-mile long-distance path, starts at the pretty little village of Edale, crossing Kinderscout, the Peak District's highest point, and ending at Kirk Yetholm on the Scottish borders.

For places to visit in the area check the location atlas
at the end of the book.

The old bridge at Three Shires Head
in the Dane Valley.

SHERINGHAM, NORFOLK   North Norfolk Railway   Map 9 TG14

Steam hauled trains operate here on certain days during the summer, with 'Santa Specials' during December. There's a great collection of steam locomotives and rolling stock too, some in various stages of renovation. See the Brighton Belle and some ex-Great Eastern Railway main-line engines. There's a museum of railwayana, plus souvenirs and a bookshop.

☏(0263) 822045, Talking Timetable (0263) 825049
Located: At Sheringham Station.

Open: Station, Easter–Oct daily 10–5 (or later). Trains run daily in Aug, but on certain days only Easter–Oct, check for specific dates.
Admission: *30p (children & senior citizens 15p). Steam trains £2 return (children £1, senior citizens £1.60).
☐ 🅿 ⅋ & shop

SHERWOOD FOREST, NOTTINGHAMSHIRE   Map 8 SK55

There is little left of the vast forest which once covered the land here, but what remains is very interesting and varied. The most famous tree is the Major Oak, over 30 feet in girth and believed to be about 500 years old. If it is the legend of Robin Hood which brings you here, the visitor centre at Edwinstowe tells the story.

☏Mansfield (0623) 823202
Located: Visitor centre, ½ mile north of Edwinstowe on B6034.

Open: Visitor Centre all year daily from 10.30; closes at 5pm Mar–Sep & 4pm Oct–Feb.
Admission: free.
P. ☐ & shop (closed Bank Hols)

SKEGNESS, LINCOLNSHIRE   Skegness Natureland Marine Zoo   Map 9 TF56

Sea lions, seals and penguins are the special feature of the Marine Zoo, but other attractions include a tropical house, aquarium and a Floral Palace of exotic plants where tropical birds can be seen in free flight. There's a pets corner too, Wild Fowl Pool, tropical butterflies and an Animal Brass Rubbing House.

☏(0754) 4345
Located: In North Parade, The Promenade.

Open: Apr–May & Sep 10–5; Jul–Aug 10–7; Oct–Mar 10–4.30. (Closed 25–26 Dec & 1 Jan.)
Admission: £1.60 (children & senior citizens 80p under 3 free).
☐ & (no disabled toilet) shop

SOLIHULL, WEST MIDLANDS   National Motorcycle Museum   Map 7 SP17

Give the younger generation a glimpse of the Golden Age of motor-cycling! This display of immaculately restored British machines spans eighty years and represents the work of a hundred different factories.

☏021-704 2784
Located: Coventry Road, Bickenhill (Off A45 close to M42 junction 6, not far from National Exhibition Centre).

Open: daily except Xmas Day 10–6.
Admission: £2.50 (children & senior citizens £1.75).
P. ☐ & shop ⅋

SOMERLEYTON, SUFFOLK   Somerleyton Hall   Map 5 TM49

Originally Tudor, this mansion was rebuilt in Anglo-Italian style in 1846, and its magnificent state rooms contain superb furniture, tapestries and paintings. In the 12-acre grounds – ablaze with azaleas and rhododendrons in Spring – you can follow a nature trail, explore the famous maze or, on the days when it is operating, take a ride on the miniature railway.

☏Lowestoft (0502) 730224
Located: Off B1074.

Open: Easter–Oct: before Spring Bank Hol Thu & Sun 2–5.30; after Spring Bank Hol, Sun & Tue–Fri 2–5.30.
Admission: £2.20 (children £1, senior citizens £1.60).
P. ☐ ⅋ & shop ⅋

SPALDING, LINCOLNSHIRE Springfields Gardens Map 8 TF22

Visit Spalding in springtime to see an amazing 25-acre carpet of colour – a magnificent bedding display with over 200,000 plants and more than a million bulbs set around lawns, lake and glass-houses. This year's Flower Parade will take place on 7th May, and floats will remain on show for the following two days. There are also Gardeners' Days Out on the 17th July and the 14th August, and a Vintage Vehicle Day.

☎(0775) 4843
Located: On eastern outskirts of town off A151.

Open: Apr–Sep daily 10–6.
Admission: £1.50 (accompanied children free). Special events £2.00.
P. ☕ ♿ shop & garden centre 🐕̸

STOKE-ON-TRENT, STAFFORDSHIRE Chatterley Whitfield Mining Museum Map 7 SJ84

A guided underground tour of the mine's workings is obviously the most thrilling part of a visit to this museum, but there is much of interest to be seen on the surface too – in the lamproom, steam winding engine room, colliery canteen and exhibition galleries.

☎(0782) 813337
Located: Near Tunstall.

Open: daily, summer 10–5, last tour 4pm. (Phone for winter opening times)
Admission: £2.95 (children 5–16 £1.85, senior citizens £2.35). Family tickets £8.50.
P. ☕ ♿ (surface only) shop 🐕̸ (underground)

STOKE-ON-TRENT, STAFFORDSHIRE Wedgwood Museum and Visitor Centre Map 7 SJ84

This "living museum" is part of the Barlaston factory; demonstrations in the craft manufacturing hall and film shows in the cinema help visitors to appreciate the traditional skills involved in the production of Wedgwood ware. There is a fine art gallery, and the museum displays a comprehensive collection of the works of Josiah Wedgwood from 1750.

☎(0782) 204141 or 204218
Located: at Barlaston, 5 miles south.

Open: Mon–Fri 9–5, Sat 10–4. Closed 25 Dec & 1 Jan.
Admission: £1.50 (children & senior citizens 75p). Family tickets (2 adults & 2 children) £3.
P. ☕ ♿ shop 🐕̸

STOWMARKET, SUFFOLK Museum of East Anglian Life Map 5 TM05

The best introduction to this fascinating open-air museum would be to take a wagon ride around the river valley site, with 'Remus' the resident Suffolk Punch horse pulling you along. You'll pass several recontructed buildings including the newly-opened Boby Building, which houses six craft workshops, videos of a cooper and basket maker and a filmshow in Bioscope cinema. Displays include scenes of Victorian domestic life, gypsies, farming and industry. Another great attraction is the pair of Burrell ploughing steam traction engines (1879) – the only surviving pair in the world.

☎(0449) 612229

Open: Apr–Oct, Mon–Sat 11–5, Sun 12 noon–5 (6pm Jun–Aug).
Admission: *£1.50 (children & senior citizens £1).
P. ☕ ⛱ ♿ shop

for STRATFORD-UPON-AVON see opposite page

SUFFOLK WILDLIFE AND RARE BREEDS PARK, SUFFOLK Map 5 TM58

You'll find exotic wild animals and birds as well as a full range of rare breeds of cattle, pigs and poultry here at the Suffolk Wildlife and Rare Breeds Park. There are amusements for children as well as a miniature steam and diesel passenger railway.

☎**Lowestoft (0502) 740291**
Located: 2½ miles south of Lowestoft.

Open: Easter–end Oct, daily 10–6.
Admission: *£2 (children £1.30, senior citizens £1.80).
P. ☕ ⛱ ♿ shop

for SWINFORD see page 104

The Heart of Shakespeare Country

For more than three centuries visitors have come to this pleasant Midland market town to pay homage to the memory of England's great dramatist and poet. Stratford means Shakespeare, and the 'Shakespeare industry' now makes it second only to London as a tourist magnet.

Historic buildings from every era since the Middle Ages line the streets here. Those most closely connected with the playwright, including the house where he was born, are cared for by the Shakespeare Birthplace Trust. Among them is Hall's Croft, home of his daughter Susanna and her husband Dr John Hall. Shakespeare himself spent his last 19 years at New Place, a house that was later demolished, but the site has been restored as an Elizabethan knot garden. Next to it stands the timbered house of Thomas Nash, first husband of Shakespeare's granddaughter Elizabeth Hall, who was his last direct descendant.

Many visitors complete their Shakespeare pilgrimage by a visit to Holy Trinity Church, beside the Avon. The parish register records Shakespeare's baptism, and here, in the chancel, he lies buried with his wife and eldest daughter.

A walk through Stratford's street will reveal much of interest that is quite unconnected with Shakespeare: 16th-century Harvard House, linked with the famous American university; the ancient Guild Chapel; the Arms and Armour Museum; the Stratford Motor Museum, where vintage cars and motorcycles are displayed; and the bustling Friday street market. A popular and relaxing pastime after a few hours' sightseeing is to hire a rowing boat on the Avon, overhung by willows and populated by graceful swans.

☆STAR ATTRACTIONS

Royal Shakespeare Theatre

Opened in 1932, this theatre replaced the first Memorial Theatre, which had burned down six years earlier. Today the prestigious Royal Shakespeare Company performs in three theatres. The main auditorium, reserved for Shakespeare's own work; the new Swan Theatre stages plays by his contemporaries; The Other Place staging mainly modern drama. Well worth seeing on a visit to the theatre is the RSC Collection, whose permanent and temporary displays illustrate the staging of Shakespeare's plays down the ages, and include some of the RSC's own costumes and props. Backstage tours are available at set times on most days and may be booked in advance.

☎(0789) 296655 ext 215
Located: Waterside.

Open: ✳RSC Collection Mon–Sat 9.15–6.30, Sun 12–5.
Admission: ✳RSC Collection £1 (children & senior citizens 50p). Backstage & exhibition tours £2.20 (children & senior citizens £1.80). P. ♿ (ground floor & grounds only) Shop 🍴

Shakespeare's Birthplace

Around half a million visitors a year cross the threshold of this timber-framed house where Shakespeare was born in 1564. The living quarters have been restored and furnished much as they would have been in his day, whilst the workshop where his father carried on his trade as a glover is now a museum illustrating the playwright's life and work. His school desk is among the exhibits. Graffiti on the walls of the room where he was born include the names of illustrious past visitors – Walter Scott, Robert Browning and Izaak Walton among them. Next to the birthplace is the modern Shakespeare Centre, headquarters of the Birthplace Trust.

☎(0789) 204016
Located: Henley Street.

Open: Apr–Oct Mon–Sat 9–6, Sun 10–6; (closes 5pm in Oct); Nov–Mar Mon–Sat 9–4.30, Sun 1.30–4.30. Closed Good Fri am, Xmas & New Year's Day am.
Admission: ✳£1.50 (children 60p). ♿ (ground floor & gardens only) Shop 🍴

SWINFORD, LEICESTERSHIRE   Stanford Hall   Map 4 SP57

Set on the banks of the Avon, this 1690's William and Mary house contains interesting paintings and antique furniture, whilst walled rose gardens and an old forge stand outside. Its appeal is not limited to lovers of gracious living, however, for members of the family interested in early technology will want to examine the replica of Percy Pilcher's flying machine of 1898 and to visit the motor cycle museum; the craft centre, open most Sundays, the nature trail or fishing may well appeal to others. A number of car and motorcycle rallies are held here during the year.

☎Rugby (0788) 860250
Located: 1 mile east of Swinford.

Open: Easter–Sep Thu, Sat & Sun 2.30–6, also Bank Hol Mon and Tue. House 2.30–6. Grounds/museum/craft centre/shop/ cafeteria from 12 noon Bank Hol & event days.
Admission: House & grounds £1.90 (children 90p). Grounds only £1 (children 50p). Museum 75p (children 35p).
P. ☯ ♿ (grounds only) shop ⚔ (in house)

THURSFORD GREEN, NORFOLK   Thursford Collection   Map 9 TF93

Here you are offered a glimpse of the working life of a bygone age, reflected in ploughing engines, farm machinery, traction engines and a 2' gauge steam railway. The lighter side of those times is not forgotten, however, for the collection includes Savage's Venetian Gondola Switchback ride, fairground, street and barrel organs, and a Wurlitzer cinema organ which is played by the country's leading organists in a series of midsummer musical evenings beginning at 8pm each Tuesday. There are also live musical shows given each day.

☎Thursford (032877) 477
Located: 6 miles north-east of Fakenham.

Open: Good Fri–Oct daily 2–5.30pm (except Jul & Aug 11–5.30).
Admission: ✳£2.30 (children 4–14 £1, under 4 free, senior citizens £2).
P. ☯ 🚉 ♿ shop ⚔

TWYCROSS, LEICESTERSHIRE   Twycross Zoo Park   Map 4 SK30

Though this collection of large animals is particularly noted for its range of primates, including gorillas, orang-utans and chimpanzees, it also has a modern reptile house and numerous exotic birds. Children will also enjoy visiting Pets Corner or trying out the adventure playground.

☎Tamworth (0827) 880250
Located: 1½ miles north-west of Twycross, off A444.

Open: daily (except Xmas Day); 10–6 summer; 10–4 winter.
Admission: ✳£2.30 (children £1.10, senior citizens £1.50). Car park 20p.
P. ☯ (licensed in summer only) ♿ shop ⚔

WANSFORD, CAMBRIDGESHIRE   Nene Valley Railway   Map 4 TL09

For a trip back in time, take a ride on a standard-gauge steam train that runs between Wansford and Peterborough. The line has a small museum of railway memorabilia and an international array of steam locomotives and stock. Special events are arranged throughout the year, including 'Santa Specials' during December.

Also see entry for Ferry Meadows Country Park under PETER-BOROUGH.

☎Stamford (0780) 782854 talking timetable ☎Stamford (0780) 782921
Located: At Wansford Station just off southbound carriageway of the A1, 8 miles west of Peterborough.

Open: Apr–Oct Sat & Sun; Jun, Jul & Aug also Wed & Thur; plus Bank Hols from May.
Admission: £3.50 return (children 5–16, disabled & senior citizens £1.75).
P. ☯ (licensed) ♿ shop

WARWICK   Warwickshire   Map 4 SP26

A Riverside Stronghold at the Heart of England

The story of this ancient town begins just over 1,000 years ago, when a castle was built here beside the Avon by Ethelfleda, daughter of Alfred the Great. A Norman fortress followed, but most of the massive castle that remains Warwick's crowning glory dates from the 14th century. Parts of the medieval town can still be seen in High Street, Mill Street, Bridge End and Castle Street. Another treasure is the Beauchamp Chapel of St Mary's Church, one of the country's finest medieval chapels. The centrepiece is the beautiful carved tomb of Richard Beauchamp, a former Earl of Warwick.

Several museums portray aspects of Warwick's history. The old market hall is home to the Warwick Museum. There are two military museums, or, for a glimpse into everyday life of yesteryear, visit St John's House, a fine Jacobean mansion where a reconstructed Victorian schoolroom is among the displays. Movie Memorabilia has a collection of costumes, props and artwork from Hollywood film studios, or you can hire a Sinclair C5 to drive in St Nicholas' Park, where other family activities include an indoor pool, the Peter Pan Railway, a helter-skelter and boat trips on the Avon.

☆*STAR ATTRACTIONS*

Lord Leycester Hospital

This delightful and much-photographed group of half-timbered buildings, some as many as 600 years old, incorporates Warwick's original West Gate, part of the town wall. The 15th-century Guildhall and the Chapel of St James also form part of the complex. Since 1571 the Lord Lycester Hospital has been a different home for ex-servicemen – originally 12 'brethren' and a 'master' – who still sometimes wear their traditional costumes.

☎(0926) 492797
Located: High Street.

Open: summer Mon–Sat 10–5.30; winter Mon–Sat 10–4. Closed Good Fri & Xmas.
Admission: ✱£1 (children 50p).
☐ (Easter–Sep only) & (ground floor only) Shop

Oken's House and Warwick Doll Museum

This Tudor house was the home of Thomas Oken, a Warwick tradesman and benefactor who died in 1573, leaving money to numerous local causes, ranging from schools and road repairs to a trust fund from which poor people still benefit today. His house now contains an outstanding collection of dolls of the past two centuries, and other toys, games and books are also on show.

☎(0926) 495546 & 491600
Located: Castle Street.

Open: Mar–Dec daily 10.30–5; Jan & Feb Sat & Sun 10.30–5.
Admission: 70p (children 50p).
Shop ⴲ

Warwick Castle

This stunning combination of mighty fortress and opulent stately home is one of England's most popular attractions. It stands in lovely riverside grounds where peacocks strut, and where the 'Red Knight' sometimes patrols on horseback. Overlooking the Avon are the state rooms, including the awe-inspiring great hall, and private apartments. These have been restored as the setting of a royal house-party that took place here in 1898, complete with waxwork figures of the Prince of Wales, Lady Warwick and other members of Victorian high society. In stark contrast is the castle dungeon and gruesome torture chamber. Visitors also have access to Guy's Tower and the Clarence Tower, flanking the fine gatehouse, and to the Watergate Tower – home, by tradition, of the castle ghost.

☎(0926) 495421
Located: Castle Hill.

Open: daily, Mar–Oct 10–5.30; Nov–Feb 10–4.30. Closed Xmas.
Admission: £4 (children £2.75). Family ticket £12.
P. ☐ (licensed) ⴲ & (garden only) shop ⴲ

WELLS-NEXT-THE-SEA Wells and Walsingham Light Railway Map 9 TF94

The Wells and Walsingham Light Railway boasts the longest 10¼ inch gauge railway in Britain. Here you can enjoy a trip on the four-mile route, noted for wild flowers and butterflies, between Wells and Walsingham.

Located: Wells Station, Sheringham Rd (A149); Walsingham Station, Egmere Rd.

Open: Good Fri–Sep daily.
Admission: return £2.50 (children £1.50); single £1.50 (children £1).
P. ⊐ shop

WESTON PARK, SHROPSHIRE Map 7 SJ81

This fine 17th-century mansion set in beautiful grounds with three lakes and vast parkland has many other attractions to satisfy family interest: a miniature railway, butterfly farm, woodland adventure playground, aquarium and a studio pottery. Special exhibitions and events are organised throughout the year, including horse trials, point-to-point, the Town and Country Fayre and the Midland Game Fair.

☎Weston-under-Lizard (095276) 207
Located: 7 miles west of Junction 12 on M6 & 3 miles north of Junction 3 on M54.

Open: Easter Sat; weekends & Bank Hols Apr, May & Sep; daily Jun & Jul (except Mon & Fri); daily Aug. Grounds 11–5, house 1–5.
Admission: *Park, £1.80 (children & senior citizens £1.30). House 75p (children & senior citizens 50p).
P. ⊐ (licensed) ┬┴ & shop

WEST RUNTON, NORFOLK Norfolk Shire Horse Centre Map 9 TG14

The ideal place for the pony-struck! There are nine breeds of mountain and moorland ponies, as well as a collection of draught horses. Also to be seen are bygones from the working life of the horse: horse-drawn machinery, wagons, carts, photograhic displays, talks and a video. There are harnessing and working demonstrations, and riding school activities.

☎(026375) 339

Open: Easter–Oct Sun–Fri, daily in Aug, 10–5. Shire horse demonstrations 11.15 & 3.15.
Admission: £2 (children & senior citizens £1).
P. ⊐ ┬┴ & (no disabled toilet) shop

WEST STOW, SUFFOLK West Stow Country Park and Anglo Saxon Village
Map 5 TL87

A hundred and twenty five acres of grass and heathland, with river and lake, make West Stow Country Park a pleasant place in which to walk. It also contains a unique reconstruction of an Anglo Saxon village on the site where excavations have shown that a settlement stood in about 500AD. The project has been fully researched, and the replica huts have been built using the same materials, methods and tools as the originals. The Park will hold its Open Day on 19 June 1988.

☎Culford (028484) 718
Located: 6 miles north-west of Bury St Edmunds, off A1101.

Open: Apr–Oct Tue–Sat 2–5, also Sun & Bank Hols 11–1 & 2–5.
Admission: 60p (children 30p, senior citizens 50p).
P. ┬┴ & (ground floor & grounds only) shop

WORKSOP, NOTTINGHAMSHIRE Clumber Park Map 8 SK57

This is one of Britain's most popular country parks, formerly the landscaped grounds of a palatial mansion and before that a tract of heath on the edge of Sherwood Forest. The mansion is gone now, but there remains the two garden temples, a Palladian bridge and the superb Clumber Chapel. The park is now devoted to leisure activities with bicycles for hire, riding permits and angling on the 85-acre serpentine lake. There is a planned nature walk, part of which follows Europe's longest double lime avenue of 1,296 trees.

Located: 4½ miles south-east of Worksop.

Open: park at all times, Chapel afternoons only.
Admission: a charge is made for vehicles.
P. ⊐ & (including fishing platforms) shop

Northern England

The spine of England, the bleak mountain chain
of the Pennines, divides the northlands into two,
as it was once divided between the red rose of the
Lancastrians and the white rose of York.

To the east lie Yorkshire, Durham and
Northumberland with great cities of two eras: the
medieval grandeur of York and Durham and the
Victorian splendours of Leeds and Newcastle.
Surrounding these cities are enormous wide
landscapes and some of the greatest medieval
monuments of England. From the North York
Moors are spectacular views out to the North Sea;
further west the magnificent Yorkshire Dales are
inhabited sparsely by people, more profusely by
sheep.

Cross the Pennines and you come to another
country. Lancashire is historically dominated by
industry, its cities inspired by Victorian self-
assurance. Much is changing as the area moves
into the post-industrial revolution, but in
Salford's art gallery you can see it as it once was
through the eyes of the artist L.S. Lowry.

Yet further west is the Cheshire countryside, rich,
kempt and rural with fine black-and-white
'magpie' buildings and the ancient city of Chester.
To the north is the breathtakingly beautiful Lake
District and the wild moorland county of
Cumbria.

From east to west the area is bordered by the
astonishing Hadrian's Wall, built by the Romans
to protect their outposts from the Scots.

BAMBURGH, NORTHUMBERLAND   Bamburgh Castle   Map 12 NU13

Dating back to the 12th century and restored in the 18th–19th
centuries, the imposing Castle stands in a magnificent setting
on a long, rocky ridge overlooking a broad sandy beach. In the
keep there is an impressive exhibition of armoury and weapons
including a loan collection from the Tower of London. This
was the first castle in Europe to succumb to gunfire during the
Wars of the Roses.

☎(06684) 208

Open: Apr–last Sun in Oct, daily from 1 pm.
Admission: ✻£1.60 (children 60p, senior
citizens £1.20).
P. ⌑ ႕ (ground floor only) shop ⅟

BEACON FELL COUNTRY PARK, LANCASHIRE   Map 7 SD54

The distant mountains of Snowdonia, the Ribble Estuary and
Blackpool Tower all feature in the panoramic views to be had
in clear weather from the 873 ft summit at the centre of this
country park, set on the western edge of the Forest of
Bowland. There was a beacon on the fell as long ago as
AD1002, and for many centuries this site remained part of the
chain of beacons built in prominent places and lit to warn of
impending danger such as the approach of the Spanish
Armada.

Today the area consists mainly of coniferous forest and open
moorland, with boggy hollows here and there betrayed by
clumps of rushes and nodding white, fluffy heads of cotton
grass. Footpaths criss-cross the moor and woodlands, and a
scenic drive runs right round the perimeter of the park. It
really is a beautiful place to spend a day.

**Located: 8 miles north of Preston, 5 miles
from A6 on unclassified road.
Information centre situated ¼ mile off
the fell, but well signposted.**

Open: Country Park at all times, Information
Centre daily.
P. ⌑ (Information Centre) ⊼ nature trail
viewpoint

BEAMISH, CO DURHAM   North of England Open-Air Museum   Map 12 NZ25

First of the open-air museums, and winner of the European
Museum of the Year Award in 1987, Beamish illustrates in
fascinating detail the Northern way of life around the turn of
the century. The 200 acres of reconstructed buildings,
appropriately furnished, are grouped into distinctive areas, and
visitors are carried from one to the other by a tram from the
museum's transport collection. The Town, with its Georgian
houses, has a car park, Co-operative shops, printer's workshop, inn and stables, whilst Home Farm surrounds a
traditional farmhouse with agricultural machinery, implements
and livestock. You can take a guided tour of a drift mine in
The Colliery, and The Railway Area features a rebuilt country
station, goods shed, weighbridge house, signal box and steam
locomotives. Special events planned for 1988 include a
Geordie's Heritage Day on 17 July and a Steam Day and
Commercial Vehicle Event on 4 September.

☎Stanley (0207) 231811
**Located: Off A693 & A6076 roads.
Signposted from A1(M) Chester-le-Street
intersection.**

Open: Apr–Oct daily 10–6; Nov–Mar daily
(except Mons) 10–5. Last admission always
4pm.
Admission: Summer £3.30 (children & senior
citizens £2.30); Winter £1.95 (children &
senior citizens £1.25).
P. ⌑ (licensed summer only) ⊼ shop

Symbols
☎ telephone number
P. parking on the premises
⌑ refreshments available
⊼ picnic area
႕ accessible to wheelchair-bound visitors
⅟ no dogs
✻ indicates 1987 details

BEDLINGTON, NORTHUMBERLAND   Plessey Woods Country Park   Map 12 NZ28

While strolling through the woodlands which form the core of this lovely park, it is hard to believe that industrial Tyneside is less than ten miles away. Visitors who follow the history trail, one of several colour-coded trails here, are shown how mining, milling, quarrying and forestry have all been major sources of employment here at one time or another.

Another route through the park, opening up entirely new vistas, is to follow the riverside trail. The River Blyth is only a few miles from its source here, but being fed by a number of smaller rivers and streams, it becomes a major river by the time it reaches the sea at Blyth. In the park it winds through dense woodland and provides a rich wildlife habitat. These are but two of the trails marked out in the park to enable you to enjoy your visit.

Located: entrance on A192 Morpeth road, 1½ miles south-west of Bedlington.

Open: all year.
Admission:
P. ▭ ⊼ Information centre

BEVERLEY, HUMBERSIDE   Museum of Army Transport   Map 8 TA03

A unique collection of British Army transport, once used on road, rail, sea and air will thrill youngsters of all ages. Some seventy vehicles are displayed here, mostly in tableaux representing the vehicle's role. There is a Land Rover rigged for a parachute-drop, some locomotives, a Blackburn Beverley transport and a Beaver aircraft.

☎Hull (0482) 860445
Located: in Flemingate.

Open: daily 10–5. (Closed Xmas day.)
Admission: £1.80 (children 3–16, senior citizens 90p). Children under 16 must be accompanied by an adult.
P. ▭ ⊼ & shop ⋔

for BLACKPOOL see page 110

BOLAM LAKE COUNTRY PARK, NORTHUMBERLAND   Map 12 NZ08

The combination of large mature deciduous and coniferous trees, open grassland, rhododendrons, and a shallow lake makes this country park an outstandingly beautiful place to spend a day out. To go with all this there is a great variety of wildlife, particularly birds.

The easiest place to see the birds is in the small upper car park where large numbers congregate waiting to be fed. Most will come to the hand, and they include blue tits, great tits, marsh tits, and nuthatches.

A system of footpaths winds through the park and gives visitors the opportunity to see some of the mammals which live here, particularly red squirrels. These delightful animals are a special feature of the park. They will even come into the car park to feed on the bird food.

Located: 2 miles north of Belsay on unclassified road off A696; 7 miles south-west of Morpeth.

Open: all year.
P. ⊼ nature trail

for BRADFORD see page 111

BLACKPOOL Lancashire Map 7 SD33

Playground of the North

More than any other resort, Blackpool is Britain's mecca of holiday entertainment. Everyone has heard of the Tower and the Golden Mile, but Blackpool's beaches and promenades stretch for some seven miles, and much of this coastline is backed by a bewildering array of seaside attractions that has to be seen to be believed.

Lacking nothing in the way of traditional family seaside facilities, Blackpool simply has more of them than anywhere else. There is not one pier but three, complete with theatres, amusements, shops and refreshments; four dance halls, 11 cinemas, 26 bowling greens, 77 tennis courts and 16 children's playgrounds. Old favourites like donkey rides, Punch and Judy, and of course, Blackpool rock, are never very far away, and no other resort can match Blackpool's 11-mile seafront tramway – the first and last of its kind in Britain. Set against these are all the space-age attractions: the sensational rides of the Pleasure Beach; the indoor seaside of the Sandcastle Leisure Centre; Splashland at the Derby Pool, where sound and visual effects give swimming a new meaning as you enter the 'Black Hole' or the 'Dragon's Cave'. Even the most traditional of Blackpool's attractions – the autumn Illuminations – has not escaped 1980s influences. Fibre optics, lasers and computer control have made the five-mile stretch even more dazzling, with amazing new features every year.

A retreat from the seafront hurly-burly is the 256 peaceful acres of Stanley Park, with its formal gardens and conservatories, woodlands and large lake.

☆ STAR ATTRACTIONS

Blackpool Tower

Blackpool's unmistakable mascot is 518 ft high and the lift ride to the top is not to be missed, for the views stretch for miles on a fine day. The entertainment complex at the foot of the Tower includes the famous Tower Ballroom, the Undersea World Aquarium and Europe's largest static circus. There is also an adventure playground and the Tiny Tots Soft Play Area.

☎(0253) 22242
Located: Promenade.

Open: *Easter–Oct daily 9.30am–11pm & weekends in winter. Circus performances Jun–Oct daily.
Admission: fee payable.
🚻 ઙ Shop

Blackpool Zoo Park

Giraffes, zebras, kangaroos and elephants are just a few of the 500 creatures to be seen at this well-landscaped modern zoo near Stanley Park. Most of the animals are in spacious moated pens or enclosures. A favourite with younger visitors is feeding time for the sea-lions and penguins each morning and afternoon. There is also a children's playground and a miniature railway.

☎(0253) 65027
Located: East Park Drive.

Open: daily, summer 10–6; winter 10–5 (or dusk if earlier). Closed Xmas.
Admission: £1.80 (children & senior citizens 90p).
P. 🚻 (licensed) 🍴 ઙ shop ⚲

Pleasure Beach

Roller-coasters, a big dipper, various water rides and the Space Tower are just a few of many attractions at this lavish 40-acre amusement park. As an alternative to rides that make your hair stand on end, the Pleasure Beach also offers skating and ice spectaculars at the Ice Drome, discos, shows, and a choice of bars and restaurants.

☎(0253) 41033
Located: Promenade.

Open: Easter week from 11am; then Mon–Fri from 2pm, Sat & Sun from 11am until Spring Bank Hol; Spring Bank Hol–early Nov daily from 11am.
Admission: charges for each individual attraction
🚻(licensed)

BRADFORD, W YORKS National Museum of Photography, Film & Television

Map 7 SE13

There is much to do and see and many experiences to enjoy on the five levels of this museum: see how a camera works in a human-size model, try your skills at operating a TV camera, conjure up portraits in early photography studios, go behind the scenes of a newspaper picture section, and see the work and skill of photographers past and present. A very special experience is to see one of the films on Europe's biggest screen: five storeys high, stretching to the limits of your vision. There is also a programme of films on Tuesday, Wednesday, Saturday and Sunday evenings in the Bradford Playhouse and Film Theatre. Telephone for the programme.

☎(0274) 727488
Located: Prince's Way.

Open: Tue–Sun 11–6, special exhibitions open until 7.30. Open Bank Hol Mon, except May Day.
Admission: *Museum free. Cinema, day time £2.50 (children £1, senior citizens £1.50); evening £3.50 (children £1.75, senior citizens £2.50).
P. ☕ ⛩ ♿ shop 🚫🐕 (except guide dogs)

BURY, GT MANCHESTER East Lancashire Railway & Bury Transport Museum

Map 7 SD81

How about a memorable day out with the magic of steam! Then take a 4½ mile journey on the East Lancashire Railway which runs between Bury and Ramsbottom – a further 4 miles is to be added soon to extend the line to Rawtenstall. The railway offers the ideal way to discover the delights of the Upper Irwell Valley, an area set in the heart of the West Pennines, and steeped in the history of early industrialisation.

The Transport Museum is ideally situated in the former Castlecroft railway warehouse at Bury, which dates back to the 1840s. This working museum houses a growing collection of locomotives, coaches and other rolling stock necessary for operating the line. Historic road vehicles are also on display here including a number of buses and lorries.

☎061-764 7790
Located: Bolton Street Station, Bury.

Open: Sat, Sun & Bank Hol Mons, Easter–October. Reduced timetable during Nov & Santa Specials in Dec.
Admission: *Museum free. Train fare 70p; £1.20 return (children 20p, 40p return). Accompanied children under 5 free.
P. ☕ (Bury Station & Buffet cars on trains) ♿ (station area only) shop

CARLTON, NORTH YORKSHIRE Carlton Towers **Map 8 SE62**

The 17th century Yorkshire home of the Catholic Dukes of Norfolk was remodelled in the 18th–19th centuries. The state rooms were designed by James Francis Bentley, architect of Westminster Cathedral in London. There is interesting furniture, paintings and examples of heraldry and exhibitions of uniforms and coronation robes worn by the family. You can see the Priest's Hole where the priest was hidden when Catholics were persecuted. Free entry to the parkland and rose garden.

☎Goole (0405) 861662

Open: *May–Sep Suns & Bank Hols.
Admission: *£1.75 (children under 5 free, children & senior citizens £1).
P. ☕ shop 🚫🐕 (except guide dogs)

CARNFORTH, LANCASHIRE Steam Railway Museum **Map 7 SD47**

Carnforth is a must for all railway enthusiasts! For it was once the meeting point of three of the old railway company lines, and now the home of the Steamtown Railway Museum. The engine shed, covering some thirty-seven acres, is home to a collection of Industrial and Mainline locomotives. They have been brought here, not only from Great Britain, but also from France and Germany and include the magnificent *Flying Scotsman*. The museum also contains a wealth of items of railway interest.

☎(0524) 734220

Open: daily Apr–Oct 10–6 (8pm in Aug); Nov–Mar Sat & Suns only 11–4.
Admission: £2 (children £1), includes steam ride. Handicapped admitted free.
P. ☕ ⛩ ♿ (limited) shop

CHARNOCK RICHARD, LANCASHIRE   Magical Kingdom of Camelot   Map 7 SD51

A magical theme park where legends come to life. Only one payment allows the use of over 80 rides and attractions, with many under cover, as the fun goes on even in the rain. Visit the whole of Camelot from the back of a Flying Dragon or take Guinevere's Swan Ride through Merlin's Magic Mountain. Watch a jousting tournament or interview a knight after one of their spectacular shows of daring and chivalry. Try out your balancing skills on the Grail Trail rope bridge or, if you're too small, enjoy a ride on a cheerful ladybird. Too much to do in a day? You can stay just outside the Park Hall – a complete holiday complex with hotels, holiday village and caravan park.

☎Eccleston (0257) 453044
Located: Off the M6 at junction 27 northbound or 28 southbound. Well-signposted.

Open: Apr–Sep, daily, 10–6.
Admission: Adults & children £4.45
P. ⌷ (licensed) & shop & garden centre ✳

for CHESTER see opposite page

CHOLMONDELEY, CHESHIRE   Cholmondeley Castle Gardens   Map 7 SJ55

Beautiful ornamental gardens surround this 19th-century castle, the home of the Marquess of Cholmondeley, (pronounced Chumley). They include an ancient private chapel, an attractive lakeside picnic area and a variety of rare breeds of farm animals.

☎(082922) 383
Located: 7 miles west of Nantwich, on A49

Open: Easter Sun to end Sep Suns & Bank Hols only, 12 noon–5.30.
Admission: £1.50 (children 50p, senior citizens £1).
P. ⌷ 🍴 shop & plants for sale ✳ (except on leads)

DACRE, CUMBRIA   Dalemain   Map 12 NY42

Dalemain was originally a medieval pele tower which was added to in Tudor times and completed in 1750 with a Georgian façade. The result is an elegant stately home with a fascinating interior including oak panelling, Tudor plasterwork and Chinese wallpaper. The Westmoreland and Cumberland Yeomanry Museum is housed in the tower, and a Countryside Museum is set in the 16th-century cobbled courtyard. An adventure playground allows children to let off steam while parents enjoy the historic gardens.

☎Pooley Bridge (08536) 450

Open: Easter Sun–mid Oct Sun–Thu 11.15–5. Last entry 5pm.
Admission: £2 (children 5–16 £1). Family ticket £5. Gardens only £1.50 (children & disabled free).
P. ⌷ (licensed) 🍴 & (ground floor & gardens only) shop & garden centre ✳

DELAMERE, CHESHIRE   Delamere Forest   Map 7 SJ57

The extensive Delamere Forest is all that now remains of the great Forest of Mara and Mondrum that stretched from Nantwich to the Mersey in Norman times. The original natural forest has gone, but in its place are extensive plantations of pine trees, mostly managed by the Forestry Commission. Here the Commission has laid out a variety of well signposted walks among the dense pine woods where peace and tranquillity can soon be found.

The Cheshire Sandstone Trail, a walking route which follows a sandstone ridge for 14 miles, runs through the woodlands at Delamere. Half a mile west of Delamere Station, a 1½ mile forest trail has been laid out. It starts from the Forestry Commission Visitor Centre, where a display on the forest's history and management can be seen.

Located: 9 miles north-east of Chester; 1 mile north of Delamere, off B5152

P. 🍴 viewpoint

for ELLESMERE PORT see page 115

CHESTER Cheshire Map 7 SJ46

The Ancient and Loyal City

'Ancient and loyal' indeed, Chester has 1900 years of history and long-standing links with the monarchy. For a long time it was one of the country's foremost towns – first as one of Roman Britain's three legionary fortresses and a base for the Roman fleet. Throughout medieval times it was the chief port of the North-West, until the Dee silted up and the nearby village of Liverpool began to take over its trade. The mayor of Chester still holds the title Admiral of the Dee, though the river is better known today for its salmon than its shipping.

Much of the town was given a face-lift by the Victorians. The wealth of black-and-white buildings for which Chester is noted were mostly either built or restored by them. The town hall, elegant Grosvenor Bridge and much-photographed Jubilee Clock above the Eastgate all appeared in the 19th century. Yet much of Chester is far older. The street plan is still basically Roman, as are parts of the city walls. Excavations just outside the east wall have revealed one of Britain's largest Roman amphitheatres. The cathedral, greatly restored a century ago, was originally an Anglo-Saxon abbey. The castle, rebuilt as a barracks in the 18th century, has medieval origins, and the famous Rows – the galleried two-tiered shops in Eastgate Street, Bridge Street and Watergate Street – were already here by the Middle Ages.

Aspects of Chester's history are vividly brought to life by films and exhibitions at two heritage centres – the Chester Heritage Centre, in St Michael's Church, and the Chester Visitor Centre, where exhibits include a life-size reconstruction of a section of the Rows as they looked in Victorian times.

☆STAR ATTRACTIONS

Chester Zoo and Gardens

A nocturnal house, a parrot house and a walk-through aviary are among the sights at this popular zoo. Some of the outdoor enclosures can be seen on waterbus tours, and fences and bars are kept to a minimum to ensure good views. Many acres of colourful gardens form part of the zoo complex.

☎(0244) 380280
Located: at Upton.

Open: daily, summer 10–5.30; winter 10–3.30. Gardens open till dusk. Closed Xmas.
Admission: *£3 (children 3–15 & senior citizens £1.50).
P. ☕ (licensed) ⛗ & Shop ✗

City Walls

Marvellous views of the city make the two-mile walk round the top of the walls well worth while. Chester's walls are the most complete of any in Britain, and are still supported by Roman foundations for much of their length. Bonewaldesthorne's Tower and the Water Tower, at the north-eastern corner, were built in the 14th century to protect the port, and the tower in the north-western corner is known as King Charles' Tower. From here Charles I watched his army's defeat at the Battle of Rowton Moor in 1645.

Grosvenor Museum

Chester's Roman fortress is brought vividly to life through imaginative models and numerous archaeological finds, and there is one gallery devoted to the Roman Army. Paintings, coins and silver are also on show and there is a reconstructed period house with Victorian and Georgian room settings.

☎(0244) 313858
Located: Grosvenor Street

Open: Mon–Sat 10.30–5, Sun 2–5pm. Closed Good Fri & Xmas.
Admission: free.
& (ground floor only) Shop ✗

DURHAM   County Durham   Map 12 NZ24

Norman Stronghold of the North

Set high on a sandstone outcrop in a great loop of the River Wear, Durham possesses a grandeur rivalled by few English cities, yet is small enough to be explored on foot. Cathedral and castle rub shoulders on the hilltop, and around them wind streets of handsome houses and steep alleys, locally known as vennels, which run down towards the river.

The castle is one of several historic buildings in Durham that are now part of the University – students still live in the massive keep, rebuilt in 1840. For over 700 years the castle was the seat of the Prince Bishops of Durham and the powerful holders of this office – unique in English history – ruled Durham as a city-state. The Bishops of Durham kept this status – in name at least – until 1836.

Two famous historic figures are buried in the Cathedral, one is St Cuthbert, who died in AD687. Durham's first cathedral was built in the late 10th century to house his shrine. His contemporary, the Venerable Bede, lived in Jarrow, but his remains were also brought to Durham.

A good introduction to Durham's story is a visit to the Heritage Centre; the Saxon and Norman city is portrayed in the University's Archaeology Museum; a third museum, which incorporates an arts centre for concerts and exhibitions, is devoted to the history of the Durham Light Infantry.

☆*STAR ATTRACTIONS*

Durham Cathedral
Claimed as Europe's finest Norman building, this great church was largely completed within 40 years of the laying of its foundation stone in 1093. The fine nave is supported by massive round stone pillars seven feet thick, embellished by bold Norman carvings. Another remarkable feature is the rib-vaulted ceiling – never before used successfully on a grand scale. Sadly, much of the cathedral's medieval woodwork and sculpture were destroyed in the 17th century. However, many fine examples of even earlier craftsmanship, including the oak coffin of St Cuthbert, are on display in the Treasury and monks' dormitory in the cloisters. Illuminated manuscripts, Anglo-Saxon carved stonework and some unique pieces of early embroidery may also be seen here.

☎(0385) 62367

Open: Cathedral, daily Jun–Aug 7.15am–8pm; Sep–May 7.15am–5.45pm. Treasury, Mon–Sat 10am–4.30pm, Sun 2–4.30pm.
Admission: donations, charge for Treasury.
⌨ & Bookshop

Oriental Museum
Part of the University's School of Oriental Studies, this is Britain's only museum devoted to the art and archaeology of the East. Paintings, ceramics, carvings, bronzes and ivories are among the exhibits. The collection is very wide-ranging, with displays from all periods and cultures, from Egypt to Japan.

☎091-374 2911
Located: University of Durham, Elvet Hill.

Open: Mar–Oct Mon–Sat 9.30–1 & 2–5, Sun 2–5; Nov–Feb Mon–Fri only 9.30–1 & 2–5. Closed Xmas & New Year.
Admission: *50p (children & senior citizens 30p).
P. Shop ⴲ

ELLESMERE PORT, CHESHIRE   Boat Museum   Map 7 SJ37

Situated in an historic dock complex at the junction of the Shropshire Union and Manchester Ship Canals, the Museum has a magnificent collection of over 50 craft ranging from a small weedcutter to a 300-ton coaster, and visitors may go on board some of them. Features include a blacksmith's forge, a docker's cottage, exhibitions of canal life and a boat trip.

☏051-355 5017
Located: Dockyard Road.

Open: Apr–Oct daily 10–5; Nov–Mar 10–4 (except Fri). Closed 23–26 Dec.
Admission: ✱£2.50 (children £1, senior citizens £1.50).
P. ⌂ ⊼ & shop

ELSHAM, HUMBERSIDE   Elsham Hall Country Park   Map 8 TA01

Never a dull moment for the children (or adults) with an adventure playground, nature trails and quizzes; Domestic animals to visit, fish to feed and a bird and a butterfly garden; pony trekking by arrangement. There is also an art gallery, a shop with craftsmen at work on occasions and Brass Band concerts on Sundays.

☏Barnetby (0652) 688698
Located: off M180 via the A15 Humber Bridge junction

Open: Easter–Oct weekdays 11–5.30, Sun & Bank Hols 11–6.30; Oct–Easter Sun 11–4 (Closed Good Fri & Xmas day).
Admission: ✱Easter–Oct £1.80 (children 90p). Oct–Easter £1.50 (children 80p). Children under 3 free.
P. ⌂ ⊼ & shop ✱ (ex car park)

GRIZEDALE, CUMBRIA   Visitor and Wildlife Centre   Map 7 SD39

Operated by the Forestry Commission, the Centre illustrates the changing face of Grizedale from its original wild state to the present day. Circular waymarked walks range from the 1½ mile Millwood Habitat Trial, with its section for the disabled, to the 9½ mile Silurian Way, and there are also waymarked cycle routes. Look out for woodland sculptures, watch wildlife from observation hides, and visit the Theatre in the Forest, the conservation tree nursery and the forest shop.

☏Satterthwaite (022984) 373

Open: Easter–Oct daily 10–5.
Admission: Free
P. ⌂ ⊼ & shop & garden centre

for HADRIANS WALL see page 116

HAREWOOD, WEST YORKSHIRE   Harewood House & Bird Garden   Map 8 SE34

This magnificent house – basically 18th-century, with some 19th-century alterations – is the home of the Earl and Countess of Harewood. Its splendid grounds, landscaped by Capability Brown, offer walks beside the lake or through woodland, whilst shrubs and flowers make a fine display in season. The Bird Garden and Tropical Paradise Garden include such exotic species as flamingoes, macaws, snowy owls and penguins. The house contains splendid Chippendale furniture, English and Italian paintings and fine Chinese and Sèvres porcelain; anxious moments could well be avoided by previously exhausting the children in the adventure playground!

☏(0532) 886225

Open: Apr–Oct daily from 10 am, house from 11 am. Feb Mar & Nov open Sun only.
Admission: ✱£3.50 (children £1.50). 24-hour recorded information service.
P. ⌂ (licensed) ⊼ & shop & garden centre

for HAVERTHWAITE see page 117

Not only the finest relic of the Roman occupation, Hadrian's Wall is also an unforgettable sight. The combination of its ancient stones and the wildness of the Pennine landscape creates the atmosphere, so that you could easily be convinced by local stories of ghostly legions marching through the twilight! Don't be too alarmed if you see centurions though – it could just be one of the groups of enthusiasts who meet here sometimes to recreate Roman Britain.

The wall was begun in about AD120 by order of the Emperor Hadrian, both to mark the northern boundary of his British territories and to help control the unruly Scottish tribes. It stretched 73 miles, from Bowness, on the Solway Firth, to the appropriately named Wallsend, on the Tyne, and took advantage of every vantage point on the rolling hills to aid its defence. Deep ditches were cut in a parallel line to accentuate the height of the wall, already up to 20 ft high. Seventeen large forts were built at intervals of between three and seven miles along the wall and each housed between 500 and 1000 men. Between the forts were 'milecastles' and each of these was separated from the others by a couple of signal towers. A formidable barrier indeed.

In the centuries that followed the departure of the Romans the large square stones of the wall were gradually plundered – at first in a piecemeal way for cottages and farms, but later large amounts were removed to construct the 'Military Road' following the 1745 uprising in Scotland. In spite of this a remarkable amount of the wall can still be seen, particularly in the central and eastern sections. The most impressive remains are at Housesteads where the fort of 'Vircovicium' was situated. Parts of its ramparts, gateways, granaries, barracks and headquarters can still be seen and a nearby milecastle is also well preserved. The fort of 'Corstopitum' at Corbridge is also worth a visit; Chesters Fort still shows remains of the bathhouse, bridgehead and other buildings; Carrawburgh is the site of an excavated Mithraic Temple from the 3rd century; at Chesterholm parts of the ramparts, gateways and central buildings remain. Well-preserved sections of wall can be seen at Heddon-on-the Wall, Low Braunton, Winshields Crags and Great Chesters, where there are also more fort remains.

For places to visit in the area check the location atlas at the end of the book

Remains of the Roman bath house at Cilurnum fort.

HAVERTHWAITE, CUMBRIA   Lakeside and Haverthwaite Railway   Map 7 SD38

Based at the railway station, this railway boasts two 2–6–4 class 4 Fairburn tank engines and nine other locomotives plus diesel locomotives, passenger carriages and various examples of freight rolling stock. The Engine Shed is much admired. There are train rides in the summer and at other times too, between Haverthwaite, Newby Bridge and Lakeside.

☎Newby Bridge (05395) 31594

Open: *Site daily (except 24 Dec–3 Jan and some Sats). Trains operational Good Fri–Easter Tue then May–Sep daily, also Apr & Oct but Suns only.
Admission: *£1.85 return (children 95p). Family ticket for rail/Sealink cruisers on Lake Windermere.
P. (at Haverthwaite Station) ☐ (at Haverthwaite Station) & shop

HAWORTH, WEST YORKSHIRE   Brontë Parsonage Museum   Map 7 SE03

At the top of the steep main street of this small moorland village stands the house where Charlotte, Emily and Anne Brontë, the three talented 19th-century novelists, lived as daughters of the vicarage. Today it's rooms contain such relics of family life as their father's spectacles and Bible, drawings they did as children, the sofa on which Emily died and a collection of letters. The sisters' favourite walk stretches two miles to the west – past the cemetery and along Enfield Side to the Brontë Waterfall (usually a mere trickle of water over mossy rocks) where Charlotte mourned her sisters and later caught the cold that led to her own death.

☎(0535) 42323

Open: Apr–Sep daily 11–5.30; Oct–Mar daily 11–4.30. Closed most of Feb & 24–26 Dec.
Admission: 60p (£1 Good Fri–Aug). Children 5–16 25p, senior citizens 30p (50p Good Fri–Aug).
& (ground floor only, no disabled toilet) shop ✗

HAWORTH, WEST YORKSHIRE   Keighley & Worth Valley Railway   Map 7 SE03

On this line, the history of which is traced in the railway museum, services run between Keighley (where it connects with British Rail) and Oxenhope via Haworth. Its stock of 32 steam engines and 7 diesels arouses a great deal of interest, and an Enthusiasts' Weekend will be held here during 1988, two weeks before Easter.

☎(0535) 43629 24-hour talking timetable, or 45214 for enquiries

Open: Weekend service, but daily during Jul, Aug & Spring Bank Hol week.
Admission: Fee payable
P. ☐ (buffets at three stations, licensed buffet on some trains) 吊 & shop

HAWORTH, WEST YORKSHIRE   Peniston Hill Country Park   Map 7 SE03

This park is in the heart of Brontë country, set as it is on Penistone Hill immediately above the village of Haworth, where the Reverend Patrick Brontë was curate of the church of Saint Michael and All Angels. This is where the famous sisters wrote their novels, and it is not difficult to see where their inspiration came from.

Heather moorland has a very special quality and where it is accessible, as in this country park, it brings a special range of wildlife within reach. An excellent detour from the Country Park is to Top Withins Farm or Wuthering Heights. On the way the track passes through lovely country, and to complete the Brontë connection, visit the Brontë Parsonage Museum (see entry).

Located: West of A6033 Hebden Bridge to Keighley road. Country Park is ¾ mile beyond Haworth village.

Open: all year.
P. 吊 nature trail

HELMSHORE, LANCASHIRE Museum of the Lancashire Textile Industry
Map 7 SD72

Textile mills once dominated the Lancashire skyline and here you can learn much about the industry and that time inside former mills. There are machines and displays about mill life and, in the 18th-century Higher Mill Museum, a huge rim-geared water wheel. The spinning mules, water wheel and the other machines are demonstrated regularly, so you can really understand how they worked.

☎Rossendale (0706) 226459
Located: Higher Mill, Holcombe Road.

Open: ✳Mar Mon–Fri 2–5; Apr–Jun & Oct Mon–Fri & Sun 2–5; Jul–Sep Mon–Fri 10–5 & Sun 2–5; also Sat 2–5 Jul & Aug. Also Bank Hol weekends. Closed Nov–Feb except for pre-booked parties. Dates not confirmed.
Admission: Fee payable.
P. ⌨ 🛆 ᵭ (ground floor, spinning room & gardens only), shop ⅍ (except guide dogs)

HOGHTON, LANCASHIRE Hoghton Tower Map 7 SD62

There are magnificent state rooms in this 16th-century fortified hill-top mansion. It has links with James I and you visit the King's bedchamber, the audience chamber, ballroom and other state rooms. There is a collection of dolls' houses and dolls too. In the Tudor Well House is a horse-drawn pump. Don't miss the underground passages with the Lancashire Witches' Dungeons. The gardens, lawns and grounds have lovely views of sea, moorland and mountains.

☎(025485) 2986
Located: 5 miles south east of Preston on A675.

Open: ✳Easter 2–5pm, then every Sun to end Oct 2–5pm (during week by arrangement); also Sat & Bank Hol afternoons in Jul & Aug.
Admission: ✳£1.50 (children 50p)
P. ⌨ ᵭ (ground floor & garden only) shop ⅍ (except grounds)

HOLKER, CUMBRIA Holker Hall and Park Map 7 SD37

Set in a great deer park with both formal and woodland gardens, Holker Hall has a fine collection of paintings and furniture belonging to the Dukes of Devonshire. There is much to do and see in the grounds: the Lakeland Motor Museum, a Craft and Countryside Museum and Victorian/Edwardian kitchens, the Baby Animal House. In addition there are special events. These include hot air balloon, model aircraft and historic vehicle rallies, archery competitions and horse and carriage driving trials.

☎Flookburgh (044853) 328
Located: near Grange-over-Sands.

Open: Easter Sun–end October daily (except Sat) 10.30–6. Last admission to hall & grounds 4.30.
Admission: ✳£1.65 (children £1).
P. ⌨ (licensed) 🛆 ᵭ (ground floor & gardens only) shop

HORNSEA, NORTH HUMBERSIDE Hornsea Pottery Leisure Park Map 8 TA24

The pottery is situated in 28 acres of parkland on the coast and is surrounded by activities planned to interest the whole family. There is a children's playground with a fort and bikes, a model village covering a whole acre, 200 butterflies in tropically heated greenhouses, and displays by birds of prey. There are also a number of factory shops selling seconds of pottery, footwear, luggage, clothing and household goods.

☎(04012) 2161
Located: In Rolston Road

Open: ✳Jan–Mar, Wed–Sat 10–4, 10–5 Sun; Apr–Oct 10–5 daily.
Admission: ✳Parking and ground free. Amenities charged individually or by day ticket.
P. ⌨ (licensed) 🛆 ᵭ shop

Symbols	
☎	telephone number
P.	parking on the premises
⌨	refreshments available
🛆	picnic area
ᵭ	accessible to wheelchair-bound visitors
⅍	no dogs
✳	indicates 1987 details

JODRELL BANK SCIENCE & TREE PARK, CHESHIRE   Map 7 SJ77

This scientific establishment will really capture the imagination. Children can get really involved with 'hands-on' exhibits, talking heads and videos. The Lovell 250-foot radio telescope is one of the largest fully steerable radio telescopes in the world, and there are Planetarium shows every hour. And for a breath of fresh air, there is a 35-acre tree park.

☎Lower Withington (0477) 71339
Located: 3 miles north-east of Holmes Chapel, off A535.

Open: Good Fri–Oct daily 10.30–5.30; Nov–Good Fri weekends only 2–5. Closed Xmas & New Year.
Admission: £2.50 (children 5–16 £1.25, senior citizens £2). Infants not admitted to Planetarium.
P. ☐ (licensed) ⌁ ♿ shop & garden centre ✻

KESWICK, CUMBRIA   Mirehouse   Map 11 NY22

There are strong literary connections at this 17th-century manor house with its portraits and manuscripts of Francis Bacon, Alfred Lord Tennyson and Carlyle. The house has beautiful rooms with their original furniture. The Victorian nursery welcomes children. As you walk through the grounds and along the lake shore you pass the place where Tennyson wrote much of Morte d'Arthur. There are four adventure playgrounds.

☎(07687) 72287
Located: 4 miles north-west of Keswick on A591.

Open: Apr–Oct; grounds & tea room daily 10.30–5.30; house Wed, Sun & Bank Hol Mon 2–5.
Admission: ✻Grounds 50p (children 35p); House and grounds £1.50 (children 75p).
P. ☐ ⌁ ♿ (ground floor & gardens only) ✻

KIRBY MISPERTON, NORTH YORKSHIRE   Flamingo Land   Map 8 SE77

In the grounds of the late 18th-century Kirby Misperton Hall are a 375-acre zoo and family funpark. Here you can see more than a thousand animals or take your pick from the fifty-plus rides and eight international shows included in the admission price. In fine weather it is pleasant to stroll beside the large lake, but there are plenty of under-cover attractions for rainy days too.

☎(065386) 287

Open: Apr–Sep daily 10–5 (6pm according to season.
Admission: ✻£4 (children under 5 free).
P. ☐ (licensed) ⌁ ♿ shop

KNUTSFORD, CHESHIRE   Tatton Park   Map 7 SJ77

The 19th-century Wyatt house has paintings, furniture and ceramics and an exhibition of Tatton in Victorian times. There is a huge deer park with a 1930s farm and an interesting 60-acre area of gardens which includes an authentic Japanese garden, a fernery, a rose garden and arboretum, a restored Italian garden and a medieval Old Hall. There is a fine collection of varied waterfowl too, as well as historical and woodland trails to follow.

☎(0565) 54822
Located: 3½ miles from M6 Junction 19 or M56 Junction 7; entrance by Rostherne Lodge on Ashley Road; 1½ miles north-east of Junction A5034 with A50.

Open: Park & gardens daily (except 25 Dec & Cheshire Show in late Jun). High Season: mid May–beginning of Sep; Gardens 11–5.30, (Sun & Bank Hol 10.30–6). Low Season: Apr–mid May & beginning of Sep–Oct; Garden 11.30–5. (Sun & Bank Hol 10.30–5.30), Old Hall 12–4, House 1–4 (Sun & Bank Hol 1–5), Farm 12–4. Winter: Nov & Mar; House & Farm 1–4, Suns only. Winter: Nov–Mar: Park 11–dusk, Gardens 11–4.
Admission: House £1.25, Garden 90p, Old Hall 95p, Farm 90p. Park £1 per car. An additional charge may be made at time of special events.
P. ☐ ✻ (in house) shop & garden centre. National Trust

LAKE DISTRICT Cumbria Map 11

Some of the very best of British scenery is to be found among the 900 square miles of reflective lakes, cascading waterfalls, dramatic mountains and deep valleys that are called the Lake District. This is an area that has a magnetic attraction for holidaymakers – and understandably so. Even though this largest of our National Parks can and does get very crowded in the summer, the narrow and meandering roads become very congested and it can also be wetter than anywhere else in England, somehow it doesn't seem to matter; the sheer beauty of the place, and its infinite number of attractions, prevail.

It is not surprising that so lovely an area should have attracted some of our greatest poets and writers. William Wordsworth spent most of his life at Grasmere (where he is also buried) and at Rydal – and both of the houses in which he lived are open to the public. The poet Robert Southey made his home in Keswick, as did Coleridge and Walpole and children's author and artist Beatrix Potter lived to the west of Windermere in the beautiful village of Sawrey. For lovers of the great outdoors this area offers the ultimate in walking, climbing and even mountaineering. The lakes – some great and some small – also offer a host of attractions – angling, sailing, rowing, powerboating, waterskiing as well as travelling on the steamships which operate on the two largest lakes – Windermere and Ullswater. In the winter when the lakes are frozen it is possible to ice-skate and the sport of curling is also popular. The best way to get to know this area is obviously on foot, and there are an infinite number of walks to suit all energy levels – from a leisurely stroll to dizzier heights like the 3,210 ft Scafell Pike (England's highest point), Great Gable or Helvellyn – the most popular of the Lake District's climbs.

For those in search of less strenuous activities there are beautiful towns and villages. Kendal, the gateway to the Lake District, is a lovely town with grey limestone houses and the ruins of a castle that was once the home of Catherine Parr, the last wife of Henry VIII. At Brockhole on Windermere in a beautiful rambling lakeside mansion, an excellent introduction to the Lake District is given to visitors including the geology, history and even customs of the area. Grasmere is the place where the traditional Grasmere Sports, the English equivalent of the Highland Games have been held each August since 1852. Unusual sports here include Cumberland and Westmoreland wrestling, fell racing, pole leaping and hound trailing (in which specially bred hounds compete to follow an aniseed-scented trail).

For places to visit in the area check the location atlas at the end of the book.

The restored Victorian steam yacht Gondola makes regular pleasure trips around Coniston Water

LEEDS, WEST YORKSHIRE   Leeds Industrial Museum   Map 7 SE33

The unique early 19th-century mill which houses the museum stands on an impressive island site. The mill can also be reached from the Leeds and Liverpool Canal and can be visited as part of a history trail along the Kirkstall Valley. There are working and stationary exhibits of water wheels, locomotives, engines and machinery for the textile, clothing and printing industries. There is also a 1920's cinema.

☎(0532) 637861
Located: Armley Mills, Canal Road.

Open: *Apr–Sep, Tue–Sat 10–6, Sun 2–6 (last admission 5pm); Oct–Mar Tue–Sat 10–5, Sun 2–5 (last admission 4pm). Closed Mons except Bank Hols.
Admission: *60p (children & senior citizens 25p).
P. ⅂ & shop ✗

LEEDS, WEST YORKSHIRE   Middleton Colliery Railway   Map 5 TQ85

This railway was, in 1758, the first to be authorised by Act of Parliament and the first, in 1812, to use steam locomotives successfully. There are industrial locomotives and rolling stock in use. Each weekend in season steam trains travel from Tunstall Road roundabout (near Junction 45 on the M1) to Middleton Park, where there is also a picnic area, fishing, a nature trail and play area. Special Santa trains on Sundays in December from 11 am to dusk.

☎(0532) 710320
Located: Moor Road, Hunslet.

Open: Easter to end Sep Sat 2.15–4.30, Sun 2–4.30; also Bank Hol Sun & Mon 11–4.30.
Admission: entrance to the site is free. Return ride on railway 80p (children 40p).
P. ⅂ & (with assistance) shop

LEIGHTON HALL, LANCASHIRE   Map 7 SD47

The extensive grounds of this neo-Gothic mansion has a large collection of birds of prey. Weather permitting, there are regular flying displays at 3.30 pm each afternoon. The house has a fine interior with early Gillow furniture and Lilian Lunn model figures.

☎Silverdale (0524) 701353 or 734474
Located: 3 miles north of Carnforth, off A6.

Open: May–Sep 2–5 (last admission 4.30). Closed Sat and Mon except Bank Hol Mons.
Admission: House & grounds £1.80 (children under 15 £1).
P. ▢ ⅂ & (ground floor) shop ✗ (except park)

LEVENS, CUMBRIA   Levens Hall   Map 7 SD48

This fine Elizabethan mansion which was added to a 13th-century pele tower (a border defence tower) has fine paintings and furniture, but some people may be more drawn to its unique steam engine collection. The topiary garden is very special too. It was laid out in 1692 and still follows that plan nearly three centuries later. There are play and picnic areas.

☎Sedgwick (05395) 60321

Open: Easter Sun–mid Oct Sun–Thu 11–5. Steam collection 2–5.
Admission: Gardens only £1.30 (children 65p, senior citizens £1.20). House & garden £2.50 (children £1.25, senior citizens £2).
P. ▢ (licensed) ⅂ & (gardens only) shop & garden centre ✗ (except car park)

LEYLAND, LANCASHIRE   British Commercial Vehicle Museum   Map 7 SD52

How were goods delivered to the shops in grandparents' and great-grandparents' day? For a complete history of the commercial vehicle from the horse-drawn era to the present day, the British Commercial Vehicle Museum aims to represent the lot. Indeed, it is the largest museum of its kind in Europe.

☎(0772) 45101
Located: In King St.

Open: Apr–Sep Tue–Sun 10–5; Oct & Nov weekends only 10–5. Also open Bank Hols.
Admission: *£1.25 (children & senior citizens 65p).
P. & shop ✗

121

LIVERPOOL, MERSEYSIDE   Croxteth Hall and Country Park   Map 7 SJ39

Set in a 500 acre park, the former home of the Earl of Sefton has displays of furnished rooms with costume groups on the theme of an Edwardian country house party. In the grounds there is a Victorian walled garden, a farmyard with interesting rare breeds of farm animals and a miniature railway. There are special events most weekends during the season. Croxteth has a highly acclaimed educational service.

☎051-228 5311
Located: At Croxteth, 5 miles north-east of the city centre.

Open: Easter–Sep daily 11–5. Some facilities open out of season so telephone to find times. *Admission:* *Hall, Farm & Walled Garden £1.50 (children and senior citizens 75p). Country park free.
P. ⌂ ⼌ ⅓ (ground floor, farm and gardens only) shop ⅓ (except in country park)

LIVERPOOL, MERSEYSIDE   Merseyside Maritime Museum   Map 7 SJ39

In the restored 19th-century dock area is this large multi-acre museum. The Boat House, Pilotage Building, Piermaster's House, Cooperage (barrel making shop) and Albert Warehouse are all open. There are displays about the Port of Liverpool and life on the Mersey today, floating craft (including Sir Alec Rose's *Lively Lady* in which he sailed single handed around the world) and outdoor exhibitions and demonstrations of such maritime skills as sail-making, net-making and ropework. There are also replica brasses from such famous ships as the *Victory* and the *Titanic* from which you can make rubbings.

☎051-709 1551
Located: Albert Dock

Open: *daily 10.30–5.30 (last tickets 4.30). Closed 1 Jan, Good Fri, 24–26 Dec. Maritime Park closed Nov–Apr. *Admission:* £1 (children & senior citizens 50p). P. (charged) ⌂ (licensed) ⅓ (limited) shop ⅓

MALHAM, NORTH YORKSHIRE   Map 7 SD86

Malham, really, is more a landscape than a village. Three of Yorkshire's most celebrated natural features lie within relatively easy walking distance: Malham Cove, the huge white limestone cliff, semicircular in shape and looking like a giant amphitheatre, its cliff-face 240 ft high with breathtaking overhangs; the dramatically impressive rock bowl of Gordale Scar, where the water hurls itself down a 250 ft ravine, up which you can climb when the water is not in spate; and finally Malham Tarn, a 153-acre moorland lake. Also near Malham passes the 250-mile long distance pathway, the Pennine Way.

The Yorkshire Dales National Park Centre is located in the village and for the family who walks together and anyone who enjoys or wishes to explore Malham or the beautiful Yorkshire Dales National Park, a trip to the visitor centre will provide a great deal of information to stimulate your interest. There is an audio-visual theatre, interpretative displays, maps and guides.

Visitor Centre ☎ **Airton (07293) 363**

Open: Apr–Oct daily, mid morning to late afternoon. *Admission:* free
P. ⅓

MALTON, NORTH YORKSHIRE   Eden Camp   Map 8 SE77

You can have a most unusual outing to this 'prisoner of war' camp devoted to the story of the Home Front experiences of World War II. There is a 1940's street, the shops showing wartime fashions and rations. There are audio-visual displays on the Black Out, the Blitz and a U-boat under attack at sea. To round off your visit you can sing-along with 1940's favourites in the Music Hall.

☎(0563) 69777
Located: At the A64 junction to Pickering.

Open: mid Feb–Xmas 10–5. *Admission:* *£2.50 (children & senior citizens £1.50). P. ⌂ shop

MANCHESTER, GREATER MANCHESTER   Gallery of English Costume
Map 7 SJ89

In this famous collection of costume, you can see four centuries of fashion and changing styles of everyday clothes and the accessories which went with them. The display brings us up to the present day. The exhibition changes at regular intervals and no one period is constantly on view.

☎061-224 5217
Located: Platt Fields, Rusholme.

Open: daily (except Tue) 10–6, Sun 2–6; Nov–Feb closes at 4pm.
Admission: free
P. (limited) ᶑ (ground floor only) shop ✴

MANCHESTER, GREATER MANCHESTER   Museum of Science and Industry
Map 7 SJ89

One of Britain's fastest growing museums is sited in the world's oldest railway station. It includes the National Electricity Gallery with an exhibition on power. The Manchester Air and Space Gallery shows aviation history and space exploration. You can also see steam and internal combustion engines, printing and textile machinery, optical equipment, a display on paper making, and stationary locomotives and rolling stock. New exhibitions include 'The Making of Manchester' and 'Underground Manchester' and towards the end of 1988 the new Science Centre will be open with interactive displays which explain scientific principles. There are regular demonstrations of machines at work and special events and changing exhibitions.

☎061-832 2244
Located: Lower Byron Street, off Liverpool Road Castlefield.

Open: daily 10–5 (last admission 4.30). Closed Christmas Day.
Admission: ✳£1 (children, senior citizens & registered disabled 50p).
P. ⌑ (licensed) ᶑ (ground floor) ✴ shop

MANCHESTER, GREATER MANCHESTER   Museum of Transport   Map 7 SJ89

The museum, which is run by volunteers, tells the story of public transport in the area. There are over 50 old buses and other vehicles, and displays of photographs, tickets and other transport memorabilia. Various special events and rallies are held too.

☎061-205 2122
Located: Boyle Street, Cheetham.

Open: Apr–Oct Wed, Sat, Sun and Bank Hols 10–5.
Admission: 70p (children & senior citizens 30p). Family ticket £1.50.
P. ⌑ ᶑ shop

MARTIN MERE, LANCASHIRE   Wildfowl Trust   Map 7 SD41

The Wild Fowl Trust has 360 acres in part of the old marsh and has created open water habitats there. On the small ponds and extensive lake you may see over 1600 wild fowl from all over the world. Among the special visitors are pink-footed geese and whooper swans from Iceland, pintail and teal from northern Europe and, especially exciting, Bewick's swans all the way from Siberia, and three flocks of flamingoes! The Norwegian Log Visitors' Centre has an exhibition gallery. There is a nature trail for the visually handicapped with a free taped commentary.

☎Burscough (0704) 895181
Located: West of A59 at Burscough Bridge Station and signposted from A565 at Mere Brow.

Open: ✳daily 9.30–5.30 (or dusk). Closed 25 Dec.
Admission: ✳£2 (children under 4 free, 4–16 £1, senior citizens £1.30).
P. ⌑ ⴹ ᶑ (except gallery) shop ✴

MIDDLEHAM, NORTH YORKSHIRE   Middleham Castle   Map 7 SE18

The great 12th-century keep of Middleham Castle gives one a very real impression of the strength of a castle. Much of the rest of the castle was built over the next two centuries. There are good explanations of the history, buildings and structure of the castle, where that controversial figure Richard III spent much of his time.

☎(0969) 23899

Open: mid Oct–mid Mar Mon–Sat 9.30–4, Sun 2–4; mid Mar–mid Oct Mon–Sat 9.30–6.30, Sun 2–6.30.
Admission: ✳75p, (children 35p, senior citizens 55p).
English Heritage

MIDDLESBROUGH, CLEVELAND   Captain Cook Birthplace Museum
Map 8 NZ42

The museum, which is close to the place where the famous explorer was born, traces his early life as a farm labourer and shows what life was like on the 18th-century sailing ships on the epic voyages which Captain Cook undertook. From the museum you can follow a 'trail' through 'Captain Cook Country' which takes you to his school, his work place at Staithes and so on through his life in the area. In the grounds of the museum there is a parakeet aviary, a collection of tropical plants and various animals and fowl in small paddocks.

☎(0642) 311211
Located: 3 miles south of Middlesborough on A172 at Stewart Park, Marton

Open: ✱Summer 10–5.30 daily. Winter 9–4 daily. Closed 25 Dec & 1 Jan.
Admission: Fee payable.
P. ☐ & shop ✹

MORECAMBE, LANCASHIRE   Frontier Land Western Theme Park
Map 7 SD46

All you'd expect from an action-packed wild west town, from rope-spinning cow-pokes to street shoot-outs. The excitement extends to some heart-stopping rides, like the Log Flume, 'the wettest, wildest water ride ever', the Waltzer, the Santa Fe train and the Stampede steel roller coaster. There's an all-weather Fun House for kids, and parents can look on from The Crazy Horse Saloon.

☎(0524) 410024
Located: South-west of Morecambe on A5105

Open: Easter week & each weekend to Spring Bank Hol, then daily to end Sep. Also weekends in Oct.
Admission: Day £4.99, evening (after 6pm) £3.20. Ride tickets 40p (some rides need 2 tickets). Kiddies amusement park; day £2.99, evening £1.99. Family passes available.
P. ☐ (licensed) ⊼ & shop

MORECAMBE, LANCASHIRE   Marineland
Map 7 SD46

There are alligators on show here and also fresh-water and salt-water fish both tropical and cold waters. Throughout the day there are displays by the delightful dolphins and huge sea lions.

☎(0524) 414727
Located: Stone Jetty, Promenade.

Open: Easter–Oct daily from 10.30.
Admission: fee payable.
Shop

NEWBY HALL AND GARDENS, NORTH YORKSHIRE
Map 8 SE36

The interior of this late 18th-century house was designed by the great Robert Adam. It contains important statuary and Gobelin tapestries. The 25 acres of garden include an adventure playground and a miniature railway among its attractions.

☎Boroughbridge (0901) 2583
Located: 4 miles south-east of Ripon.

Open: Hall & Gardens, Easter–Oct daily. Hall 12–5, Gardens 11–5.30. Last entry 5pm. Closed Mon except Bank Hol Mons.
Admission: House & gardens £3 (children & disabled £1.50, senior citizens £2.70). Gardens only £1.70 (children & disabled £1.30, senior citizens £1.60). All prices subject to alteration.
P. ☐ (licensed garden restaurant) ⊼ & (ground floor & gardens) shop & plant stall ✹

NEWTON, NORTHUMBERLAND   Hunday Countryside Museum
Map 12 NZ06

A fine display of agricultural bygones including a collection of over 250 tractors and engines, and a range of hand tools, harness and dairy equipment. There's a water mill, joiner's and blacksmith's shops, a farmhouse kitchen and many domestic items. Added attractions are a narrow-gauge railway, animals and a soft play area.

☎Stocksfield (0661) 842553
Located: At West Side (¾ mile north of A69).

Open: Apr–Sep daily 10–5.
Admission: £1.90 (children & senior citizens 80p).
P. ☐ (summer only) ⊼ & (ground floor) shop ✹

PICKERING, NORTH YORKSHIRE   North Yorkshire Moors Railway   Map 8 SE78

Eighteen miles of railway history through the heart of the spectacular North York Moors National Park. The line runs betwen Pickering and Grosmont, while Newtondale Halt is the ideal stopping off place for access to the forest and some lovely walks. 'Santa Trains' are run during December.

☎(0751) 72508
Located: At Pickering Station.

Open: Apr–beginning of Nov on most days.
Admission: Peak (late Jun–early Sep) £5 (children £2.50); family (2 adults 1 child) £11, additional child to max of 4 £1. Offpeak £4.50 (children £2.30 & senior citizens £3); family £10.
P. ▱ 🍴 shop

PRESCOT, MERSEYSIDE   Knowsley Safari Park   Map 7 SJ49

In the drive-through reserves of this Safari Park, children will take pleasure in identifying such traditional favourites as lions, tigers, rhinos, elephants and monkeys. Pets Corner provides an opportunity to meet the more cuddly species at close quarters, and there is an amusement park where they can let off steam.

☎051-430 9009

Open: Game reserves, Mar–end Oct; other attractions Easter–end Sep; daily 10–4.
Admission: *£6 per saloon car including all occupants. Minibus passengers £1.80 (children 3–15 & senior citizens £1).
P. ▱ (licensed) 🍴 ᵹ 🍴 (in game reserves – kennels provided)

RAVENGLASS, CUMBRIA   Ravenglass and Eskdale Railway   Map 6 SD09

A seven-mile ride from Ravenglass to Eskdale will take you through some exceptionally beautiful scenery, but when the narrow-gauge steam railway was first built in 1875 its purpose was the more mundane one of carrying iron ore; the development of the line is traced in the railway museum at Ravenglass. Today, both steam and diesel engines are used, pulling a range of wagons and passenger coaches.

☎(06577) 226

Open: Trains operate late Mar–Oct daily. Reduced service all winter (except pre-Xmas).
Admission: *Return fare £3.60 (children £1.80).
Eskdale Explorer Ticket, 2 adults & 2 children, or 3 adults, including Railway Museum & unlimited travel for the day, £9.
P. ▱ 🍴 ᵹ shop

RIPON, NORTH YORKSHIRE   Fountains Abbey   Map 8 SE37

In a very beautiful valley setting, with a landscape garden laid out in the 18th-century with a lake, you come to the imposing ruin of one of the best preserved 12th-century abbeys in Europe, founded by the Cistericans in 1132. There is a small museum and the site is well signposted and explained. The park has splendid vistas, a 400-acre deer park with about 300 fallow, red and sika deer and geese, ducks and coot on the lake. The more formal gardens have statuary, temples and man-made ponds, canals and waterfalls. There are various events through the year including Easter Egg Rolling and the annual Boxing Day pilgrimage from Ripon Cathedral to Fountains Abbey.

☎Sawley (076586) 333
Located: 2 miles south-west off B6265.

Open: Abbey and gardens all year. Nov–Mar 10–5 or dusk if earlier (closed 24 & 25 Dec). Apr–Sep 10–7; Jul & Aug 10–8; Oct 10–6 or dusk if earlier.
Admission: £1.90 (children 90p).
P. ▱ ᵹ shop
National Trust

SALFORD, GT MANCHESTER   Salford Museum and Art Gallery   Map 7 SJ89

Founded in 1850, this is one of the oldest public museums in Britain. The art gallery has an unrivalled collection of the works of the artist L.S. Lowry who lived in the area. The museum, among other exhibits, offers the very special treat of Lark Hill Place: a typical northern street at the turn of the century splendidly reconstructed with shops, homes and transport of the period.

☎061-736 2649
Located: The Crescent, Peel Park.

Open: Mon–Fri 10–5, Sun 2–5. Closed 25–26 Dec, 1 Jan & Good Fri.
Admission: Free.
P. ⌷ & shop ⚐

SANDTOFT, HUMBERSIDE   Sandtoft Transport Centre   Map 8 SE70

This developing transport museum specialises in the preservation of trolleybuses, several of which have been restored and operate on the centre's own overhead wiring circuit. There are over 60 vehicles including motorbuses and other items of transport interest from Britain and the Continent.

☎Doncaster (0302) 771520

Open: Etr–Sep, Suns & Bank Hols 12–6.
Admission: £1 (children & senior citizens 50p). Family car £2.50.
P. ⌷ ⊼ & (no disabled toilet) shop

SCUNTHORPE, HUMBERSIDE   Normanby Hall   Map 8 SE81

Built in 1825, the fine Regency mansion of Normanby Hall contains a delightful display of costume and furniture. The house is surrounded by some 350 acres of magnificent parkland, with lawns, gardens, deer park and nature trails for the more energetic visitors. The stable complex includes an interesting Countryside Interpretation Centre, a pottery and a blacksmith's workshop, while the new Normanby Park Farming Museum is due to open during 1988.

☎(0724) 720215
Located: Normanby Country Park, 5 miles north of Scunthorpe on B1430.

Open: Apr–Oct, Mon–Fri 10–12.30 & 2–5.30, Sun 2–5.30; Nov–Mar, Mon–Fri 10–12.30 & 2–5, Sun 2–5. Closed Good Fri, Xmas & New Years Day.
Admission: *60p (children & senior citizens 30p).
P. ⌷ (Apr–Oct) ⊼ & (ground floor & grounds only) shop ⚐ (except guide dogs)

SHEFFIELD, SOUTH YORKSHIRE   Abbeydale Industrial Hamlet   Map 8 SK38

One of the earliest examples of an exhibition based on our industrial heritage, Abbeydale is a unique, restored scythe and steel works of the late 18th-century. There is a crucible, steel furnace, a water-powered tilt forge and grinding wheel, and other machines showing production from raw materials to finished product. There are also some workers' cottages to give you an idea of life in those days. There are working days when the machinery is demonstrated and a Craft Fair (contact the Museum for details).

☎(0742) 367731
Located: In Abbeydale Road South

Open: Mon–Sat 10–5, Sun 11–5.
Admission: *80p (children & senior citizens 40p). On working days 90p (children & senior citizens 45p).
P. ⌷ (Apr–Oct) & (ground floor only) shop ⚐

SHEFFIELD, SOUTH YORKSHIRE   Sheffield Industrial Museum   Map 8 SK38

The displays here describe the industrial development of Sheffield over four centuries. There is working machinery, and film and slide shows which present the wide variety of goods made in Sheffield in the past and today. You can watch traditional cutlery craftsmen at work using the time honoured hand skills of Sheffield's most famous industry.

☎(0742) 722106
Located: Kelham Island, Alma Street.

Open: Wed–Sat & Bank Hol Mons 10–5, Sun 11–5. Closed 25 Dec.
Admission: 80p (children & senior citizens 40p, disabled free).
P. ⌷ & (ground floor only) shop ⚐ (except guide dogs)

SHUGBOROUGH, STAFFORDSHIRE   Shugborough Hall   Map 7 J92

Still the home of the present Earl, photographer Patrick Lichfield, the mansion and grounds are in a beautiful setting with parkland and formal gardens containing temples and follies. The house has a fine collection of paintings, ceramics and furniture. The County Museum in the old servants' quarters gives a fascinating insight into 19th century-Staffordshire life. The original kitchens, butler's pantry, brewhouse and laundry room are beautifully restored. Of special interest is the Park Farm which uses historic agricultural equipment and has rare breeds of farm animals.

☎Little Haywood (0889) 881388
Located: 5 miles east of Stafford, off A513

Open: Apr–Sep daily including Bank Hol Mon, 11–5; Oct–24 Dec daily 11–4.
Admission: Entry to estate £1 per car. Mansion £1.50 (children £1); Museum £1.50 (children £1); Farm £1.50 (children £1); All-in-ticket £4 (children £2).
P. ⌨ & (ground floor only) shop
National Trust

SKELTON, CUMBRIA   Hutton-in-the-Forest   Map 12 NY43

A pele tower built in 14th-century against forays from over the Borders was added to between the 17th–19th centuries. The house has tapestries, pictures and furniture. There are fine specimen trees in the grounds and an ornamental lake and nature trail.

☎(08534) 500

Open: all Bank Hol Suns & Mons and Thu, Fri, Sun May–Sep, 1–4. Grounds open daily dawn-dusk.
Admission: House £2 (accompanied children free, senior citizens £1.80). Grounds £1 (children 50p).
P. ⌨ shop ✶ (in house)

SOUTHPORT, MERSEYSIDE   Model Village and Model Railway   Map 7 SD31

There is a working 3″ gauge railway running through the village with its buildings and figures made on a scale of 1:12. The village is in a pretty garden setting with a lake and waterfalls.

☎(0704) 42133 or (051) 639 4729
Located: The Promenade.

Open: ✶Mar–Oct daily 9.30–dusk (weather permitting).
Admission: ✶90p (children 45p, senior citizens 60p).
⌨ & shop garden centre

SOUTHPORT, MERSEYSIDE   Southport Zoo   Map 7 SD31

The Zoo has a varied collection of large and small mammals including lions, leopards and a lynx and, everyone's favourites, the chimpanzees. There are duck and flamingo pools and various aviaries. The Zoo has recently added an aquarium, a reptile house, an alligator beach and a mandrill house.

☎(0704) 38102
Located: Princess Park.

Open: all year (except 25 Dec) 10–6 in summer, 10–4 in winter.
Admission: £1.50 (children 90p). Special rates for handicapped.
⏆ & shop

SOUTHPORT, MERSEYSIDE   Steamport Transport Museum   Map 7 SD31

Actually linked to the British Rail system by 1000 foot of standard gauge track, this large Museum has several railway and industrial locomotives. There is also a large collection of local buses, tramcars, traction engines and other old vehicles. There are special events through the year, including the Santa Steam Special in December.

☎(0704) 30693
Located: In Derby Road.

Open: ✶Jun–mid Sep 1–5pm; July–Aug 11–5. Weekends & Bank Hols May–Sep 11–5; Oct–Apr 2–5pm.
Admission: ✶Non-steam days £1.20 (children 80p, senior citizens £1). When 1 loco is in steam £1.40 (children £1, senior citizens £1.20); 2 locos in steam £1.50, children £1, senior citizens £1.30); 3 locos in steam £1.60 (children £1, senior citizens £1.40).
& ⌨ (Sun) & shop

STYAL, CHESHIRE   Quarry Bank Mill and Styal Country Bank   Map 7 SJ88

This beautifully preserved Georgian cotton mill and village is an award-wining working museum. There are demonstrations of hand spinning and weaving and there is a truly magnificent iron water wheel. The Apprentice Hall is opening in 1988. Much of the 250-acre estate is now a Country Park.

☎Wilmslow (0625) 527468
Located: 2 miles north-west of Wilmslow near M56 Exit 6, off B5166.

Open: Oct–Mar Tue–Sun 11–4; Apr–May Tue–Sun 11–5; Jun–Sep daily 11–5. Open Bank Hol Mons. Country Park open all year during daylight hours.
Admission: £2.50 (children £1.75). Family ticket £7.
P. ⌑ (licensed) ⊼ shop ⴱ
National Trust

TARLETON, LANCASHIRE   Leisure Lakes   Map 7 SD42

Ninety acres of picturesque woodland and heath provide the setting for a fun outdoor day. Take a bucket and spade – the sandy beaches are ideal for children – there's a boating lake and sailboard facilities. This is the perfect place for a picnic, and The Brewers free house serves a pub menu.

☎Hesketh Bank (0772) 813446

Open: all year 8am–8pm
Admission: *75p (children 50p). Dinghies & canoes £1.50, fishing £1.60, sailboarding £2.
P. ⌑ (licensed) ⅋ shop

WASHINGTON, TYNE AND WEAR   Wildfowl Trust   Map 12 NZ35

A combination of ponds and low woodland by the River Wear attracts a wide variety of species of birds, some familiar and some rare. A nature trail winds through woodland and a hide overlooks a feeding station where you may see tits, an occasional great spotted woodpecker, pheasants and other visitors. The shallow wader pond attracts various wading birds. There is also a large collection of ducks, swans and geese with examples from every continent.

There are free natural history films most days in the lecture theatre. From the inside viewing gallery there is an excellent view over part of the main collection area.

☎(091) 416 5454

Open: *all year daily 9.30–5.30 or dusk if earlier. Closed 24 & 25 Dec.
Admission: *£1.80 (children under 4 free, children 80p, senior citizens £1.20).
P. ⌑⊼⅋ shop ⴱ

WHITBY, NORTH YORKSHIRE   Bram Stoker's Dracula Experience   Map 8 NZ81

This is not an experience for the nervous! The exhibition follows the original scary Dracula Story with "horror lurking in the swirling mist". There are static and moving displays of vampires, shipwrecks, the threatening large black dog and finally a re-enactment of Dracula's ghastly end. You have been warned!

☎(0947) 601923
Located: At 9 Marine Parade.

Open: Easter holidays, May–Sep daily, & weekends in Oct, 10–5.
Admission: £1.50 (children and senior citizens 50p).
shop

WIGAN, LANCASHIRE   Wigan Pier   Map 7 SD60

For a flavour of turn-of-the-century industrial Wigan, the Pier complex offers an educational centre and exhibition housed in canal-side warehouses. See Trencherfield, a textile mill boasting the world's largest working mill engine, and a replica of the original Pier. The complex is split in two and linked by waterbus.

☎(0942) 323666

Open: daily 10–5. Closed Xmas
Admission: £2 (children & senior citizens £1).
P. ⌑ (licensed) ⅋ (except steam engine) shop ⴱ

WILLASTON, CHESHIRE   Wirral Country Park   Map 7 SJ37

Step into the booking hall at Hadlow Road Station, near Willaston on the Wirral peninsula, and you are back in the 1930's. The timetables, tickets and furnishings are all authentic. On the platform are milk churns and wooden trolleys. The atmosphere is so real that you expect to hear the hiss of steam and the whistle of a train. But there are no trains!

In fact, this preserved railway station is one small part of a 12 mile-long Country Park that follows the long-disused railway from West Kirkby to Hooton. There are numerous access points to the park, as well as car parks, picnic sites, a number of visitor centres, and a Ranger service.

Located: on West side of Wirral Peninsula, west of the A540. The Willaston section is east of the A540, and south of the B5133.

Open: all year daily.
P. 🚻

WINDERMERE, CUMBRIA   Lake District National Park Visitor Centre   Map 7 SD49

The Visitor Centre is situated in a 19th-century house in 32 acres of garden. It sets out to introduce you to the Lake District and all its pleasures and opportunities. There are audio-visual displays, films, a 'Living Lakeland' exhibition and information centre. Daily lake launch trips in summer and garden tours on Wednesday and Friday from May to September. There is a lakeshore nature trail and compass course and a play area. Special events in the summer includes 'Teddy bear Picnics' and World of Beatrix Potter activities.

☎(09662) 6601
Located: At Brookhole on A591.

Open: late Mar–early Nov from 10am, closing time varies with the season.
Admission: £1.20 (children under 5 free, 5–18 60p).
P. 🍴 🚻 & (ground floor & part gardens only) shop

WINDERMERE, CUMBRIA   Steamboat Museum   Map 7 SD49

The Museum has a unique and delightful collection of Victorian and Edwardian steamboats and other sail and steam boats which used to ply the Lakes. Many of them are still in working order and afloat. There are also displays about life on and around Lake Windermere. In the summer there are special events, such as a model boat regatta and steamboat rally, and boat trips on the lake.

☎(09662) 5565
Located: In Rayrigg Road

Open: *Apr–Oct Mon–Sat 10–5, Sun 2–5.
Steam trips subject to availability and weather Mon–Sat.
Admission: fee payable.
P. 🍴 🚻 & shop

AA

DAY TRIPS NORTH WEST ENGLAND

A variety of day trips are presented in this colourful and practical guide. Beautiful countryside, popular seaside resorts, historic towns and picturesque villages are all included, together with a wealth of maps and street plans.

YORK   North Yorkshire   Map 8 SE65

A Jewel among Medieval Cities

Practically every era of the past 2000 years has made its mark on York, but it is a strongly medieval feel that prevails. The city walls, the Minster and most other churches, many timber-framed buildings and the narrow streets that contain them were all here by the 15th century.

From its very beginnings, York has figured prominently in England's history. As the capital of Britannia Inferior – all Roman Britain north of the Trent – it was a key Roman stronghold. Roman fortifications provided the foundations for the fine walls that ring the city today, offering superb views from the wall walk, nearly three miles long. A 150ft stretch of Roman wall survives almost intact near the remarkable ten-sided Multangular Tower, itself a Roman building dating from about AD300.

Later, York became a great Viking trading centre – Jorvik. There was a harbour on the Foss, and a busy market. Recent excavations have revealed much about the city at this time, and were the inspiration for the exciting Jorvik Viking Centre.

The Norman period left few lasting traces in York. Two wooden castles built by William the Conqueror soon fell, one of them to be replaced in the 13th century by Clifford's Tower, all that remains today of York Castle.

Most of the Minster as it stands today was built between 1220 and 1472, a time of great prosperity for York. It was England's second largest provincial city and was especially known for its glass-painters, whose work still graces the Minster and other city churches. Craftsmen were protected and controlled by the guild companies, who left fine medieval buildings such as the Merchant Adventurers' Hall and the Merchant Taylors' Hall, as well as the Guildhall, which was reconstructed after bomb damage in World War II.

In the 18th century York became a social centre as well as a coaching town. There are still many fine Georgian buildings such as the Assembly Rooms and Fairfax House, which is open to the public and furnished in period style. The 18th century also saw the beginnings of what is still York's main industry – sweet-making. The firms that later became Rowntrees and Terry's were founded at this time by Quaker families in the city. A different 18th-century legacy is the story of Dick Turpin, the highwayman reputed to have ridden his horse Black Bess from London to York in 15 hours, an almost impossible feat. Crime did not pay for Turpin, for he was hanged in York in 1739 and was buried in St George's Churchyard.

A century later the railway arrived; the first train to London ran in 1840, and by 1877 York had one of Europe's grandest stations. Today York is home to the National Railway Museum. Other museums with 19th-century roots include the Yorkshire Museum, set in the grounds of ruined St Mary's Abbey. Exhibits here portray the geology and early history of York, and included a good Roman collection.

☆𝓢𝓣𝓐𝓡 𝓐𝓣𝓣𝓡𝓐𝓒𝓣𝓘𝓞𝓝𝓢

Castle Museum

Fifty years old in 1988, this imaginative folk museum stands on the site of York Castle, in a building that was once a prison. A reconstruction of Kirkgate, a cobbled Victorian street complete with stagecoach, hansom cab and authentic shopfronts, is perhaps the star exhibit. There is also an Edwardian street and park, period room settings including a 1953 sitting room, and a new gallery called 'Every Home Should Have One' – a collection of domestic gadgets of the past century.

Jorvik Viking Centre

The sight, sounds and smells of more than 1000 years ago are brought to life at this unique reconstruction of a Viking town. Archaeologists excavated for five years here beneath the Coppergate shopping precinct, and their discoveries, including complete houses and workshops, clothing and tools, a wharf and a market, have been pieced together to tell Jorvik's story. Visitors are transported through the exhibition in 'time cars' with accompanying commentary. Part of the display is a reconstruction, in situ, of the archaeological dig itself.

National Railway Museum

Locomotives, carriages, signals, posters, signboards and a model railway are among the many items of railway memorabilia recapturing 150 years of railway history here, from the first horse-drawn trains to the prototype of the Intercity 125. Queen Victoria's opulent saloon and the *Mallard* – holder of the world steam speed record – are also on display.

York Minster

The largest medieval church in England, the Minster celebrated its 500th anniversary in 1972 by the completion of a major restoration programme. Four of its predecessors were destroyed by fire, a hazard which has struck repeatedly – most recently in 1984, after the south transept was struck by lightning. A masterpiece of Gothic architecture, the Minster took some 250 years to complete, and is noted for its beautiful stained glass – more than half the medieval stained glass surviving in England is in the Minster's windows. The Undercroft Museum contains finds from the Minster's predecessors, as well as a collection of silver and other treasures.

The York Story

Tableaux, tapestries and slide-shows recall 1900 years of York's social and architectural development at this fine heritage centre. The setting is a 15th-century church, which was specially adapted and opened in 1975 to commemorate European Architectural Heritage Year. In addition to the modern audio-visual technology, a planned heritage walk around the city is also available here.

☎(0904) 653611
Located: Tower Street.

Open: Apr–Oct Mon–Sat 9.30–6.30, Sun 10–6.30; Nov–Mar Mon–Sat 9.30–5, Sun 10–5. Last admission 1 hour before closure. Closed Xmas and New Year's Day.
Admission: ✳£2.25 (children & senior citizens £1.15). Family ticket £7.
P. ⌨ ♿ (ground floor only) shop 🍴

☎(0904) 643211
Located: Coppergate.

Open: daily, Apr–Oct 9–7; Nov–Mar 9–5.30.
Admission: £2.75 (children under 16 £1.35, senior citizens £2).
♿ Shop 🍴 (except guide dogs)

☎(0904) 21261
Located: Leeman Road.

Open: Mon–Sat 10–6, Sun 11–6. Closed Xmas and New Year's Day.
Admission: £1.50 (children, senior citizens & disabled 75p). Family ticket £4.
P. ⌨ 🚃 ♿ Shop 🍴

Open: daily.
Admission: donations; charge for Undercroft Museum, Chapterhouse & Central Tower (when open)

☎(0904) 68632
Located: In St Mary's Church, Castlegate.

Open: all year Mon–Sat 10–5, Sun 1–5pm. Closed Xmas & New Year's Day.
Admission: ✳80p (children & senior citizens 40p). Joint ticket with Castle Museum £2.50 (children & senior citizens £1.25). Family ticket £7.
Shop 🍴

YORKSHIRE DALES AND MOORS   North Yorkshire   Maps 7 & 8

Sweeping down from the Pennines is a vast area of hills and dales criss-crossed by dry stone walls where pretty limestone villages nestle comfortably along river valleys. This is the Yorkshire Dales National Park which covers 680 square miles from Skipton in the south up to Stainmore Forest in the north and from Sedbergh westwards to Great Whernside. This National Park encompasses not only the finest, but also the most awesome of the Dales scenery – where the massive limestone rock formation gives some areas a 'lunar landscape' feel. Nowhere is this truer than at Malham – a village set among rugged limestone rocks. At Malham Cove, just a mile north of the village, a giant natural amphitheatre has been formed as the result of land movements that took place millions of years ago – the result is spectacular. Once the river fell in a great torrent down the cliff face here, but now it has gone underground and appears at a more leisurely pace at the foot of the cove. The Dales – Swaledale, Wensleydale, Wharfdale, Littondale and Ribblesdale – offer a superb array of footpaths. Visitors to this area will be spoilt for choice of pretty villages, old churches and abbeys and fascinating castles – some ruined and some restored, to visit. There are villages such as Aysgarth, Wensleydale's prettiest, which has a series of waterfalls which thunder down limestone steps in a glorious woodland setting. Grassington – Upper Wharfedale's principal village, with its medieval bridge and cobbled market square, is another typical Yorkshire hamlet. There are old abbeys, like the 12th-century Bolton Abbey which is magnificently placed, like a piece of stage scenery by the River Wharfe, and castles, like that at Richmond, from the top of which one of the finest views in the north of England can be found. To the east of the Dales is another area of exceptional beauty which is also one of our oldest National Parks – the North Yorkshire Moors National Park which coveres 550 or so square miles. These northern moors, which start from behind the coastal strip between Scarborough and Staithes, embrace wild and desolate moorland crossed by tiny roads, steep, secluded valleys, market towns and villages and an intriguing array of old abbeys, churches and castles all the more romantic because, like the dramatic Rievaulx Abbey near Helmsley, they are often in ruins. This is a fine area for touring by car, for walking, angling and sailing as well as for riding on the steam and diesel railway which runs for 18 glorious miles between Pickering and Grosmont through the very heart of the North Yorkshire Moors National Park.

For places to visit in the area check the location atlas at the end of the book.

Hikers look out across the North York Moors from the summit of Beacon Hill

Wales

Entering Wales is like coming into a foreign country for all the road signs are in both Welsh and English and in places Welsh is spoken by old and young alike.

Wales is a country of marked contrasts. It is an enchanted land with much that is magical: wild mountains reflected in calm lakes, long sandy beaches or a rugged coastline often of a breathtaking grandeur.

To the south is the lovely Wye Valley and Tintern Abbey; further west, Cardiff, capital of Wales, with its extraordinary castle and the 'Valleys' where coal has been wrenched from the earth though now the scars are healing. Beyond is the beauty of the Gower Peninsula and the magnificent Pembrokeshire coastline.

Travel northwards to the lovely mountain area of the Brecon Beacons or the gentle, fertile country around Carmarthen, or west to the village of St David's with its venerable cathedral and the shrine of the Welsh patron saint.

In the far north the peaks of Snowdon and Cader Idris dominate the scene; even from the sandy beaches there are wonderful views of the mountains. While the great castle of Caernarfon, one of the best preserved in Britain, gives a real sense of castle life long ago.

ABERCRAF (Abercrave), POWYS   Dan-yr-Ogof Showcaves   Map 3 SN81

You can have a guided tour through the passages of this, the largest showcave complex in Western Europe. You'll see some of the largest stalactites and stalagmites in the country. Britain's first archaeological showcave is here, and children will love the model Dinosaur Park. There is also a dry ski slope.

☎Abercrave (0639) 730284
Located: 3 miles north of Abercraf on the A4067.

Open: Easter–Oct daily from 10: for winter opening please telephone.
Admission: £2.85 (children £1.85, senior citizens £2.50).
P. ☐ ⊼ shop & information centre

for ABERSYTWYTH see opposite page

BALA, GWYNEDD   Cyffdy Farm Park   Map 6 SH93

Here are animals in abundance: farm animals, including rare breeds, waterfowl and llama. There's a pets' corner, children's playground and donkey cart rides; a farm trail, nature trail, fishing and pony hire. Demonstrations are held of traditional farming crafts: butter making, spinning, shearing and dog handling; and fresh produce to take home.

☎Llanuwchllyn (06784) 271
Located: 3 miles south-west of Parc.

Open: *Easter–Oct. Winter opening by arrangement.
Admission: *£1.80 (children 90p).
P. ☐ (cafe Jun–Aug only) ⊼ ♿ (ground floor only) shop & garden centre

BANGOR, GWYNEDD   Penrhyn Castle   Map 6 SH57

This splendid neo-Norman castle was built far too late (c1820–1845) to have any defensive purpose. It is in a wonderful position between the Menai Strait and Snowdonia. It has interesting Norman-style furniture and fine pictures. There is also an industrial railway and a museum of dolls. The grounds have a woodland area and a Victorian walled garden.

☎(0248) 353084
Located: 3 miles east of Landegai on A5122.

Open: Apr–Oct daily except Tue, 12–5 (last admission 4.30); 11–5 Jul–Aug.
Admission: £2.20 (children £1) Gardens only £1.10 (children 50p). Family ticket £5.40
P. ☐ ♿ ♥ (except guide dogs)
National Trust

BARRY, SOUTH GLAMORGAN   Porthkerry Country Park   Map 3 ST16

Fossil-rich limestone cliffs, rising to 150ft, and a lofty viaduct built in 1898 for the Vale of Glamorgan Railway, are dramatic features of Porthkerry Country Park. Here, oak and ash dominate clifftop woodlands, where springtime's primroses, violets and bluebells give way to wild strawberries during the summer months. Oystercatchers and gulls, searching the smooth shingle shore, are frequent sights too.

Porthkerry is said to be named after Ceri ap Caid, a local ruler in the pre-Christian era. It also witnessed the first Norman invasion of South Glamorgan, in 1093. Other links with the past include the remains of a kiln where lime was burned to make fertiliser, and a 19th-century sawmill overlooked by Mill Wood.

Located: on the coast, 2 miles west of Barry.

Open: all year.
P. ☐ ⊼ shop

for BEAUMARIS see page 136

University Town by the Sea

The largest town in mid Wales, Aberystwyth is the focal point for a vast area of wild country around it. Yet despite being an important administrative and shopping centre, its atmosphere is still that of a genteel seaside resort and university town – roles it took on in the 19th century.

A Victorian appearance disguises the town's much earlier beginnings. Pen Dinas, the hill overlooking Aberystwyth from the south, was topped by a Celtic hillfort many centuries before the appearance of the monument to Wellington that crowns it today. In 1277, Edward I chose the headland between the two beaches as the site for a castle. Its ruins now stand in pleasant gardens from which views extend over Aberystwyth's sweeping bay, backed by its promenade. The cheerful colour-washed seafront houses of Marine Terrace overlook the sadly truncated remnant of the 800ft-long pier that was built in 1865.

Near the pier stands the university's first building, an extravaganza of Victorian Gothic. It was built as a hotel in 1860 by Thomas Saving, a railway entrepreneur who planned to offer free holidays here to people buying return tickets from London. His scheme collapsed, and ten years later the building was sold to become the University College of Wales. Today, the University campus is on Penglais Hill, behind the town. Also here is the imposing building of the National Library of Wales.

South of the castle, where the rivers Rheidol and Ystwyth meet the sea, is the harbour. Once busy with shipments of coal and lead, it is now a quieter place, frequented by pleasure craft and fishing boats. Deep-sea angling is a popular pastime with visitors. Aberystwyth's other leisure facilities include an indoor swimming pool, tennis courts, an 18-hole golf course and the Penglais Sports Centre.

☆STAR ATTRACTIONS

Aberystwyth Cliff Railway and Camera Obscura
Advertised as 'a conveyance for gentlefolk since 1896', this is Britain's longest cliff railway. Its cars ascend the 1-in-2 slope of Constitution Hill at a stately pace of four miles per hour, offering a panorama of the town and the bay. At the top are tea-rooms – a new Camera Obscura – a darkened viewing gallery with a special lens system which focuses details of the view on to a screen. Energetic passengers may take the footpath and nature trail down to Clarach Bay.

☎(0970) 617642
Located: Promenade (northern end):

Open: Easter–Oct daily 10–6.
Admission: fee payable

Ceredigion Museum
This folk museum is set in a restored Edwardian theatre, the Coliseum. Its carefully preserved atmosphere makes a unique setting for displays featuring the paraphernalia of local trades and crafts, from farming to lead-mining and from weaving to carpentry. A reconstructed 19th-century cottage interior is among the exhibits.

☎(0970) 617911
Located: Terrace Road.

Open: Mon–Sat 10–5.
Admission: free.

Vale of Rheidol Railway
No visitor to Aberystwyth should miss the hour-long trip up the valley to Devil's Bridge on this delightful line, British Rail's only narrow-gauge steam railway. Opened in 1902 to carry lead from mines up the valley, as well as passengers, the 12-mile line offers spectacular views. At Devil's Bridge, do not miss the waterfalls and the three remarkable bridges, stacked vertically one above the other, in the narrow gorge of the Afon Mynach.

☎(0970) 612378
Located: Terminus at the British Rail station in Alexandra Road.

Open: Easter–Oct. Telephone for details of train times.
Fare: payable
P. ⌓ 👭 shop

BEAUMARIS, GWYNEDD   Beaumaris Castle   Map 6 SH67

This last of the Welsh castles to have been built by Edward I in the 14th-century still looks much as it did in his day. It is surrounded by a water-filled moat and has its original small dock to which supplies were brought to the castle by sea. From the rampart walk you have a clear view of the whole castle and its beautiful surroundings.

☎(0248) 810361

Open: mid Oct–mid Mar Mon–Sat 9.30–4, Sun 2–4; mid Mar–mid Oct Mon–Sat 9.30–6.30, Sun 2–6.30. *Admission:* fee payable
P. ⅂⊼ shop
Cadw: Welsh Historic Monuments

BEAUMARIS, GWYNEDD   Beaumaris Gaol   Map 6 SH67

You can understand just how harsh prison conditions were in Victorian times when you visit this old gaol, built in 1829. You see the prisoners' cells, a unique treadmill and the condemned man's final walk to the scaffold. The courthouse is also open and there is an exhibition illustrating prison life.

☎(0248) 810921

Open: May–Sep, daily 11–6
Admission: 70p (children & senior citizens 35p). Family tickets available.
& (ground floor only) shop ⊬

BEAUMARIS, GWYNEDD   Museum of Childhood   Map 6 SH67

This museum will delight all generations. It is a century and a half of children's toys and pastimes: about 1500 items displayed in eight rooms. Early visual and audio equipment plays ever hour. The art gallery has paintings and prints of children, and samplers, and needlework pictures made by children long ago. There are dolls, games, trains and cars, musical boxes, magic lanterns, push toys, cycles and prams, and children's furniture. There is even a whole room devoted to savings boxes. It is a fascinating place for young and old alike.

☎Menai Bridge (0248) 712498
Located: 1 Castle Street.

Open: daily Mon–Sat 10–6, Sun 12–5. Closed Xmas & 2nd week Jan to 2nd week Mar.
Admission: £1.50 (children 75p, senior citizens £1, children under 5 free.). Family ticket £4.
& (ground floor only) shop ⊬

BEDDGELERT, GWYNEDD   Sygun Copper Mine   Map 6 SH54

This unique 19th-century copper mine is a British Tourist Authority award winner, and is set deep in the spectacular scenery of the Gwynant Valley. The centre contains fascinating artefacts discovered during excavation work and a continuous audio-visual presentation about the mine.

☎(076686) 595

Open: guided tours Apr–Oct daily 10–6 (last tour 5.15).
Admission: £2.10 (children £1.30, senior citizens £1.65)
P. ⌕ ⅂⊼ shop

BLAENAU FFESTINIOG, GWYNEDD
Ffestiniog Pumped Storage Scheme   Map 6 SH64

Visit the first hydroelectric pumped storage power station to be built for the Central Electricity Generating Board! This fascinating example of modern technology will enthrall adults and junior scientists alike. Set against the spectacular background of the old slate quarries, it was opened by Her Majesty the Queen in 1963.

The Information Centre contains an exhibition of the scheme and a cinema, while guided tours can also be arranged. There is a picnic area and walks to enjoy.

☎(0766) 830310
Located: off the A496 at Tanygrisiau, near Blaenau Ffestiniog

Open: Easter–Oct 10–4.30.
Admission: ✳£1.25 (children 70p, senior citizens 80p).
P. ⌕ ⅂⊼ & (ground floor of power station & Information Centre only) shop ⊬

BLAENAU FFESTINIOG, GWYNEDD   Gloddfa Ganol Slate Mine   Map 6 SH64

Visit the world's largest slate mine! Take the quarryman's railway and explore this real working mine, see the massive machinery and the splitting of the slate. Also featured are an exciting Land Rover Safari and a variety of interesting museums, including a narrow gauge railway centre.

☎(0766) 830664

Open: Easter–Sep Mon–Fri 10–5.30. Also Suns mid Jul–end Aug.
Admission: ✱£2.20 (children £1.10).
P. ☞ (licensed) 🌲 shop

BLAENAU FFESTINIOG, GWYNEDD   Llechwedd Slate Caverns   Map 6 SH64

The world of the Victorian slate miner is recreated here in two exciting subterranean tours. Travel on the miner's underground tramway and explore the deep mine on foot. Music, light and sound are used to help you relive the atmosphere of times long past.

☎(0766) 830306

Open: end Mar–Oct daily from 10am, last tour 5.15.
Admission: ✱free to surface. Mine tours £2.35 (children £1.50, senior citizens £1.90).
P. ☞ (licensed) 🌲 & (mine tour by special arrangement) shop ⚒ (underground)

BLAENAVON, GWENT   Big Pit Mining Museum   Map 3 SO20

An exciting journey 300ft underground where you experience the environment of the Welsh coalminers. Equipped with helmet, lamp, and emergency air, you will be guided through the narrow tunnels of the mine. On the surface an absorbing collection of exhibits include a reconstructed miner's cottage. Stout shoes and warm clothes are recommended.

☎(0495) 790311

Open: Mar–Dec daily (except 24–26 Dec). First underground tour 10am, last tour starts 3.30pm.
Admission: underground tour & surface ticket £3.25 (children £2.25, senior citizens £3). Surface only £1.25 (children 75p, senior citizens £1).
P. ☞ 🌲 & (underground possible by prior arrangement only) shop ⚒ (underground or cafeteria).

for the BRECON BEACONS see page 138

BRYNSIENCYN, ANGLESEY   Anglesey Sea Zoo   Map 6 SH46

Ever picked up a live lobster? You can in the 'touch me' room at Anglesey Sea Zoo. You can also lift rocks, with care, in search of crabs. Elsewhere in the zoo you can come close to a conger eel or marvel at the grace of shoals of herring and sand eels. When you have seen the great variety of sea creatures here it might surprise you to learn that they are all to be found around the British coastline. Mum will no doubt appreciate the first-class seafood shop.

☎(024873) 411
Located: at the Oyster Hatchery.

Open: mid Feb–early Nov, daily 10–5
Admission: £1.95 (children 95p, senior citizens £1.50).
P. ☞ & shop

BURY PORT, DYFED   Pembrey Country Park   Map 2 SN40

Opened in 1980, this 520-acre country park on the eastern shore of Carmarthen Bay, caters for a remarkably wide range of activities and interests. They include land yachting and parascending on the seven-mile sweep of Cefn Sidan Sands, horse-and-carriage rides, pony trekking, orienteering and four nature trails – one of which is suitable for disabled visitors. Among the other facilities are barbecue sites and guided walks, but many visit Pembrey just to relax on the dune-backed beach, which is patrolled by lifeguards during the summer months.

off A484, 1 mile west of Burry Port.
Located: all year

Open: charged
P. ☞ 🌲 visitor centre

for CAERNARFON see page 139

Stretching between the Black Mountain of Dyfed in the west and the Black Mountains of Powys and Gwent in the east are the 519 square miles of wild and beautiful countryside that are now protected as the Brecon Beacons National Park. This is an area of sharp contrasts: The massive contoured Beacons (so called because of their use as sites for signal fires) rise up in great crests, like waves about to break, before falling away sharply in sheer 600ft precipices. The Beacons preside over great sweeping valleys, heather-covered uplands and high moorlands where vast flocks of sheep and pretty wild Welsh mountain ponies roam freely, and where wild plant, animal and bird life abounds and thrives.

The two principal towns of this area are Abergavenny and Brecon. Abergavenny, a market town on the River Usk surrounded by mountains, is the gateway to the Brecon Beacons National Park. It is a town with many buildings dating back to Tudor times, the ruins of an 11th-century castle, and is an excellent centre for walking, pony trekking and fishing. Brecon, set at the confluence of the rivers Usk and Honddu, is also an attractive old market town and like Abergavenny is an excellent centre for walking, pony trekking and fishing. Within Brecon are the ruins of a medieval castle and a part 13th-century fortified cathedral, and the town is a good place to hunt for antique bargains and local craft for sale in its many inviting shops. To the west of Brecon, at Libanus, is the Mountain Centre from which there are panoramic views of the Beacons. The Centre can supply all the information about this area that any visitor could possibly wish for, and there is also a buffet where refreshments are served.

No stay in this area is complete without a visit to some of the fantastic caves. Just north of Abercraf visitors can be treated to a magical mystery tour through the illuminated caves of Dan-yr-ogof that will take them past stalagmites and stalagtites, weird and wonderfully-shaped rock formations and underground lakes. There are many ways of getting to know this area – by car, on foot or on horseback, but one of the most pleasurable must surely be by riding on the Brecon Mountain Railway. The starting point of this narrow gauge railway is at Pant, on the outskirts of Merthyr Tydfil. From here the train runs for two miles to Pontsticill, through glorious countryside with breath-taking views across the lake to the Brecon Beacons.

For places to visit in the area check the location atlas at the end of the book

The borderland Vale of Ewyas is noted for its religious sites.

CAERNARFON, GWYNEDD   Caernarfon Castle   Map 6 SH46

Edward I planned this huge castle in the 13th-century as a seat of royal government and a palace for the Prince of Wales. It is splendidly preserved to this day. It has a series of 13 towers linked by curtain walls and within there are two large baileys. Caernarfon has been described as a work of 'unparalleled architectural magnificence'. You can go up to the roof of the great Eagle Tower and get a panoramic view of the whole castle and the surrounding country. The rampart walk of the great southern curtain wall should not be missed either. Birthplace of Edward II, the first Prince of Wales, and site of the present Prince's investiture in 1969, there are exhibitions about the castle and its history, including a display about the Princes of Wales. There is also a display of arms and armour and the Royal Welsh Fusiliers Museum is in the Queen's Tower.

☎(0286) 77617

Open: mid Mar–mid Oct Mon–Sat 9.30–6.30, Sun 2–6.30; mid Oct–mid Mar Mon–Sat 9.30–4, Sun 2–4. Also open from 9.30 on Suns between Apr & Sep.
Admission: fee payable.
P. shop
Cadw: Welsh Historic Monuments

CALDICOT, GWENT   Caldicot Castle and Countryside Park   Map 3 ST48

A restored Norman border castle with several museum displays and featuring personal stereo cassette tours. The surrounding Countryside Park has an exciting adventure playground to please the children, and a special barbecue site.

☎(0291) 420241
Located: on B4245

Open: Mar–Oct, Mon–Fri 11–12.30 & 1.30–5, Sat 10–1 & 1.30–5, Sun 1.30–5. Park open all year.
Admission: £1 (children & senior citizens 50p). Countryside Park free.
P. ☕ ⊼ & (grounds only) shop

for CARDIFF see page 140

CARDIGAN, DYFED   Cardigan Wildlife Park   Map 2 SN14

A pleasant family day out can be spent ambling around this beautiful park, with its unusual mixture of animals. Children will love the tunnel to the disused slate quarries. See the ancient art of coracle fishing demonstrated on several weekday afternoons. Mums and Dads can relax at the café, while youngsters amuse themselves in the adventure playground.

☎(0239) 614449
Located: entrance near Cilgerran village, off A478.

Open: daily 10–sunset (last admission 5.30).
Admission: ✳£1.50 (children and senior citizens 75p).
P. ☕ (licensed, seasonal) ⊼ & (excluding some trails) shop ✸ (except guide dogs)

CERRIGYDRUDION, CLWYD   Llyn Brenig Information Centre and Welsh Water Authority Estate   Map 6 SH94

The Centre is set in a 2400-acre estate in which there is a 10 mile around-the-lake walk (with a certificate for those who complete it!). The nature Reserve has a nature trail and there is access to the bird hide (best viewing between November and March). There are fishing platforms with special open days for disabled fishers, and sailing and canoeing opportunities. Unique to the Centre is its archaeological trail. There is also a Welsh/English language exhibition on the geology, archaeology, natural history and history of the region.

☎(049082) 463

Open: Apr–mid Oct daily 8–6; mid Oct–Mar Mon–Fri 8–4. (Access in winter may be limited by snow; cross country skiing is then available.)
Admission: Free except for canoeing, sailing and fishing.
P. ☕ (weekends Apr–Jun & Sep, daily Jul–Aug) & souvenir & fishing tackle shop (Apr–mid Oct)

for COLWYN BAY see page 141

Capital City of Wales

Cardiff has existed since Roman times at least, but it is the last 150 years that have given the city most of its present character. To the Romans it was a garrison and naval base and the Normans built a castle here, yet despite its importance in Britain's history, Cardiff remained a relatively quiet seaside town until the Industrial Revolution. With the growth of the local coal and steel industries, Cardiff increased dramatically in both size and prosperity, and by the turn of the 19th-century it was one of the busiest ports in the world.

Rebuilding during the city's prosperous years has meant that few ancient buildings are left. Notable exceptions are the cathedral at Llandaff and the medieval church of St John. But Victorian and Edwardian redevelopment has left its own fine legacy – elegant shopping arcades such as Castle Arcade, and the dignified municipal buildings of Cathays Park, set among colourful formal gardens and broad, tree-lined avenues.

Among the city's newest buildings are some well-known Welsh venues for cultural and sporting events. St David's Hall stages concerts by world-famous orchestras, pop groups and leading Welsh choirs. The Chapter Arts Centre has a theatre, two cinemas and two galleries. Then there is the National Sports Centre for Wales, the Wales Empire Pool, and – of course – Cardiff Arms Park, known and respected throughout the rugby-playing world.

☆ STAR ATTRACTIONS

Cardiff Castle

Traces of Roman walls, together with a fine Norman keep standing on the original mound, testify to the antiquity of Cardiff Castle. However, it is the dramatic additions of the 19th-century that impress most visitors. The living quarters are a fairy-tale showpiece, with murals, carvings, tiles and stained glass in a riot of exotic pattern and dazzling colour. Two of the most stunning features are the Moorish room and the banqueting hall. All this is the work of William Burges, the young architect commissioned to transform the neglected castle in 1865 by its wealthy owner the Third Marquis of Bute. The castle's more recent features include a 100yd-long sculptured mural depicting life in Roman times, and the Welsh regiment Museum.

☎(0222) 822083
Located: Castle Street.

Open: daily (except Xmas & New Year). Conducted tours Mar, Apr & Oct. Mon–Sun 10–12.30 & 2–4 (castle closes 5pm); May–Sep daily 10–12.40 & 2–5 (castle closes 6pm); Nov–Feb daily 10.30–3.15 (castle closes 4.30pm). Only short tours when functions in progress.
Admission: conducted tour all year ✳£2 (children & senior citizens £1). Short tour & Welsh Regimental Military Museum (when appropriate) £1.50 (children & senior citizens 75p). Green, Roman Wall, Norman Keep & Military Museum £1.10 (children & senior citizens 55p).
P. ⌂ & (grounds only) shop ✗ (except grounds)

National Museum of Wales

This imposing domed and colonnaded building is one of the biggest museums in Britain, internationally acclaimed particularly for its fine collection of modern European paintings and sculpture, which includes works by Cézanne, Monet, Renoir and Rodin. Other departments tell the story of Wales – its plant and animal life, geology, archaeology and industry. Exhibits range from a fine collection of early Welsh inscribed stones and carved crosses to a model coal-mine. Visitors can also see the regalia worn by Prince Charles at his investiture as Prince of Wales at Caernarfon Castle in 1969.

☎(0222) 397951
Located: Cathays Park

Open: Tue–Sat 10–5, Sun 2.30–5. Closed Xmas, New Year's Day, Good Fri & May Day.
Admission: free.
P. ⌂ & shop ✗

For The Welsh Folk Museum entry look under ST FAGANS

Welsh Industrial and Maritime Museum

Set in the heart of Cardiff's dockland, this museum opened in 1977. Machinery from coal-mines, steelworks, tin-plate mills and other South Wales industries helps to tell the story of 200 years of industrial developments in this unique area. Among many larger exhibits displayed outside on the four-acre site are a canal boat, various cranes and an industrial locomotive.

☎(0222) 481919
Located: Bute Street.

Open: Tue–Sat 10–5, Sun 2.30–5. Closed Xmas, New Year's Day, Good Fri & May Day.
Admission: free.
& book shop ✗

COLWYN BAY, CLWYD   Welsh Mountain Zoo and Flagstaff Gardens
Map 6 SH87

The site of this zoo is splendid with panoramic views over Colwyn Bay. The animals live in natural settings between garden and woodland areas. The collection includes elephants and lions, various species of deer, bears, chimpanzees, monkeys and performing sealions, reptiles, tropical birds, parrots, penguins and birds of prey. The zoo also provides a natural home for various local wildlife. During the summer months the eagles are flown completely free. 1988 is the zoo's jubilee year and there will be special events in celebration.

☎(0492) 532938

Open: all year daily 9.30–5 (9.30–4 in winter months).
Admission: £2.80 (children & senior citizens £1.40).
P. ⌂ (licensed) ⟰ & (in parts) shop garden centre ✗ (in zoo)

for CONWY see page 142

CWMCARN, GWENT   Scenic Forest Drive   Map 3 ST29

An idyllic spot for a picnic or barbecue and the kids will love the play areas. This seven-mile drive through mountain forest offers spectacular views of the surrounding countryside as far as the Brecon Beacons and the Bristol Channel. The forest, which is mainly larch, spruce and pine, has paths for the walker too, with clearly marked viewpoints.

☎Penhow (0633) 400205

Open: Good Fri–Aug daily 11–8, also Sep 11–6.
Admission: fee payable.
P. ⟰ & shop

CYNONVILLE, WEST GLAMORGAN
Welsh Miners Museum and Afan Argoed Country Park   Map 3 SS89

Witness the harsh realities of mining through the eyes of the miner. The museum contains simulated coal faces, early pit equipment and vivid reconstructions of the miner's way of life. The park, set in the heart of the Afan Valley, will enchant you with its scenic beauty and breath-taking forested walks.

☎(0639) 850564 or 850875
Located: on A4107, 6 miles north-east of Port Talbot.

Open: Mar–Oct 10.30–6; Nov–Feb Sat & Sun only 10.30–5.
Admission: 30p (children over 5 & senior citizens 15p, disabled free).
P. ⌂ ⟰ & shop ✗

DOLGELLAU, GWYNEDD   Tal-y-Waen Farm Trail   Map 6 SH71

The whole family can enjoy a day at this award-winning Welsh Hill Farm. Walk the farm trail and observe the farm animals and wild life in their own environment, and enjoy the panoramic views of the Mawddach estuary. Other attractions include pets corner, an adventure play area, pony rides, an art gallery, museum and barbecues.

☎(0341) 422580
Located: on Cader Road.

Open: May–Oct 10–5, closed Sat.
Admission: *£4 per family (2 adults & up to 3 children).
P. (licensed) ⟰ & shop ✗

FAIRBOURNE, GWYNEDD   Fairbourne Railway and Butterfly Safari   Map 6 SH61

Plenty here for the railway enthusiast on this delightful ride through sand dunes, past the impressive Cader Idris and the lovely Mawddach estuary. Its sister attraction is the magical Butterfly Safari with beautiful butterflies from all parts of the world living, feeding and breeding in a natural environment.

☎(0341) 250362
Located: Beach Road.

Open: Easter–Sep. times vary according to season or special event.
Admission: Railway; 2nd class return £2.20 (children £1.30, senior citizens £1.65) 1st class return £2.95 (children £1.75, senior citizens £2.25). Butterfly Safari; £1.30 (children £1, senior citizens £1.40).
P. ⌂ & shop

for GLYN CEIRIOG see page 143

CONWY Gwynedd Map 6 SH77

Guardian of Land and Sea

Its dramatic setting alone, with the wide Afon Conwy on one side and the foothills of Snowdonia's mountains on the other, would make Conwy a memorable place to visit. The fact that it is one of Britain's finest medieval walled towns, complete with a superb 13th-century castle, makes it a very special place indeed.

It was doubtless the strategic, not the aesthetic, possibilities of the location that made Edward I choose this spot in 1283 as the site of a major castle in his campaign to subdue the Welsh. The rocky, then inaccessible place at the mouth of the Afon Conwy would be easily defended by both land and sea. The town was ringed by a 35ft-high wall, approaching a mile round and punctuated by 21 crenellated towers. Today the wall walk on the north-west section offers marvellous views of the castle, the town and their surroundings.

The walls enclose a web of narrow streets, but only a few of the older buildings are still here. Among them are 15th-century Aberconwy House, the medieval church of St Mary, and Plas Mawr, a fine Elizabethan town house noted for its panelling and plasterwork. It is now an art gallery.

More recent additions to Conwy's townscape include the three bridges over the river. Telford's suspension bridge replaced the hazardous ferry crossing in 1826. Harmonising perfectly with the castle, it is now open to pedestrians only. The tubular rail bridge followed 22 years later, and a new road bridge was built in the 1950s. It looks across the harbour to the quay, dwarfed by the great town walls. Here fishing boats unload and pleasure craft tie up just as vessels carrying slate and other cargo did in centuries past.

☆STAR ATTRACTIONS

Aberconwy House

Probably 100 years younger than the castle, this is Conwy's oldest house. The timber-framed building, whose overhanging or 'jettied' upper storey is reached by an external staircase, is owned by the National Trust. Inside is a fascinating exhibition on Conwy through the ages.

☎(049263) 2246
Located: Castle Street/High Street.

Open: Apr–Sep daily except Tue. 11–5; Oct Sat & Suns 11–5. Last admission 4.45.
Admission: 70p (children 35p).
shop (no dogs) (except guide dogs)
National Trust

Conwy Castle

Eight massive, battlemented round towers linked by 30ft-high walls show that Edward I meant business when he built this great stronghold in 1283. It looks impregnable enough, but its forbidding exterior did not prevent Owain Glyndwr's forces from capturing in in 1401. On other occasions it withstood sieges – the last during the Civil War, when it was held for the King. Afterwards it fell into disrepair, but it has lately been restored. Four of the eight towers are topped by turrets – added protection for the royal apartments in the inner bailey. Here will be found one of the castle's most complete rooms, known as Queen Eleanor's Chapel.

☎(0492) 592358

Open: mid Oct–mid Mar Mon–Sat 9.30–4, Sun 2–4; mid Mar–mid Oct Mon–Sat 9.30–6.30, Sun 2–6.30. Between Apr & Sep also open from 9.30am on Sun. Closed Xmas & New Year's Day.
Admission: fee payable.
P. shop
Heritage in Wales

Smallest House

With a frontage measuring only 6ft wide by 10ft high, this popular tourist attraction is the house listed by the *Guinness Book of Records* as the smallest in Britain. A steep staircase links the only two rooms, which are simply furnished as a Victorian fisherman's cottage.

☎(0492) 593484
Located: The Quay.

Open: Apr–Jun & Sep–Oct 10–6; Jul & Aug 10–9.30. Visits in winter by arrangement only.
Admission: 20p (children under 5 free).
♿ (ground floor only) shop

GLYN CEIRIOG, CLYWD   Chwarel Wynne Mine and Museum   Map 7 SJ23

Go underground for a fascinating guided tour of the slate mine. There are a number of interesting exhibits on show in the museum and a video of the history of the slate industry. The mine is set in beautiful 12-acre surroundings complete with nature trail.

☎(069172) 343
Located: at Wynne Quarry, on B4500.

Open: Easter–Oct daily 10–5.
Admission: £2 (children & senior citizens £1). Family tickets available.
P. ⌷ ⊼ & (ground floor and grounds only) shop & garden centre

KIDWELLY, DYFED   Kidwelly Industrial Museum   Map 2 SN40

The museum is based at the old Kidwelly Tin Plate Works and is located in the buildings, displaying machinery from the works. Exhibition galleries tell the story of the area and its industry. There is also an exhibition on coal mining and mining machinery. In addition there is a steam crane, steam and diesel locomotives and typesetting machinery. The delightful setting by the Gwendraeth Fach River and the adventure playground help to make it an excellent outing.

☎(0554) 891078

Open: Easter–end Jun & Sep Mon–Fri 10–5, Sat & Sun 2–5 (last entry 4pm); Jul & Aug Mon–Fri 10–6, Sat & Sun 2–6 (last entry 5pm).
Admission: 75p (children & senior citizens 30p). Family ticket (2 adults & children) £1.80.
P. ⌷ ⊼ & shop

LLANBEDR, GWYNEDD   Maes Arto Tourist Village   Map 6 SH52

There is a wide variety of things to do and see in the village which is set in ten acres of beautiful gardens near the Cambrian Coast. There is an aquarium, a model village, the re-creation of an old Welsh street, and an adventure playground. In addition you can visit the Pets' Corner, the Animal House and TV film sets. There are a number of craft shops with a wide choice of products.

☎(034123) 467

Open: ✳Easter–mid Oct daily 9–6.
Admission: fee payable.
P. ⌷ ⊼ & shop

LLANBERIS, GWYNEDD   Llanberis Lake Railway   Map 6 SH56

On this line, which was originally used to carry slate from Dinoric Quarry to Port Dinorwic, you can travel on a 4 mile return journey starting near the Welsh Slate Museum. The trains are pulled by steam locomotives dating from 1889–1948 and the carriages were specially built for the railway.

☎(0286) 870549
Located: Padarn Country Park.

Open: Easter–early Oct daily, except Sat, 11–4.30 (in peak season).
Admission: ✳£2.20 (children 5–15 £1.10). Family Saver tickets available.
P. ⌷ ⊼ & (some parts inaccessible) shop

LLANBERIS, GWYNEDD   Snowdon Mountain Railway   Map 6 SH56

This, the only rack and pinion railway in Britain, was opened in 1896 and is still operated by steam locomotives. It climbs over 3000ft in 4¾ miles to the summit of Snowdon from where on a clear day you have wonderful views of North Wales and as far as the Isle of Man and the Wicklow Mountains of Ireland. The round trip takes 2½ hours including a stop of half an hour on the summit.

☎(0286) 870223

Open: Week before Easter–late Oct daily from 9am (weather permitting). No weekend services early or late season.
Admission: ✳£9.50 (children £6.50).
P. ⌷ (& licensed at summit) shop

LLANBERIS, GWYNEDD   Welsh Slate Museum   Map 6 SH 56

Dinorwic Slate Quarry was closed in 1969 and the workshops, machinery and plant were preserved to form this exciting branch of the National Museum of Wales. You can visit the fitting and erecting shops, the repair shops, the smithy, the dressing and sawing sheds, the foundry, office and messroom. The museum retains a very real atmosphere of working life.

☎**Caernarfon (0286) 870630**

Open: Easter–Sep daily, Mon–Sat 9.30–6.30, Sun 2–6.30.
Admission: £1.20 (children and senior citizens 60p).
P. 🎋 ⅅ shop
Cadw: Welsh Historic Monuments

for LLANDUDNO see opposite page

LLANDYSAL, DYFED   Maesllyn Woollen Mill Museum   Map 2 SN44

You can see how hand spinning and weaving gave way to powered machinery processes in this 19th-century woollen mill. The restored water wheel drives some of the machinery. There are displays about the industry and you can follow an interesting nature trail along the waterway. There is also a vintage wireless collection here too.

☎**Rhydlewis (023975) 251**

Open: Mon–Sat 10–6, Sun 2–6 (summer); Mon–Fri 10–5 (winter).
Admission: *80p (children 40p, senior citizens 60p).
P. ⅅ (Easter–Oct) 🎋 ⅅ (ground floor only) shop ✖ (in building)

LLANFAIR CAEREINION, POWYS   Welshpool and Llanfair Light Railway   Map 6 SJ10

The narrow gauge steam railway (2ft 6in gauge) runs the eight miles between Welshpool and Llanfair Caereinion. It has interesting Austrian and Colonial locomotives. The Mid-Wales Festival of Transport is held here in mid-July.

☎**(0938) 810441**

Open: Easter–beginning of Oct, weekends & Spring Bank Hol; mid June–early Jul also Tue, Wed & Thu; daily from mid Jul–mid Sep. Trains from Llanfair at 11, 1.45, 4.15; from Welshpool at 12.20, 3, 5.15.
Admission: *return fare, £3.90 (children under 5 free, 5–15 £1.95); Single £2.50 (children £1.25). Family ticket £8.50.

LLANGOLLEN, CLWYD   Canal Museum & Passenger Boat Trip Centre   Map 7 SJ24

A visit to this fascinating museum of Britains's great canal era offers the opportunity of a horse drawn passenger boat trip along the beautiful Vale of Llangollen. Explore the reproduction of a 19th-century coalmine. Learn the story of the water transport system through static and working models, photos, murals and slides.

☎**Chester (0244) 335180 or Llangollen (0978) 860702**
Located: The Wharf.

Open: daily Easter–Sep 10.30–5
Admission: *Museum 50p (children 30p). Horse drawn boat trips £1.30 (children 70p).
P. ⅅ (ground floor only) shop

for further LLANGOLLEN entry see page 146

Symbols
☎	telephone number
P.	parking on the premises
ⅅ	refreshments available
🎋	picnic area
ⅅ	accessible to wheelchair-bound visitors
✖	no dogs
*	indicates 1987 details

Queen of Welsh Resorts

The amenities of the 20th-century combine with Victorian seaside charm here at Wales' largest resort. The 1850s saw the transformation of a cluster of fishermen's cottages into a planned town of wide streets, canopied shops, a sweeping promenade and a fine pier – all of which still give Llandudno its unique character more than a century later.

Fine sandy beaches border both sides of the peninsula on which Llandudno stands. The North Shore is where the main seaside attractions, including the pier are situated. Something of a speciality, opposite the pier gates, is the Victorian Punch-and-Judy theatre – 'Professor Codman's Wooden-headed Follies'. The West Shore, overlooking Conwy Bay, is quieter – a fine place to watch the sunset over the Menai Straits. Also here, by the model yacht pond, is a statue of Lewis Carroll's White Rabbit from *Alice in Wonderland*. It commemorates the author's visit to Llandudno in 1862 to stay with the family of Alice Liddell, the little girl for whom he wrote the story.

Overlooking Llandudno Bay from the lower slopes of Great Orme is Happy Valley, where there are gardens, a children's playground, miniature golf and summer entertainment ranging from fireworks to an open-air theatre. Other entertainment – classical concerts, summer shows, wrestling or roller discos – is offered at the Aberconwy Centre, which also has badminton and squash courts. Llandudno's museums include the Mostyn Art Gallery and the Charden House Museum.

Visitors who like to explore might take the planned town trail (leaflet available at information offices) or one of the coach tours that depart regularly from Prince Edward Square. For a taste of the magnificent countryside inland, try a train trip up the Conwy Valley to Betws-y-coed in the heart of Snowdonia.

☆*STAR ATTRACTIONS*

Doll Museum
More than 1000 dolls from many countries and periods make up this collection. Dolls' prams, furniture and houses are also on display. One room of the museum is devoted to a large working model railway.

☎(0492) 76312
Located: Masonic Street.

Open: Easter–end Sep daily, 10–5, Sun 2–5.
Admission: ✳£1 (children 50p)

Great Orme
Towering to a height of 678ft above Llandudno and its bays, this limestone headland was the site of some of the earliest settlement in this area, including the 6th-century cell of St Tudno, the early missionary after whom Llandudno is named. Today, most of the headland is a country park, offering fine breezy walks, interesting wild flowers and the chance to watch seabirds such as kittiwakes, guillemots and fulmars. The summit, where there is an interpretive centre, can be reached by cabin-lift or tram as well as by road or footpath. The trams, which have operated every summer since 1902, can be boarded at Victoria Station, Church Walks. Happy Valley Station, above the pier, is the starting point for the cabin-lift – Britain's longest cable-car ride. Round the foot of Great Orme runs Marine Drive, a 4½-mile circular scenic route.

Open: Interpretive Centre Easter–Sep daily; Tramway May–Sep daily (except Sat) 10–5.45 (last tram out); Cabin-lift Easter–Sep daily (weather permitting).
Admission: ✳Interpretive Centre free; Tramway £1.35 (children 85p); Cabin-lift £2.90 return (children £1.45) toll payable on Marine Drive 50p.
P. ♿ 🍴

Llandudno Pier
Reaching 2296ft out into Llandudno bay, this is one of Britain's finest Victorian piers. Built in 1876, it combines 19th-century charm and elegance with up-to-the-minute facilities including amusements, a café and bar, summer shows at the Pier Pavilion, and the spine-chilling Llandudno Dungeon Waxworks.

☎(0492) 76258
Open: all year.

LLANGOLLEN, CLWYD   Llangollen Railway   Map 7 SJ24

See the beautiful Dee Valley by steam train from the restored Great Western Railway Station in the town centre, where locomotives and rolling stock are on display. Passenger trains run from here to Berwyn Station – a 3½ mile round trip. A special coach is available for the disabled. Santa and mince pie specials in December.

☎(0978) 860951 (talking timetable) or 860950
Located: at Llangollen Station, Abbey Road.

Open: Trains operating weekends from Easter–mid May & mid Sep–end Oct. Daily train service from mid May–mid Oct. Trains are steam hauled daily during Jul & Aug, most weekends & for Santa specials during Dec weekends.
Admission: *Station free; return fares 1st Class £1.80 (children 90p), 2nd Class £1.40 (children 70p). Single 1st Class £1.20 (children 60p), 2nd Class £1 (children 50p).
🛒 ♿ (ground floor) shop

LLANRUG, GWYNEDD   Bryn Bras Castle and Grounds   Map 6 SH56

Bryn Bras is a Regency period Romanesque castle with panelling, stained glass and richly carved furniture. The lovely grounds include a stream with waterfalls and pools. There are wonderful hydrangeas and rhododendrons and there are panoramic views from the woodland and mountain walks.

☎Llanberis (0286) 870210

Open: Spring Bank Hol–Sep, Mon–Fri & Sun 1–5. Mid Jul–Aug 10.30–5.
Admission: *£1.40 (children under 15 70p)
P. 🛒 shop ⚞

LLANUWCHLLYN, GWYNEDD   Bala Lake Railway   Map 6 SH82

Take a delightful 4½-mile journey by narrow-gauge steam train along the shores of Llyn Tegid (Bala Lake), through the beautiful scenery of the Snowdonia National Park. Your journey commences from Llanuwchllyn Station, and the railways boasts one of four remaining GWR signal boxes.

☎(06784) 666
Located: the Station.

Open: Easter–Oct (phone for train times & details).
Admission: *Return £2.80 (children £1.40); family saver, 2 adults 1 child £6.50, 2 adults 2 children £7.
P. 🛒 🍴 ♿ shop

LLYSYFRAN, DYFED   Llysyfran Reservoir Country Park   Map 2 SN02

The summits of Mynydd Preseli, where prehistoric men quarried monoliths for Stonehenge, gaze down on the placid waters of this 187-acre reservoir. Fishing, sailing, canoeing and other activities take place here, but pleasant walks can also be made along the shore. Rolling hills provide delightful backgrounds, and walks also reveal a rich variety of plant and animal life on land and in the water.

Llysyfran is an appropriate name for the reservoir and country park. It means 'Court of the Crows' in Welsh, and the area is indeed frequented by carrion crows, rooks, jackdaws and magpies.

Located: off B4329, 12 miles north-east of Haverfordwest.

Open: all year.
P. 🛒 🍴 visitor centre

MAESGWM, GWYNEDD   Maesgwm Visitor Centre   Map 6 SH72

Situated at the heart of the magnificent 16,000-acre Coed y Brenin Forest, the centre supplies information on the local gold mines as well as the environment, life and work of this great forest. There are 50 miles of waymarked walks, with wildlife observation hides and picnic places; guide leaflets are available for the Afon Eden Trail – a scenic riverside walk which starts here.

☎Ganllwyd (034140) 666
Located: 8 miles north of Dolgellau, just off A470.

Open: Easter week, then Whit Sun–Sep daily 10–5.
Admission: free
P. ⊡ ⅁ & shop

MARGAM, WEST GLAMORGAN   Margam Park   Map 3 SS88

Children will love this beautiful country park. Its 850 acres includes a castle and abbey, and a magnificent Orangery which is the largest building of its kind in Britain. The Margam Maze is one of the largest in Europe and an unusual Sculpture Park features the work of internationally renowned sculptors. Pony rides, boating, putting and a new adventure playground will provide hours of fun and, for the energetic, there are waymarked walks around the park. The Coach House Theatre features film shows about the park and its resident deer herd.

☎Port Talbot (0639) 881635 or 371131
Located: east of M4 Junction 38.

Open: Apr–Sep, daily 9.30–7 (last admission 5pm); Oct–Mar, Wed–Sun 9.30–5 (last admission 3pm).
Admission: ✱Apr–Sep £1 (children 5–16 & senior citizens 50p); Oct–Mar (half price). Registered disabled free.
P. ⊡ ⅁ & shop

MERTHYR TYDFIL, MID GLAMORGAN   Brecon Mountain Railway   Map 3 SO00

There are interesting locomotives from three continents on this narrow-gauge steam railway which operates in the Brecon Beacons National Park. You can follow the lovely lakeside and forest walks from the terminus.

☎(0685) 4854
Located: at Pant Station, 2¾ miles north-east of Merthyr Tydfil to the north of A465.

Open: times on application to The Brecon Mountain Railway, Pant Station, Merthyr Tydfil, Mid Glamorgan.
Admission: return fare £2.50 (children under 16 £1.25 – free when travelling with adult paying full return fare).
P. ⊡ (licensed) ⅁ & shop

MERTHYR TYDFIL, MID GLAMORGAN   Garwnant Forest Centre   Map 3 SO00

There are many attractions in the Brecon Beacons forests and the Forest Centre helps you to enjoy them. It explains the water sources, farming and forestry of the valleys in the area. Forest trails are described and there is an adventure play area.

☎(0685) 3060
Located: 5 miles north of Merthyr Tydfil, off A470.

Open: ✱Easter–Sep Mon–Sat 10.30–4.45, Bank Hol 12–6; Apr Sat & Sun 2–4; May & Sep 2–5; Jun 2–6 & Jul–Aug 1–6. At other times telephone for details.
Admission: Free
P. ⅁ & shop

NARBERTH, DYFED   Oakwood Adventure and Leisure Park   Map 2 SN11

Oakwood's 80 acres provide challenge and fun for all the family. A miniature railway ride leads to the bobsleigh run, Skyleap-free-fall and assault courses, whilst the less intrepid may prefer the miniature golf course. There's a special play area for the under-tens too, offering hours of fun in the Klondyke Gold Mine, Fort William or the ball-pool. There are also go-carts, BMX bikes and boating lakes. Browse round the Nature Pavilion, which illustrates the geology of the area, together with its flora and fauna, before following one of the nature trails, or hire a map and compass to try your hand at orienteering in the wilder areas of the complex.

☎Martletwy (083485) 373

Open: Apr–Oct daily 10–6.
Admission: £3.25 including all rides (children 3–5 £1.85, senior citizens & handicapped £2.65).
P. ⌨ 🍴 & shop ⚡

NEWCASTLE EMLYN, DYFED   Felin Geri Mill   Map 2 SN34

Dating from the 16th-century, this is one of the last watermills in Britain still to be using the original means of production to make wholemeal flour commercially. There is also a water-powered sawmill and a mill museum. In the grounds there is an adventure playground, a nature reserve and nature walks, a woodland interpretation centre and trout ponds. You can also watch craftsmen at work in their workshops. There is certainly something to appeal to every member of the family.

☎(0239) 710810

Open: Easter–Oct daily 10–6.
Admission: £2 (children under 5 free, children £1, senior citizens £1.50).
P. ⌨ (licensed) 🍴 & (grounds & gardens only) shop

NEWPORT, GWENT   Fourteen Locks Picnic Area   Map 3 ST38

Easy-going waymarked walks of 2 and 3 miles start and finish at this fascinating picnic area in an abandoned waterway, less than 3 miles from the bustling heart of Newport. The longer route goes under the M4 and climbs a low, wooded ridge overlooking the town, the shorter crosses fields and passes the Ynysyfro reservoirs. An even shorter trail, just half a mile in length, explores the canal and canal-side ponds near the Fourteen Lock Interpretation Centre.

The picnic area takes its name from a flight of locks on the Crumlin arm of the Monmouthshire and Brecon Canal. The 'staircase' enabled barges to climb 168ft in less than 1000 yards and took about two hours to negotiate.

Located: off B4591, 3 miles north-west of Newport.

Open: all year
P. 🍴 Interpretation Centre

NEWPORT, GWENT   Tredegar House and Country Park   Map 3 ST38

One of the finest country houses in Wales set in 90 acres of parkland and gardens. It has a medieval wing but is mainly 17th century. The art gallery has changing exhibitions. In the grounds there is a Visitors' Centre, craft workshops, carriage rides, an orienteering course and a brass-rubbing centre. You can fish or go boating on the lake. In the summer there are various special events.

☎(0633) 62275
Located: at Coedkernew.

Open: Grounds daily, dawn–dusk. House Good Fri–end Sep Wed–Sun & Bank Hols (guided tours every half hour from 12.30–4.30. Also Tue in school hols & weekends only in Oct.
Admission: ✳£1.50 (children 75p, senior citizens 90p). Family ticket £3.20. Grounds free.
P. ⌨ (licensed) & shop

PEMBROKESHIRE COAST NATIONAL PARK   Dyfed   Map 2

Well over a third of Pembrokeshire is designated as one of our National Parks. It is a spectacularly beautiful area, much of which is taken up by a dramatic coastline which has rugged cliffs and headlands battered daily by Atlantic rollers as well as sheltered coves, sandy beaches and offshore islands. Much of this coastline is accessible by following the 167 mile coastal path which runs from St Dogmaels in the north round to Amroth in the south. Inland wild moorland sweeps up to hills that are cut by deep river valleys. This is an area rich in prehistoric remains; in fact, the bluestones that form Stonehenge's inner ring are believed to have been taken from this area to Salisbury Plain by Bronze Age Britons. Don't miss King's Quoit, about ½ mile south west of Manorbier. This is a group of prehistoric standing stones which are capped by a massive stone which is 15ft long by 9ft wide – it is really impressive.

This part of Wales has an infinite number of coastal attractions. Apart from the glorious coastal path there are superb and sophisticated seaside resorts such as Tenby – an ancient and picturesque walled town set on a rocky promontory overlooking sandy bays, and St David's – Britain's smallest cathedral city, near which are several sweeping bays with golden sand. For sporting enthusiasts there is river and sea fishing, sailing and water skiing aplenty to be found in the area, while for nature lovers the several small offshore islands, accessible to visitors by boat, are rich in wildlife. At Caldy Island, just a couple of miles south of Tenby, the profusion of coves and beaches are home to great numbers of seabirds. Caldy Island also has a monastery where monks farm and weave as well as making chocolate and perfume. Skokholm and Skomer Islands – just off the coast from Milford Haven – are both bird sanctuaries where many species of birds can be seen. On Skomer, as well as on Ramsey Island, the grey seals which come out of the Atlantic to breed, are often to be seen.

This is an area steeped in history and there are great numbers of old churches, chapels and castles. The tiny 13th-century chapel built into the side of a cliff at St Govan's head and Pembroke's superb moated Norman castle, where Henry VII was born, are both 'musts' for visitors to this part of Wales.

For places to visit in the area check the location atlas at the end of the book.

Beautiful unspoilt coastline is preserved in the Pembrokeshire Coast National Park.

PONTERWYD, DYFED   Bwlch Nant-Yr-Arain Forest Visitor Centre   Map 6 SN78

In a spectacular location the Forestry Commission runs this Centre to help visitors understand the forest as part of the landscape and the local community and to show how it is the habitat for wildlife and provides a place for recreation. There are waymarked forest walks nearby, where, with luck, you may see foxes, hares, kestrels and other birds. The view alone is worth coming to the Centre to enjoy.

☎(097085) 694 or Crosswood (09743) 404
Located: on A44 10 miles east of Aberystwyth, 3 miles west of Ponterwyd.

Open: Easter–Sep daily 10–5 (Sat & Sun 12.30–5); closes at 6pm in Jul–Aug.
Admission: free
P. (100 yards, charge) 🌲 ⅋ shop

PONTERWYD, DYFED   Llywemog Silver-Lead Mine   Map 6 SN78

Set in the midst of the beautiful Welsh mountains is this restored mid 19th-century, water-powered silver-lead mine. You can follow the miner's trail, visit the audio-visual unit and underground drift mine – with a floodlit cavern – and see interesting working machinery. Restoration work is continuing and is fascinating to watch.

☎(097085) 620
Located: 10 miles east of Aberystwyth on A44.

Open: Easter–Aug daily 10–6, Sep 10–5, telephone for Oct opening times.
Admission: £1.80 (children under 5 free, 5–15 80p, senior citizens £1.50)
P. ☕ 🌲 ⅋ (ground floor & gardens) shop

PORTHMADOG, GWYNEDD   Festiniog Railway   Map 6 SH53

Take the journey of a lifetime! This historic narrow-gauge railway negotiates some of the most beautiful, exciting and remote parts of the Snowdonia National Park. Refreshments are available from the licensed buffet cars as you relax and enjoy the magnificent scenery rolling by. Some of the steam locomotives have served the line for over 100 years.

☎(0766) 512340 or 831654 (timetable & fares on request).

Open: daily service late Mar–early Nov & also 26 Dec–1 Jan & weekends in Mar.
Admission: charges vary according to distance travelled. 3rd class fare Porthmadog to Ffestiniog £6.80 return.
P. ☕ (licensed) ⅋ shop

PORTMEIRION, GWYNEDD   Map 6 SH53

Portmeirion is a fantasy fairytale land of pastel-coloured buildings with domes and spires set amid acres of lush sub-tropical gardens and edged by secluded sandy beaches. This Italianate dream village was created by Welsh architect, Sir William Clough Ellis, over a 50-year period up to 1976. Children will also enjoy a specially-designed children's play-ground and, of course, the ice-cream parlour. For those tempted to stay for more than a day, the village also has a hotel and self-catering cottages.

☎Porthmadog (0766) 770228
Open: Apr–Oct daily 9.30–5.30
Admission: £1.80 (children 75p)
P. ☕ (licensed) 🌲 ⅋ (ground floor & gardens only) shop

Symbols	
☎	telephone number
P.	parking on the premises
☕	refreshments available
🌲	picnic area
⅋	accessible to wheelchair-bound visitors
🐕	no dogs
✳	indicates 1987 details

PUMPSAINT, DYFED   Dolaucothi   Map 2 SN64

The National Trust's Dolaucothi Estate, set amid wooded hillsides overlooking the beautiful Cothi valley, is famous for its Roman gold mines. Gold was mined here soon after the Roman conquest of Wales and around AD80, probably to provide bullion for imperial mints in France and Rome. There are tours of the mines of varying lengths. These show the opencast workings and the ingenious aqueduct system installed by the Roman miners to bring water to wash and separate the ore. Gold was mined here intermittently until 1939. The Visitor Centre and walks provide information on the history and geology of the mine, and underground tours are also available mid-summer.

A circular estate walk, taking about an hour, has also been laid out here by the Trust.

☎(05585) 359
Located: south of Pumpsaint, off A482 between Llanwrda & Lampeter.

Open: estate walk at all times. ✳Gold mines; mid Apr–late Oct daily including Bank Hols 10–5. Underground guided tours mid Jun–mid Sep, every ½hr 10–5. Last admissions 5pm.
Note Tour lasts about 1hr, involving rugged, climbing; helmets with lights provided; stout shoes recommended.
Admission: ✳Surface visit & underground tour £2.50 (children & senior citizens £1.25). Visitor Centre & surface tour £1.25 (children & senior citizens 70p).
P. ⟊ shop ✳ (underground)
National Trust

RHOOSE, SOUTH GLAMORGAN   Wales Aircraft Museum   Map 3 ST06

Enthusiasts will enjoy this collection of 30 aircraft featuring a Vulcan Bomber. Snacks are available in the Viscount airliner and children can sit in the cockpit of a Sea Hawk. Engines, photographs, models and historical items are also displayed in this privately owned museum situated adjacent to the airport.

☎(0222) 757767
Located: at Cardiff (Wales) Airport.

Open: ✳Jun, Jul & Aug daily 11–5.30. Remainder of year open Sun only 11–6 (or dusk).
Admission: ✳80p, children 6–16 & senior citizens 40p, children under 5 & disabled free.
P. ⟊ (summer only) ♿ (ground floor only) shop

ST FAGANS, SOUTH GLAMORGAN   Welsh Folk Museum   Map 3 ST17

The fascinating open-air museum is set in the 100 acres of parkland of St Fagan's Castle (open). The museum depicts the life and culture of Wales. There are more than 20 reconstructed buildings showing the evolution of building styles and living conditions. The resident stonemason and carpenter continue to work and you can watch them at their age-old skills. There is a reconstructed tannery, tollgate, cockpit, chapel and Victorian school. In the work areas there is a water-powered woollen mill, an 18th-century smithy, a saddler, a cooper and a woodturner's shop, and you can watch the traditional craftsmen at their work. Cattle, sheep and poultry complete the rural scene. Gallery exhibitions show agricultural life, costume and culture of Wales. Special events include a traditional Welsh country fair over the May Day holiday with over 100 events for all the family.

☎Cardiff (0222) 569441

Open: Apr–Oct daily 10–5; Nov–Mar Mon–Sat 10–5. Closed 24–26 Dec, 1 Jan & Good Fri.
Admission: £2 (children £1, senior citizens £1.50)
P. ⟊ (licensed) ⟊ ♿ shop ✳ (in house)

ST FLORENCE, DYFED   Manor House Wildlife & Leisure Park   Map 2 SN10

Collections of wild animals, exotic birds, reptiles and fish share their 12-acre park with a leisure complex guaranteed to amuse even the most demanding child. The adventure playground features a giant astraglide, a go-kart track, model railway and radio-controlled models. Watch out for Zoo Month in July when a famous television personality will spend a day at the Park.

☎Carew (06467) 201

Open: Easter–Sep daily 10–6.
Admission: £1.40 (children & senior citizens 80p).
P. ⟊ (licensed) ⟊ ♿ shop & garden centre ✳

151

SCOLTON, DYFED   Scolton Manor Museum & Country Park   Map 2 SM92

There are 40 acres of magnificent grounds, rich in fine trees and ornamental shrubs, surrounding this elegant Georgian mansion. Just the place for youngsters to go exploring; and the tree trail and nature trail provided make a fun visit an educational one too! The mansion, stables and large exhibition hall provide a comprehensive display on the history and natural history of Pembrokeshire. The first Saturday in August sees all the fun of the Pembrokeshire Country Fair.

☏Clarbeston (043782) 328
Located: on B4329, 5 miles north of Haverfordwest.

Open: Country Park open all year. Museum May–Sep only, Tue–Sun & Bank Hols 10.30–6.
Admission: ✶50p (children & senior citizens 25p).
P. (400 yds) ⬜ ⅂⊼ ♿ (ground floor & gardens only) shop ⽥

for SNOWDONIA NATIONAL PARK see opposite page

SOLVA, DYFED   Solva Nectarium   Map 2 SM82

Exotic butterflies from the rain forests of India and Malaysia, and from the Amazonian jungles can be seen here flitting around in a tropical setting. In the insect gallery you can learn about the life of a butterfly from pupae stage to maturity.

☏St Davids (0473) 721323

Open: Easter–Sep. Mon–Sat 10–6, Sun 2–6 (last admission 5pm).
Admission: £2 (children 5–14 £1, senior citizens £1.50).
⬜ (licensed) ⅂⊼ shop ⽥

TAL-Y-CAFN, GWYNEDD   Bodnant Gardens   Map 6 SH77

There are splendid views of Snowdonia and down over the River Conwy from this beautiful 80-acre garden. it boasts a magnificent collection of rhododendrons, camellias, magnolias, shrubs and trees. Much of the garden is steep, but there are many steps.

☏(Tyngroes) (049267) 460
Located: 8 miles south of Llandudno & Colwyn Bay on A470. Entrance ½ mile along Eglwysbach Road.

Open: mid Mar–Oct daily 10–5. Last admission 4.30.
Admission: £1.90 (children 95p)
P. ⬜ ♿ ⽥ (except guide dogs)
National Trust

TINTERN, GWENT   Tintern Abbey   Map 3 SO50

Founded as a Cistercian abbey in 1131, the extensive ruins in a splendidly picturesque setting in the Wye valley are amongst the most beautiful in Britain. There is an exhibition describing the history of the abbey since its foundation which helps you to interpret the ruins fully. Tintern is a lovely and romantic place to visit.

☏(02918) 251

Open: mid Mar–mid Oct Mon–Sat 9.30–6.30 Sun 2–6.30; mid Oct–mid Mar Mon–Sat 9.30–4, Sun 2–4.
Admission: fee payable.
P. ⅂⊼ shop ⽥
Cadw: Welsh Historic Monuments

TYWYN, GWYNEDD   Narrow Gauge Railway Museum   Map 6 SH50

In this little museum is a brilliant display of narrow gauge locomotives and who can resist the opportunity to sit in the cab of the Victoriam steam locomotive 'Jubilee 1897' and operate the controls?

☏(0654) 710472
Located: at Wharf Station.

Open: end Mar–Oct 10–5 daily. Winter by arrangement.
Admission: 30p (children 10p).
P. (100 yds) ⬜ (at Wharf Station) ♿ (ground floor only) shop ⽥

See next entry.

for further TYWYN entry see page 154

The 840 square miles of great mountains and forests, tumbling rivers, cascading waterfalls and beautiful coastline that make up the Snowdonia National Park are among the most breath-taking areas in the British Isles. The ruling force of this region is, of course, the mountain that gives its name to the National Park – Snowdon; at 3560ft Snowdon is the highest mountain in England and Wales. This is a part of the country that really does have something for everyone, irrespective of their age and interest. For lovers of the great outdoors there is excellent fishing, pony trekking, skiing, canoeing and sailing. The opportunities for walking and climbing in this area are superb – infinitely varied and to suit all energy levels. Snowdon is obviously the main attraction and there are a number of routes to its summit. For the less energetic the Snowdon Mountain Railway runs from Llanberis (at the heart of the beautiful Llanberis Pass) to the very top of Snowdon where there is a restaurant and shop, as well as some of the finest views to be found anywhere in the country. Gilfach Ddu, (near the departure point of the Snowdon Railway) is the place from where the narrow gauge Llanberis Lake Railway starts. Its trains run by the eastern shore of Llyn Padarn giving passengers fine views over Snowdonia along the way. The pleasures associated with the mountains, forests, lakes and rivers of this region are obviously paramount, but the many attractive towns and villages are equally deserving of exploration. Caernarfon, the ceremonial capital of Wales and dominated by its castle, is the place where Prince Charles was invested as Prince of Wales. Bangor is the cathedral and university city of North Wales. On a smaller scale there is Beddgelert (named after Gelert, the dog belonging to Llewellyn the Great. Legend has it that the Prince killed his dog in a fit of temper and today thousands of people come to visit Gelert's grave). Beddgelert is situated where three valleys meet and is surrounded by the most beautiful of mountain and forest scenery, further enhanced by the rushing rivers Glaslyn and Colwyn. Betws-y-coed, situated in the Gwydyr Forest, is another excellent centre for exploring Snowdon. Not far from this village are the Swallow Falls, the magical Fairy Glen and the Conwy Falls – a 'must' for visitors to this area. Within the Snowdonia National Park are about 25 miles of coastline and Penmaenmawr and Llanfairfechan are just two of the resorts that have fine beaches and plenty of seaside amusements.

For places to visit in the area check the location atlas at the end of the book.

Moel Siabod towers over the Gwydyr Forest in this fine walking country.

153

TYWYN, GWYNEDD   Talyllyn Railway   Map 6 SH50

Take a splendid family excursion on the oldest 2ft 3in gauge railway in the world. The line runs for 7¼ miles to Nant Gwernol, where there are pleasant forest walks by tumbling streams. Stop at Dolgoch to see the spectacular waterfalls and mountainside scenery, or Abergynolwyn for refreshments.

☎(0654) 710472
Located: at Wharf Station.

Open: regular daily service end Mar–Oct (except Fri in Oct). Also 26 Dec–1 Jan daily. Timetables available.
Admission: ✱ fares for return journey £3. Family ticket (2 adults, 1 child) £7; (2 adults, 2 children) £7.50.
P. (100 yds) ⌷ 🍴 ⚹ (ground floor & on trains by prior arrangement) shop

USK, GWENT   Gwent Rural Life Museum   Map 3 SO30

Run by volunteers in a charming old Malt Barn, the museum has a collection of lovingly restored objects of rural Wales. There are wagons and farm machinery, and a display of the four seasons of the country including tools and machinery and dairy equipment. In the adjoining cottage there are numerous household bygones and tools of craft skills.

☎Usk (02913) 3777 or Tredunnock (063349) 315
Located: Malt Barn, New Market Street.

Open: Apr–Sep daily, Mon–Fri 10–12.30 & 2–5, Sat–Sun 2–5; Mar & Oct closed Sat; Nov–Feb Mon–Fri only. Closed Xmas.
Admission: 80p (children & senior citizens 40p).
⚹ (ground floor & yard only) shop

WOLVESNEWTOWN, GWENT   Model Farm Folk Collection and Farm Centre
Map 3 ST49

Everyday rural life from Queen Victoria's time onward is on show in this late 18th-century cruciform barn. There is also a Victorian bedroom and a medical display. In the grounds you can see rare breeds of poultry and follow a nature trail with a children's quiz. There is in addition an audio show, craft workshops and a picture gallery.

☎(02915) 231
Located: 1½ miles off B4235 at Llangwm.

Open: ✱Apr–Sep daily 11–6; Oct–Nov weekends only.
Admission: fee payable.
P. ⌷ (licensed) ⚹ (ground floor & grounds only) shop

WREXHAM, CLWYD   Erddig   Map 7 SJ35

There is much to see in this 17th-century house and its gardens. The house has a great deal of its original furniture and the laundry, bakehouse, sawmill and smithy have all been restored to working order. The garden has been restored to its 18th-century formal design and contains many now little known varieties of fruit.

☎(0978) 355314
Located: off the A525, 2 miles south of Wrexham.

Open: Easter–mid Oct 12–5 (last admission to house 4pm, to gardens 4.30pm). Closed Fri, except Good Fri. Due to extreme fragility Tapestry & Chinese Rooms only open on Wed & Sat. Country Park & Visitor Centre Sat & Sun 10–5 (last admission 4.30).
Admission: House & garden £2.50 (children £1.20). Garden only £1.60 (children 70p). Family ticket £6.20
P. ⌷ ⚹ ✻
National Trust

SCOTLAND

Glens, lochs, heather, haggis, bagpipes, tartans, Rabbie Burns, castles, golf, salmon and deer, and wild majestic scenery spring to mind when we think of Scotland. These are all symbols of this small but diverse nation.

To the south and east are the Lowlands with lush pasturelands; to the north and west are the Highlands, rugged and romantic, with people who still speak Gaelic, one of the world's oldest languages.

The towns and cities have much to offer the visitor. Edinburgh alone has more than a dozen museums and galleries. Glasgow is becoming one of the most exciting cities in Europe. Yet not far from any urban area is open country. In the south there are rolling hills, heather and lonely beaches. There are stately homes, ruined abbeys and ancient fortresses. To the north are the last truly wild places of Britain – sometimes stark but never lacking in grandeur. Along the ruggedly indented west coast sea lochs bring the sights and sounds of the ocean into the land and remind one that nowhere in Scotland can we ever be more than 40 miles from the sea.

And off the shores of the Highlands are the Scottish Islands: to the north beyond John o' Groats lie the Orkneys and Shetlands; to the west it is not far over the sea to Skye, but further to the Western Isles.

ABERLADY, LOTHIAN   Myreton Motor Museum   Map 12 NT47

Myreton offers a glimpse into an era when motoring, and road transport in general, was an elegant pastime. Here you'll see cycles from 1863, cars and motorcycles from 1896, as well as a collection of advertising posters, enamel signs and other period memorabilia. There are also commercial vehicles and military vehicles from World War II.

☎(08757) 288

Open: daily, 10–6 summer; 10–5 winter. Closed Xmas Day.
Admission: £1 (children under 16 30p).
P. & (ground floor only) ✝

AUCHINDRAIN, STRATHCLYDE   Auchindrain Open-Air Museum   Map 10 NN00

To visit Auchindrain is to step back in time and see what life was like for a Highland community. There is evidence that this township was inhabited in neolithic times. Buildings standing today span the centuries, from the Cottar's House, a labourer's house of the 1700s, to the Colt House, a modern house (1950s) built for the last township inhabitant.

☎Furnace (04995) 235
Located: 5½ miles south-west of Inveraray on the A83.

Open: Apr, May & Sep, Sat–Thu 11–4; Jun–Aug daily 10–5.
Admission: ✱£1.50 (children and senior citizens £1), family ticket £4.
P. ⌂ ⟰ shop

AUCHTERARDER, TAYSIDE   Strathallan Aircraft Museum   Map 11 NN91

This fine collection of vintage aircraft is predominantly from World War II. Take grandad along and he can tell you stories of the escapades of planes like the Lancaster and the Lysander. There are special air displays during the summer.

☎(07646) 2545
Located: 4 miles north-west of Auchterarder off B8062.

Open: ✱Apr–Oct, daily 10–5.
Admission: fee payable.
P. ⌂ ⟰ & shop ✝ (except in car park)

AVIEMORE, HIGHLAND   Aviemore Centre   Map 14 NH81

One day won't be long enough to sample all that this leisure, sport and conference centre has to offer. There is a wide range of recreational and entertainment facilities, including cinema/theatre, ice rink, saunas, artificial ski slope, go-karts, discos and restaurants. Within the grounds of the centre is the Aviemore Bird Garden featuring pheasants, waterfowl, owls and domestic poultry, many of which are rare and endangered species. There is also the Craigiellachie National Nature Reserve. A mixture of beach woodland and moorland, this 642-acre nature reserve rises to over 1700ft. A mile-long nature trail begins at Loch Puladelern and offers some spectacular views of the Cairngorm Mountains. You'll also find some interesting insects, notably certain species of moth that inhabit the beech trees.

☎Aviemore (0479) 810624, Bird Garden: Aviemore (0479) 811259

Open: all year, daily 10am onwards. Bird Garden 10–6 (subject to weather conditions in winter). Nature Reserve at all reasonable times.
Admission: Free. Charge for facilities. Bird Garden £1 (children 50p). Nature Reserve free.
P. ⌂

for AYR see opposite page

BALLOCH, STRATHCLYDE   Balloch Castle Country Park   Map 10 NS38

Balloch Castle Country Park is perfectly situated on the shore of Loch Lomond. A large area of grassland, ideal for picnics, is surrounded by extensive woodlands. There are wonderful views of the loch from the castle terrace, a walled garden, nature and tree trails. There is a Countryside Ranger service.

☎Alexandria (0389) 58216

Open: Visitor Centre Apr–Sep daily 10–6. Country Park 8–dusk. Garden 10–9 (4.30 winter).
Admission: free.
P. &

for BARCALDINE see page 158

Royal Burgh in Burns Country

This attractive market town and fishing port is also one of Scotland's most popular seaside resorts. Safe, sandy beaches stretch for more than two miles, offering plenty of traditional seaside pastimes as well as fine views across to the island of Arran. Early-morning strollers on the beach may encounter race-horses being exercised – a reminder that Ayr has long been Scotland's main racing centre. It is also something of a golfers' mecca: The internationally famous courses at Turnberry, Troon and Prestwick all lie within a few miles along the coast.

The town itself is steeped in associations with Scotland's national poet, Robert Burns, whose statue stands near the station. He was born at nearby Alloway. Today visitors from all over the world come to see the cottage of his childhood and the places he wrote about. He was baptised at the Auld Kirk of Ayr, a 17th-century church famous for its three galleries – the Merchants' Loft, the Sailors' Loft and the Traders' Loft. The church was built with money contributed by Oliver Cromwell as compensation for the 12th-century church of St John, which he had incorporated into the citadel he built here. Only the church's tower remains, one of Ayr's most prominent landmarks.

Almost as old as St John's Tower is the famous Auld Brig o'Ayr, which was for centuries the only bridge over the River Ayr here. It was threatened with demolition at the turn of the century, but Burns enthusiasts and the people of Ayr raised £10,000 to restore it, and it was reopened in 1910. Today it is open only to pedestrians.

Other landmarks in the town include the neo-gothic Wallace Tower, built in 1832 to commemorate Sir William Wallace, champion of Scottish independence. Near it is the Tam o'Shanter Museum. Ayr's other notable museum, the Maclaurin Art Gallery, stands in Rozelle Park, where there is also a lake and nature trails.

☆STAR ATTRACTIONS

Alloway

Now a southern suburb of Ayr, Alloway was a village two miles from the town when William Burns built himself a cottage here in 1757. Two years later his eldest son, Robert, was born, and here the family lived until he was seven. Now furnished and equipped as it would have been at that time, the house is a museum in memory of the poet. Some of his possessions, and editions of his works, are among the exhibits. Burns' later life is portrayed in audio-visual presentations at the new Land o'Burns Centre, a pleasant walk away from the cottage. Nearby is Alloway's 'auld haunted kirk' – already a ruin when Burns was a child. Beside the Auld Brig o'Doon stands the classical Burns Monument, built in 1823 and set in pleasant gardens embellished by sculptures of characters from Burns' works.

🕾Burns Cottage (0292) 41215, Burns Monument (0292) 41321, Land o'Burns Centre (0292) 43700

Open: Burns Cottage and Monument Jun to Aug 9–7 (Sun 10–7); Sep–Oct 10–5 (Sun 2–5); winter 10–4 (closed Sun). Land o'Burns Centre Oct–May daily 10–5, Jun & Sep daily 10–5.30, Jul and Aug 10–6.
Admission: Burns Cottage & Monument £1 (children 50p). Land o'Burns Centre free, but audio-visual theatre 40p (children 20p).
Burns Cottage: P. ⌨ (Apr–Oct) & shop
Burns Monument: P. & (grounds only) Shop
Land o'Burns Centre: P. ⌨ ⅄ & shop

BARCALDINE, STRATHCLYDE   Sea Life Centre   Map 10 MN94

Sea life as you've never seen it before! Modern technology and materials enable you to get really close to a whole variety of sea creatures – see huge cod, octopus and seals from a special underwater observatory.

☎**Ledaig (063172) 386**

Open: *Apr–Oct daily 9–6 (until 8pm in Jul & Aug).
Admission: *£1.85 (children £1, senior citizens £1.20).
P. ☐ (licensed) 🍴 & shop ✻

BLAIR ATHOLL, TAYSIDE   Atholl Country Collection   Map 14 NN86

An interesting collection of artefacts and photographs shows how the villagers and glen folk of these parts spent their daily lives from the middle of the 19th-century. There is the blacksmith's 'smiddy', the crofter's stable and byre, and even a glimpse of his living room with its box bed. The vet and gamekeeper, road and rail services, the school, the kirk and the importance of flax growing and spinning to the economy of the district are all featured, and children will gain particular enjoyment from the fact that many items can be picked up and examined.

☎**(079681) 232**

Open: Easter & late May to mid Oct daily 1.30–5.30pm; also Jul & Aug weekday mornings from 9.30am.
Admission: 50p (children 25p).
P. 🍴 & shop

BLAIR ATHOLL, TAYSIDE   Blair Castle   Map 14 NN86

Dating back to the 13th century, this castle is still the home of the Duke of Atholl, the only man in Britain today to have his own private army – the Atholl Highlanders. Thirty-two rooms of exhibits trace Scottish life from the 16th to 17th century, displaying beautiful furniture and fine collections of paintings, china, lace, arms and other unique treasures. Magnificent grounds, surrounded by the rolling hills of Perthshire, contain a deer park, and there are nature trails and pony trekking facilities here. During 1988 the Atholl Gathering and Highland Games takes place here on 29 May, with the Atholl Highlanders' Parade on the preceding day; other events include a Charity Day (7 July), Scouts' Jamborette (18–29 July), Grand Highland Concert (21 July), Horse Trials (28 August) and the Glenfiddich World Piping Championship (29 October).

☎**(079681) 207**

Open: end Mar–mid Oct Mon–Sat 10–6, Sun 2–6; Sun Jul & Aug noon–6. Last admission 5pm.
Admission: £2.50 (children £1.50, senior citizens £2). Family ticket £7.50.
P. ☐ (licensed) 🍴 & (ground floor & grounds only) shop ✻ (except in grounds)

BLAIR DRUMMOND, CENTRAL   Blair Drummond Safari Park   Map 11 NS79

Here's a chance to experience the excitement of a safari by driving through the Game Reserves where wild animals roam freely. Alternatively, you could take a Jungle Cruise and view them from the safety of a safari boat. Pets Corner allows children a chance to get really close to the Park's safer inhabitants. Excess energy can be spent in the adventure playground or on the giant astraglide. Cinema 180 offers a breathtaking experience in 3D film and the whole family will be amused by the performing seals in the Aquatic Mammals show.

☎**Doune (0786) 841456**
Located: on A84 between Doune & Stirling, close to M9 exit 10.

Open: *Easter to early Oct daily, 10–4.30 (last admission).
Admission: *£3 (children & senior citizens £2, children under 3 yrs free).
P. ☐ (licensed) 🍴 & (except Cinema) shop ✻ (kennels at entrance)

BOAT OF GARTEN, HIGHLAND   Strathspey Railway   Map 14 NH91

There can be no more leisurely way to enjoy the five-mile stretch of countryside from Boat of Garten to Aviemore than to be chugging along on a steam train. The 20-minute journey can also begin at Aviemore.

☎(047983) 692

Open: on specific days between Easter & Oct. Telephone for details.
Admission: Basic return fare £2.40 (children 5–15 half fare). Family fares available.
P. ☕ (on train) shop

CARRBRIDGE, HIGHLAND   Landmark Visitor Centre   Map 14 NH92

Children will probably head straight for Landmark's fabulous adventure playground where they can enjoy the thrill of a 50ft-long tube slide, swing through the air Tarzan-style, ride on Scotland's largest monorail or lose themselves in the puzzling paths of the giant woodland maze. After all that action, however, they'll be ready for one of the Pine Forest Trails, either to the Nature Centre where they will be introduced to the wildlife of the forest, or to the Tree Top Trail which leads through the magnificent pines to a height of 20ft. The Highland Sculpture Park offers plenty of 'hands-on' experience with the works of Britain's best-known sculptors in wood, stone, steel and bronze, in this attractive woodland setting. The history of the region, and of the clans' struggle for survival is documented in an exhibition and a multi-vision filmshow entitled 'The Highlander'.

☎(047984) 614
Located: off A9 between Inverness and Aviemore.

Open: Summer 9.30am–9.30pm: winter 9.30–5.
Admission: ✱£1.85 (children £1.10).
P. ☕ (licensed) ⟗ ↿ shop & garden centre

CAWDOR, HIGHLAND   Cawdor Castle   Map 14 NH84

School lessons on Shakespeare's *Macbeth* will take on a new meaning after a visit to Cawdor Castle, home of the Thanes of Cawdor since the 14th century. Although this fairy-tale castle has a fascinating history, it is by no means just another cold monument to the past. Today it is the warm and friendly home of the present Lord and Lady Cawdor. The castle grounds offer beautiful lawns and gardens, nature trails and mini-golf or putting.

☎(06677) 615
Located: on the B9090 off the A96, between Inverness and Nairn.

Open: May–2 Oct daily 10–5.30 (last admission 5 pm).
Admission: ✱£2.40 (children 5–15 £1.30, senior citizens & disabled £2); Family ticket £7. Gardens, grounds & nature trails only £1.20.
P. ☕ (licensed) ⟗ ↿ (ground floor & gardens only) shop ✝

CRATHES, GRAMPIAN   Crathes Castle and Gardens   Map 15 NO79

Crathes Castle is a most attractive building with a double square tower dating from 1533. The interior is famed for its magnificent 16th-century ceiling paintings. The beautiful garden is a composite of eight smaller ones enclosed by 200-year-old yew hedges. Children will love the nature trails and these are also suitable for wheelchair users.

☎(033044) 525
Located: 3 miles east of Banchory on A93.

Open: Castle Easter & May–Sep, daily 11–6; also all weekends in Apr & Oct. Last tour 5.15. Gardens & grounds open daily 9.30–sunset.
Admission: Castle, Garden & Grounds £2.70 (children £1.35). Grounds & Castle £2.10 (children £1.05). Grounds & Garden £1.90 (children 95p). Grounds 90p (children 50p).
Visitor Centre ☕ shop
National Trust for Scotland

159

CULZEAN, STRATHCLYDE   Culzean Castle and Country Park   Map 10 NS21

Robert Adam designed this magnificent castle which dates mainly from 1777. The interior has many attractive features including the Round Drawing Room, a splendid oval staircase and some fine plaster ceilings. The Eisenhower Presentation explains General Eisenhower's association with the castle. Culzean Country Park was opened in 1970 and was Scotland's first country park. The Reception and Interpretation Centre will tell you all you need to know to enjoy your day out here and there is a ranger naturalist service with guided walks, talks and filmshows in summer. In all, there are 563 acres of grounds to explore at Culzean, including a walled garden, an aviary, swan pond, orangery and camellia house.

☎Kirkoswald (06556) 274
Located: 4 miles north of Kirkoswald.

Open: Castle: Apr, Sep & Oct daily 12–5 (10–6 Easter week); May–Aug daily 10–6 (last admission ½ hour before closing). Park open all year. Visitor centre Apr, Sep & Oct, daily 10–5; May–Aug, daily 10–6.
Admission: Castle £2 (children & senior citizens £1). Park – pedestrians free, cars £3.50.
P. ⌸ & (Country Park)
National Trust for Scotland

DALKEITH, LOTHIAN   Edinburgh Butterfly Farm   Map 11 NT36

Deep in a jungle of exotic plants and tropical pools you'll find some of the world's most exquisite butterflies, all flying free so that you might appreciate their brilliant colours and delicate markings at close quarters. If this seems all too pretty for those with a penchant for creepy crawlies – little brothers won't be disappointed. The Butterfly Farm is also home to a number of unusual and dangerous insects such as the scorpion and the tarantula – just don't show Mum!

for DUMFRIES see opposite page

☎031-663 4932
Located: at Dobbie's Melville Garden Centre, 1 mile north on A7.

Open: Apr–Oct, daily 10–5.30 (10–5 Sat & Sun).
Admission: ✳£1.75 (children under 5 free, children & senior citizens £1. Family tickets £5.
P. ⌸ 🛆 & shop & garden centre ✳

DUNS, BORDERS   Manderston   Map 12 NT75

Manderston is a magnificent Edwardian country house on which no expense was spared. You'll see here the only silver staircase in the world, and sumptuous staterooms decorated in Adam style using the finest craftsmanship and materials. The massive basement give the visitor a glimpse of life 'below stairs' at the turn of the century. The home of the Palmer family, Manderston is also the site of Britain's first biscuit-tin museum displaying an unusual collection of tins produced by Huntley and Palmer's over the last 100 years. Don't miss the magnificent marble dairy in the immaculate formal gardens.

☎(0361) 83450
Located: 1¼ miles east of Duns off A6105.

Open: mid May–late Sep, Sun & Thu 2–5.30. Also open Bank Hols.
Admission: ✳House and gardens £2.20. Gardens only £1.
P. ⌸ & (ground floor & gardens only) shop

Symbols
☎   telephone number
P.   parking on the premises
⌸   refreshments available
🛆   picnic area
&   accessible to wheelchair-bound visitors
✳   no dogs
✳   indicates 1987 details

Queen of the South

The county town of old Dumfriesshire is actually two towns in one. Dumfries and Maxweltown, on opposite banks of the River Nith, were amalgamated only in 1929. Dumfries was created a royal burgh as early as 1186, and for a long time it was in the thick of the battles and raids that resulted from the unrest between England and Scotland. Not until the 18th century did it settle down to a comparatively peaceful existence, and many buildings in the town date from this period. They include the Midsteeple, built in 1707, the year in which the English and Scottish crowns were united. This complex of municipal buildings, including a prison and a courthouse, has on its wall a table of distances – a reminder of the days when cattle drovers took their stock to markets as far afield as Huntingdon.

The shadow of Robert Burns falls over much of South-West Scotland, and Dumfries is no exception. Here the poet spent the last five years of his life, and here 10,000 mourners are said to have attended his furneral in 1796. He is buried, with his wife and five sons, in an elaborate Grecian-style mausoleum in St Michael's churchyard. The 18th-century Old Town Mill, beside the Nith, has recently been opened as a Burns interpretation centre, with an exhibition and film on Burns and Dumfries. Among the displays is a scale model of the town when Burns lived here.

☆STAR ATTRACTIONS

Burns House
Burns and his wife, Jean Armour, moved to Dumfries in 1791 after giving up their farm at nearby Ellisland. They moved to this house in 1793, and here the poet died on 21 July 1796. Jean lived here until her death in 1834. The house contains original manuscripts of Burns' works as well as some of his personal belongings.

☎(0387) 55297
Located: in Burns Street.

Open: All year (except Sun & Mon Oct–Mar) Mon–Sat 10–1 & 2–5, Sun 2–5.
Admission: 50p (children 25p).
Shop

Dumfries Museum and Camera Obscura
The focal point of this museum is the tower of an 18th-century windmill. It was converted into an observatory in the 1830s, when the camera obscura was installed on the top floor. Here, panoramic views of Dumfries and its surroundings are thrown onto a table-top screen. The museum collections portray the history of the people and landscape of the area from earliest times, with sections on subjects as diverse as Victorian everyday life and the flora and fauna of the Solway Firth.

☎(0387) 53374
Located: in Church Street.

Open: Museum and camera obscura Apr to Sep Mon to Sat 10–1 and 2–5, Sun; museum only Oct to Mar Tue to Sat 10–1 and 2–5.
Admission: museum free; camera obscura 50p (children 25p).
P. & shop

River Nith
The river that sweeps in a great bend round the centre of Dumfries offers pleasant waterside walks and several features of interest. It is spanned by four bridges, among them the six-arched Old Bridge, which has been here for over 500 years. Built into one end of it is Old Bridge House, which dates from 1660 and is now open as a museum with a series of period rooms, including Victorian kitchens and an early dentist's surgery. Downstream from here is the Caul, a weir built in the 18th century to power the riverside grain mills. Salmon can sometimes be seen leaping here as they swim up the river to spawn. Nearby, in the park on the western bank, yet still in the heart of the town, is an enclosure of fallow deer. To the north of the town a specially planned Burns Walk runs beside the river.

Open: Old Bridge House Apr to Sep Mon to Sat 10–1 and 2–5, Sun 2–5.
Admission: free.

EDINBURGH   Map 11 NT27

The Athens of the North

For sheer beauty and historical interest Edinburgh, crowned by its massive castle, is certainly one of the richest cities in Britain; it is justly deserving of its popular title of the 'Athens of the North'. Edinburgh is a delicious mixture of old (medieval) and new (Georgian). The old part of Edinburgh is clustered around the castle, which sits on a rocky promontory overlooking the spires and turrets of the beautiful old buildings below. From the castle a succession of streets, known as the 'Royal Mile', run past stately buildings and the cathedral, or 'high kirk', of St Giles, to the Palace of Holyroodhouse, still the official royal residence in Scotland today. Princes Street, with its many fine shops on one side of the street and the beautiful public gardens on the other, is the hub of the city. To the north of Princes Street is the network of elegant streets, squares and crescents that is known as New Town; so called because it was one of the first examples of town planning. This is a city that can entertain a visitor for weeks; it has numerous museums and galleries, many of which can compare with those in London. There are galleries containing everything from old masters, like those on view in the National Gallery of Scotland and the National Portrait Gallery, to the more *avant garde* works to be found in the new National Gallery of Modern Art. There are many museums too, ranging from the National Museum of Antiquities, that explains much of Scotland's history, to the Waxworks Museum and the Museum of Childhood. Among all this history visitors also have the very best of 20th-century facilities – excellent shops and eating houses, superb sports amenities like the Commonwealth Pool, Meadowbank Stadium and the dry ski slopes at Pentland, still within the city limits. There is the Usher Concert Hall – a regular venue for the Scottish National Orchestra and the more intimate Queens Hall, while the Playhouse is often used for opera and the Kings Theatre and Lyceum for live theatre.

For three weeks of each summer Edinburgh springs into festival mood for the Festival of Music and Drama when the city becomes a showcase for music, dancing, drama and exhibitions. During this time the Military Tattoo, a military extravanganza set to music, takes place on the Castle Esplanade against the dramatic backcloth of the floodlit castle.

The Low Defence on the eastern side of Edinburgh Castle.

☆STAR ATTRACTIONS

Edinburgh Castle
The Castle sits on a great mound of volcanic rock high above the city, and from its battlements are superb views of Edinburgh and the Forth River. The oldest of the Castle buildings is the tiny but lovely St Margaret's Chapel which dates from Norman times. Near the chapel is Mons Meg – a famous 15th-century cannon once used for Royal salutes. Salutes, including the daily 'one o'clock gun', are still fired from the castle today only using more modern cannon. The buildings of the Castle form three sides of a square with the fourth side taken up by the Scottish National War Memorial. Don't miss the magnificent Great Hall, built by James IV, which has a fine collection of armour, the Crown Room, which houses the Honours of Scotland (Scotland highest accolade), and the crown, sceptre and the Sword of State – probably the oldest royal regalia in Europe.

Open: all year daily (except 1–4 Jan); Apr–Sep 9.30–5.05, Sun 10.30–5.05; Oct–Mar 9.30–4.20, Sun 12.30–3.35.
Admission: *£2 (children & senior citizens £1). Family £4.
P.
Ancient Monument

Palace of Holyroodhouse
The façade of this majestic and historic royal palace, founded in the 11th century, mostly dates back to its rebuilding by Charles II in 1671. This is a place that has many associations with Mary Queen of Scots and Bonnie Prince Charlie. Within the Palace is an exceptional collection of Royal portraits, tapestries and fine furniture and the 13th-century ruins to the north-east of the main building are both beautiful and of great interest. Today, Holyroodhouse, is still the official Royal residence in Scotland used by the Queen when she comes to Edinburgh. It is here, in the Throne Room, that the Queen carries out investitures. From behind the Palace visitors can make their way from the park up the steep path to Arthur's Seat, from where there are wonderful views across the city.

☎031-556 7371
Located: in Cannongate.

Open: late Mar–late Oct (except 9–31 May) 9.30–5.15, Sun 10.30–4.30; late Oct–late Mar (except 1–4 Jan) 9.30–3.45, closed Sun. (Subject to closure for State visits).
Admission: £1.60 (children and senior citizens 80p).
& (grounds, ground floor & part of 1st floor only) shop ✹

Museum of Childhood
Edinburgh's Museum of Childhood was one of the first of its kind in the world and it provides a wonderfully nostalgic journey down memory lane for people of all ages. This museum was recently much extended and now covers five floors with displays of moving and musical toys, toy animals, toy soldiers, train sets, games, construction toys and Edwardian slot machines as well as one of the largest displays of dolls.

☎031-225 2424
Located: in High Street.

Open: Mon–Sat 10–6 (5 Oct–May) & Sun during Edinburgh festival 2–5 (Closed Xmas)
Admission: free.
& (3 floors only) shop ✹

Edinburgh Zoo
One of the finest zoos in Europe, Edinburgh Zoo is set in 80 acres of grounds from where there are panoramic views of the city and surrounding countryside. More than 2000 mammals, birds and reptiles can be seen here including the zoo's most famous inhabitants – the penguins which parade daily in the park during the summer.

☎031-334 9171
Located: Corstorphine Hill.

Open: all year. Mon–Sat 9–6, Sun 9.30–6 (closes at 5 or dusk in winter).
Admission: *£2.60 (children and senior citizens £1.30).
P. ⌂ licensed ⩕ & shop & garden centre ✹

Royal Botanic Gardens
Edinburgh's lovely Botanical Gardens celebrated for their many species of trees set among beautifully maintained lawns, also have one of the largest collections of rhododendrons to be found anywhere in the United Kingdom. There are also woodland and healthland gardens, superb rock gardens and herbaceous borders that are a blaze of colour in season. In addition to the outdoor displays there are glass houses containing exotic plants.

☎031 552 7171 ext 260
Located: Inverleith Row.

Open: all year (except Xmas Day & 1 Jan): Mon–Sat from 9am, Sun from 11am, closes 1hr before sunset in summer & at sunset in winter. Buildings open 10–5, Sun 11–5.
Admission: free.
⌂ (Apr–Sep) & shop ✹ (except guide dogs)

GLASGOW   Strathclyde   Map 11 NS56

St Mungo's City

Certainly Scotland's largest city, though never its capital, Glasgow is said to have been founded in the 6th century by St Kentigern, affectionately known as St Mungo, to whom the fine cathedral is dedicated. Until recent years, the city had a certain notoriety as a child of the Industrial Revoluation. Surrounded by coalfields, and within easy reach of the sea via the navigable Clyde, Glasgow was the ideal place for heavy industry – and all the smoke, grime and overcrowded workers' housing that came with it. But times have changed, and the city has been given a face-lift. Grand 19th-century buildings have been cleaned and restored, the notorious tenements have been cleared, and Glasgow is now acclaimed for a Victorian achitectural heritage as rich as the wealth of cultural treasures to be seen in its prestigious museums.

The city's beginnings are believed to have been on the site of the cathedral, to the east of the centre. Here St Mungo founded his church, in AD543. The saint's tomb can still be seen in the crypt of the present cathedral – the only complete medieval cathedral on the Scottish mainland. Nearby, in Castle Street, is Glasgow's oldest house, Provand's Lordship, dating from 1471. Twenty years before that, the University of Glasgow had been founded. For some 400 years its premises were in the High Street, but in 1870 its present buildings were opened, Victorian Gothic in style and set on a fine site overlooking Kelvingrove Park.

The history of the university is the subject of a display in the Hunterian Museum, founded in 1807 as the university's own collection. It owes its existence to a former student, Dr William Hunter. He collected coins, works of art, fossils, geological and zoological specimens and all kinds of curiosities, and bequeathed them to the university when he died, forming the basis of a collection which has grown considerably over the years. Another major museum in Glasgow is the city Art Gallery and Museum in Kelvingrove Park. Opened in 1902, it houses Britain's finest civic art collection, which includes work from all the main European schools, and British paintings of the past three centuries. Also here are extensive natural history and archaeology collections, with special emphasis on Scotland, and an ethnography gallery illustrating the cultures of other continents.

Kelvingrove is one of more than 70 parks and gardens in Glasgow, covering altogether some 6000 acres. Linn Park offers pleasant woodland and riverside walks, whilst Roken Glen has a famous waterfall and a loch, and is rich in bird life. Glasgow Green, beside the Clyde, is the oldest park, but more ancient by far are the remarkable fossilised tree stumps in the Fossil Grove Building in Victoria Park. Shows, carnivals, sports championships and other events enliven many of the parks at certain times of the year. Bellahouston Park has a fine sports centre and all-weather athletic centre. Glasgow's many other sporting facilities include two ultra-modern swimming pools, the Govan Fun Pool and Pollok Leisure Pool.

☆STAR ATTRACTIONS

Botanic Gardens

A herb garden and a chronological border are among the outdoor features of these 40-acre gardens beside the River Kelvin. Not to be missed are the glasshouses, especially the elegant Kibble Palace, one of the largest glasshouses in Britain. Beneath its great central dome is a remarkable collection of tree ferns, some over 100 years old and up to 45ft high. Tender plants from various temperate areas of the world grow elsewhere in the house. Other glasshouses include a palm house, an orchid house and an aquatic house, home of the giant Victoria water-lily. This extraordinary plant grows so fast that within six months of the seed being sown each year, its leaves measure up to five feet across.

☎041-334 2422
Located: off Great Western Road.

Open: gardens daily, 7–dusk; Kibble Palace daily, summer 10–4.45, winter 10–4.15; the main glasshouse summer Mon to Sat 1–4.45, Sun 12–4.45, winter Mon to Sat 1–4.15, Sun 12–4.15.
Admission: free.
P. ♿ (gardens only)

The Burrell Collection

This magnificent collection was amassed by Sir William and Lady Burrell and comprises more than 8000 items – Chinese ceramics, bronzes and jades, Near Eastern rugs and carpets, Turkish pottery and artefacts from the ancient civilisations of Iraq, Egypt, Greece and Italy. There are European paintings from the 15th to the 20th centuries including works by Rembrandt, Millet, Degas, Manet and Cezanne; European medieval art is represented by metalwork, illuminated manuscripts, ivories and two of the most important museum collections in the world of stained glass and tapestries. The collection was given to the city in 1944, but it was not until 1983 that it went on show to the public in this award-winning gallery.

☎041-649 7151
Located: in Pollok Country Park.

Open: all year daily (except Xmas Day & 1 Jan) Mon–Sat 10–5, Sun 2–5.
Admission: free.
P. ⌂ 🍴 ⅋ shop ✶ (except guide dogs)

Haggs Castle

This 16th-century house near Pollok Park is aimed very much at children. Quiz sheets, treasure-hunt cards and imaginative booklets help visitors to imagine domestic life here from the 1580s until Victorian times. There is a 16th-century kitchen, a 17th-century bedroom and a Victorian nursery complete with a rocking horse, dolls and toys. Children are encouraged to explore history through a variety of activities such as making butter and cheese, weaving, and dressing up in period costumes.

☎041-427 2725
Located: at 100 St Andrews Drive.

Open: Mon to Sat 10–5, Sun 2–5. Activity workshops mainly Sat and school hols; telephone for details. Closed Xmas Day and 1 Jan.
Admission: free.
P. 🍴 ⅋ ground floor & workshops only shop ✶ (except guide dogs)

Hunterian Art Gallery

The art collection begun by William Hunter had grown so much by 1980 that it had to be moved from the Hunterian Museum to this new gallery. Special attractions include a large collection of paintings by Whistler, as well as works by British and European masters and a growing number of 19th- and early 20th-century Scottish paintings. The gallery holds Scotland's largest collection of prints, ranging from Dürer to Hockney, shown in frequently changed exhibitions in the Print Gallery. A special feature of the Hunterian is the Mackintosh House, a reconstruction of the main rooms of the Glasgow Home of Charles Rennie Mackintosh, the innovative early 20th-century architect.

☎041-330 5431
Located: at University of Glasgow.

Open: Mon to Fri 9.30–5, Sat 9.30–1 (Mackintosh House closed 12.30–1). Telephone for public holiday closures.
Admission: free (but Mackintosh House 50p on weekday afternoons and Sat mornings).
⅋ (except Mackintosh House) shop ✶

People's Palace Museum

Glasgow's history – from St Mungo to Billy Connolly – is the theme of this colourful museum. Much of the collection dates from the 19th century, with particularly interesting displays on industries such as metal-casting, glass-making and textile manufacture. Earlier prosperity is recalled by the reconstructed office of an 18th-century Glasgow tobacco lord, as well as the first printing press for the *Glasgow Herald*. The city's political history is brought to life by displays of trade union and women's suffrage memorabilia, and there is a good collection of material on the theatre, cinema and music hall. All this is housed in a grand late Victorian building which was originally a cultural centre for Glasgow's East End.

☎041-554 0223
Located: Glasgow Green.

Open: Mon to Sat 10–5, Sun 2–5. Closed Xmas and 1 Jan.
Admission: free.
P. ⌂ ⅋ (ground floor only) shop ✶ (except guide dogs)

GLENCOE, HIGHLAND   Map 14 NN15

Whether you enter Glencoe from Loch Linnhe in the west or from the desolate Rannoch Moor to the east, it is a startling place – a short, steep-sided glen amidst spectacular mountain scenery. This is a must for tourists, famed for its massacre of 1692 and one of the best areas for hill walking and mountaineering in Scotland. There is a visitor centre with a Ranger Naturalist service. Housed in two heather-thatched cottages is the Glencoe and North Lorn Folk Museum which has some fascinating domestic and agricultural exhibits, costumes and a children's section.

☎Visitor centre: Ballachulush (08552) 307
Located: on A82 east of Ballachulish.

Open: Visitor Centre Apr–Oct 10–5.30 (9–6.30 Jun–early Sep); Folk Museum: mid May–Sep Mon–Sat 10–5.30
Admission: Visitor Centre 50p (children 25p); Folk Museum 50p (children 25p).
P. shop at museum

GLENGOULANDIE DEER PARK, TAYSIDE   Map 14 NN75

Set amid some of Scotland's finest scenery Glengoulandie affords visitors the opportunity to see its magnificent wildlife in natural surroundings. You might be lucky enough to spot a majestic red stag with full antlers against a background of heatherclad mountains or a shaggy-coated Highland cow with her golden-haired calf. Endangered rare breeds, such as the Soay and Jacob sheep, thrive in this protected habitat, as do Basil and Pooh – a pair of red foxes. Greylag geese, mallard, guineafowl and peacocks are among the many birds who make their home in this tranquil environment.

☎Kenmore (08873) 509
Located: 8 miles north-west of Aberfeldy on B846.

Open: Apr–Oct daily, 9am until 1 hr before sunset.
Admission: 50p, cars £2.
P. ⊼ shop

INGLISTON, LOTHIAN   Scottish Agricultural Museum   Map 11 NT17

The life and work of families in rural Scotland, in days gone by, is interestingly depicted by a series of tableaux and exhibits of tools, crafts and machinery. Social life and home life is covered as well as all aspects of farming. There are two big tractors outside for youngsters to sit on.

☎031-225 7534

Open: May–Sep, Mon–Fri 10–5, Sun 11–5.
Admission: free.
⌂ & shop ✗ (except guide dogs)

INVERARAY, STRATHCLYDE   Argyll Wildlife Park   Map 10 NN00

Magnificent scenery is a feature of Scotland's newest wildlife park, but there is much more to see as well. There are 100 species of swan, geese and duck – some extremely rare; also some rare owls. There is an illustrated nature walk through coniferous forest, where you might come across some deer, badger or even wildcats.

☎(0499) 2264
Located: Dalchenna.

Open: daily 9–6.30 (or dusk).
Admission: fee payable.
P. ⌂⊼ shop & garden centre

INVERARAY, STRATHCLYDE   Inveraray Castle   Map 10 NN00

This fairytale castle dates from the late 18th-century and is the ancestral home of the Dukes of Argyll. The great armoury and staterooms are well worth a visit and there are portraits by Gainsborough, Ramsay and Raeburn. There is a combined operations museum in the grounds, and the gardens are open to the public on selected weekends.

☎(0499) 2203

Open: 1st Sat Apr–2nd Sun Oct daily (closed Fri except Jul & Aug) 10–1 & 2–6; Apr–Jun & Sep–Oct, Sun 1–6, Jul & Aug daily 10–6, Sun 1–6. Last admissions 12.30 & 5.30. Woodland walks all year.
Admission: £2.20 (children up to 16 £1.10, senior citizens £1.70). Family ticket £6.
P. ⌂ (licensed) ⊼ & (ground floor only) shop ✗

KELSO, BORDERS Floors Castle Map 12 NT73

This splendid Adam building belongs to the Duke and Duchess of Roxburghe. Though built in 1721 by William Adam there were later additions by William Playfair. The handsome exterior is matched by an equally sumptuous interior with superb French and English furniture, tapestries and paintings. The grounds offer children a chance to let off steam in a purpose-built playground and there is also a magnificent walled garden.

☎(0573) 23333

Open: Easter Sun & Mon then May–Sep, Sun–Thu (alo Fri in Jul & Aug) 10.30–5.30 (last admission to house 4.45pm).
Admission: £2.20 (children 8 & over £1.30, senior citizens £1.80). Family ticket £6. Grounds only £1.25.
P. ⌑ (licensed) ⊼ Ᏸ (ground floor & garden only) shop & garden centre ⴕ (in house)

KILCHRENAN, STRATHCLYDE Ardanaiseig Map 10 NN02

Enjoying a magnificent view across Loch Awe, these beautiful gardens at Ardanaiseig are renowned for their rare shrubs and trees. Azaleas and rhododendrons also bloom in profusion here.

☎(08663) 333
Located: 3 miles north-east at end of unclassified road.

Open: ✳Apr–Oct, daily 8.30–dusk.
Admission: fee payable.
P. garden centre ⴕ

KILMARNOCK, STRATHCLYDE Dean Castle Map 10 NS43

The ancestral home of the Boyd family, this 14th- and 15th-century castle contains an outstanding collection of medieval arms, armour, tapestries and musical instruments. There are displays of family history, and of the life and works of Robert Burns. A 200-acre country park with gardens, nature trail and picnic area is part of the estate. Other attractions include a children's adventure playground, a riding school and an aviary.

☎(0563) 26401 ext 36
Located: in Dean Road.

Open: all year daily, 12–5 (closed 25 & 26 Dec, 1 & 2 Jan) Country Park dawn to dusk.
Admission: ✳£1 (children under 16 & senior citizens free). Country Park free.
P. ⌑⊼ Ᏸ (limited areas of ground floor & gardens only) shop ⴕ (in castle)

KINCRAIG, HIGHLAND Highland Wildlife Park Map 14 NH80

Brown bear, elk, arctic fox and lynx once roamed freely in the Scottish Highlands. Today, the only opportunity to see these fine creatures in a natural habitat, comes with a visit to the Highland Wildlife Park. A drive-through area houses red-deer, bison, Highland cattle, wild sheep, goats and horses while the more dangerous animals are kept in enclosures in a walk-round display area. The Park is also renowned for its collection of Scottish birds. Younger children will enjoy Pets Corner.

☎(05404) 270
Located: between Aviemore & Kingussie on the B9152.

Open: Apr–Oct daily 10–6.
Admission: ✳£6 per car (no limit on number of passengers).
P. ⌑⊼ Ᏸ (ground floor & gardens) shop ⴕ

KINGUSSIE, HIGHLAND Highland Folk Museum Map 14 NH70

Life through the ages in the Highlands is cleverly re-enacted during special Heritage in Action Days at this fascinating museum. Indoors is the Farming Museum, and examples of domestic interiors, and outside is the Open Air Museum including a Clack Mill, a Turf House and a Salmon Smoke-house plus a relaxing garden with the pleasing scent of lilac, roses and herbs.

☎(05402) 307
Located: in Duke Street.

Open: Apr–Oct, Mon–Sat 10–6, Sun 2–6, Nov–Mar, Mon–Fri 10–3.
Admission: £1.25 (children & senior citizens 65p)
P. ⊼ Ᏸ (ground floor and gardens only) shop

LANGBANK, STRATHCLYDE   Finlaystone Country Estate   Map 10 NS37

A collection of dolls from around the world will enthral all little girls who visit Finlaystone House, and they can join their brothers in the adventure playground in the grounds or go pony trekking. At Christmas it is even possible to cut your own Christmas tree here. In fact, there is something for everyone all year round at Finlaystone – from the historical interest of the house to the magnificent grounds with their woodland walks and garden centre. Watch out for the circular Celtic pavement in the formal gardens.

☎(047554) 285
Located: on the A8 1 mile west of Langbank.

Open: Woodland & gardens open all year, daily; House Apr–Aug Sun 2.30–4.30.
Admission: 80p (children 50p).
P. ⌂ (Apr–Sep, Sat & Sun 2–5) ⩒ & (ground floor) nursery garden

LANGHOLM, DUMFRIES and GALLOWAY   Craigcleuch Collection   Map 11 NY38

Housed in a baronial mansion, this unusual collection includes artefacts in wood, jade, ivory and coral, as well as hundreds of rare tribal sculptures and prehistoric stone pipes. Girls will love the doll's collection and there are also some fine Oriental paintings. The grounds offer some fine woodland walks.

☎(0541) 80137
Located: 2 miles north-west of Langholm on the B709.

Open: Easter weekend, Bank Hols & May–mid Sep, Mon–Sat 10–5.30. Other times by appointment.
Admission: £1.25 (children 50p)
P. & (ground floor only) shop ⫟

LARGS, STRATHCLYDE   Kelburn Country Centre   Map 10 NS25

Children will love it here on the Earl of Glasgow's estate overlooking the Firth of Clyde. In the grounds there is an adventure course, a stockade and the Kelburn Glen, part cultivated, part in its wild state, complete with nature trails. There are beautiful gardens, waterfalls and rare trees. Some 18th-century farm buildings have been converted to form a village square complete with craft shops, workshops, display rooms and a café. For the more energetic there is pony-trekking and a marine assault course.

☎Fairlie (047556) 685
Located: 2 miles south off A78.

Open: Easter–Sep daily 10–6; Oct–mid Feb, Sun only 11–5; mid Feb–Easter weekends 11–5.
Admission: Easter–Sep £1.80 (children & senior citizens £1.20); Oct–Easter £1 (children & senior citizens 60p)
P. ⌂ (licensed) ⩒ & shop

LAUDER, BORDERS   Thirlestane Castle   Map 12 NT54

The Maitland family have owned this magnificent Castle since the 12th century and it is still very much a family home. The state apartments are rich in Scottish history, and there are some fine 17th-century ceilings; but, it is the nursery wing with its unique collection of Victorian toys, that will capture a child's imagination. In the beautiful grounds, alongside the River Tweed, is the Border Country Life Museum which tells the story of the people, their towns and villages, and the river. There are also regular craft displays and exhibitions.

☎(05782) 430

Open: Easter, May, Jun & Sep, Wed, Thu & Sun; Jul & Aug, daily except Sat. Castle 2–5; Grounds 12–6.
Admission: £2 (children & senior citizens £1.50) Family £5
P. ⌂ ⩒ & (ground floor & gardens only) shop

LAWERS, TAYSIDE   Ben Lawers Visitors Centre   Map 11 NN64

Nestling on the slopes of Ben Lawers, Perthshire's highest mountain at 3984ft, the Visitor's Centre overlooks some of Scotland's finest scenery. The story of the mountain, which is noted for its alpine plants and interesting birdlife, is told in an exhibition and audio-visual display. Guided walks are arranged during the summer months and there are nature trails for those who'd rather be independent.

☎Killin (05672) 397

Open: Apr–May & Sep, daily 11–4, Jun–Aug, daily 10–5.
Admission: 80p (children 40p).
P.
National Trust for Scotland

LEUCHARS, FIFE   Earlshall Castle   Map 12 NO42

This fine 16th-century castle is the family home of Major
Baxter, Laird of Earlshall, and it was actually built by his
ancestor, Sir William Bruce. There are many Jacobean relics
as well as some fine furniture and a permanent display of
Scottish weapons. The garden has a stunning display of
topiary yews clipped in the shape of chess pieces. A craft
festival takes place here on 29 July to the 1st August 1988.

☎(033 483) 205

Open: Easter weekend–late Sep Thu–Sun 2–
6 (last admission 5.15pm).
Admission: £2.80 (children 5–16 £1, senior
citizens £1.50).
⌨ 🚻 & (gardens only) shop ✻ (except guide
dogs)

LOCH AWE, STRATHCLYDE   Cruachan Power Station   Map 10 NN12

An unforgettable experience – that's what is promised of a visit
to this vast underground power station. An electric bus will
take you through a tunnel into a vast cavern inside Ben
Cruachan. Here the massive power house utilises water
pumped from Loch Awe to a reservoir 1200ft up the
mountain. A Visitor's Centre on ground level features an
exhibition and, nearby, the banks of Loch Awe provide a
scenic picnic spot.

☎Taynuilt (08662) 673
**Located: 3 miles west off A85, near the
Pass of Brander.**

Open: Easter–Oct, daily 9–4.30.
Admission: £1 (children 8–16 50p).
P. ⌨ 🚻 &(grounds & Visitors Centre only)
shop ✻

LOCHGILPHEAD, STRATHCLYDE   Kilmory Castle Gardens   Map 10 NR88

These 30 acres of grounds surrounding the castle had been
the subject of much neglect until the present owners restored
them to their former 18th-century glory. Woodland walks and
nature trails allow visitors to appreciate the magnificent rare
trees and shrubs here.

☎(0546) 2127

Open: all year, daily 9–dusk
Admission: free
P. 🚻 & (gardens only) ✻

MARYCULTER, GRAMPIAN   Anderson's Storybook Glen   Map 15 NO89

Set in 20 acres of beautifully landscaped garden with waterfalls and seating areas, this magical glen has a surprise around
every corner. Fairytale and nursery rhyme characters such as
the Old Woman Who Lived in a Shoe and Goldilocks and the
Three Bears are recreated in life-size tableaux. There's a
castle, a pirate ship, swings, slides, a small farmyard and much
more to thrill and entertain youngsters – of any age!

☎Aberdeen (0224) 732941

Open: *Mar–Oct, daily 10–7.
Admission: fee payable.
P. ⌨ (licensed) & shop ✻

MELROSE, BORDERS   Melrose Abbey   Map 12 NT53

The ruins of this once magnificent Cistercian abbey must be
the most famous in Scotland, thanks mainly to the romantic
writings of Sir Walter Scott. The subject of repeated English
invasions, most of the ruins seen today date from the 15th-
century reconstruction. The heart of Robert the Bruce is
buried near the High Altar. Results of excavations in and
around the abbey can be seen in the Commendators House
which is now a museum.

Open: Apr–Sep, Mon–Sat 9.30–7, Sun 2–7;
Oct–Mar, Mon–Sat 9.30–4, Sun 2–4; closed
1 & 2 Jan, 25 & 26 Dec.
Admission: *£1 (children & senior citizens
50p)
Ancient Monument

MELROSE, BORDERS   Melrose Motor Museum   Map 12 NT53

Cars seen on our roads over the past 50 years make up the major part of this fascinating museum, one of the largest of its kind in Scotland. All of the popular makes and models are here, in running order, and many with the original paintwork and plating. There are also bicycles, motorcycles and World War II military vehicles, as well as some interesting motoring memorabilia.

☎(0835) 22356
Located: in Newstead Road.

Open: Whit Sun–Oct, daily, 10.30–5.30.
Admission: fee payable
P. & shop ✻ (except guide dogs)

MINTLAW, GRAMPIAN   Aden Country Park   Map 15 NK04

This 230-acre country park is set in open farmland and used to be part of a large estate. There are many paths and a specially developed nature trail allows visitors to appreciate the abundance of plants and wildlife to be found here. The North East of Scotland Heritage Centre is housed in a semi-circular farmstead and offers a glimpse of estate life in the 1920s. There are craft workshops regularly in use and a Farm and Field Day takes place on 12th June 1988.

☎(07712) 2857
Located: 1 mile west of Mintlaw, off A950.

Open: Park open all year. Buildings daily mid May–Sep 12–6. Heritage Centre daily May–Sep 11–5; Apr & Oct weekends only 12–5.
Admission: free
P. ☕ (table licence) ⪥ & (ground floor & gardens only) shop

MULL (ISLE OF), STRATHCLYDE   Narrow Gauge Railway   Map 10 NM73

Opened in 1983, this is Scotland's first island railway. The 10¼ inch-gauge track runs for 1¼ miles, through some superb mountain and coastal scenery, from Craignure to Torosay Castle. Journey time is 20 minutes by either diesel or steam train.

☎(06802) 494 (in season) & (06803) 389 or 472 (out of season)
Located: at Craignure (Old Pier) Station.

Open: ✳Easter week then May Day Bank Hol–late Sep. Ring for details of train times.
Admission: return £1.20 (children 85p); single 90p (children 70p). Family return £3.25.
P. (Craignure only) ☕ (Torosay Castle) & (ground floor only) shop

MULL (ISLE OF), STRATHCLYDE   Torosay Castle and Gardens   Map 10 NM73

At the end of the railway line you'll find this magnificent Victorian mansion and beautiful Italian terraced gardens covering some 11 acres, and featuring a statue walk, a Japanese garden and water garden. Inside the house there are a number of fine paintings and an interesting collection of stags' antlers. Also on show is the huge head of a prehistoric elk, which was discovered in a bog in Co. Monaghan.

☎(06802) 421
Located: Craignure.

Open: mid Apr–early Oct, daily 10.30–5.30. Gardens dawn–dusk.
Admission: fee payable
P. ☕ shop ✻ (in house)

for PERTH see opposite page

PITLOCHRY, TAYSIDE   Faskally   Map 8 SE78

This area of Forestry Commission land borders Loch Faskally and offers the family a beautiful setting for picnics and some fine woodland walks.

☎Dunkeld (03502) 284
Located: 2 miles north-west of Pitlochry.

Open: Apr–Oct, daily dawn–dusk.
Admission: free.
P. ⪥ &

for further PITLOCHRY entry see page 172

Fair City at the Edge of the Highlands

Formerly St Johnstoun – a name that lives on in its football team – Perth stands in an area that has been inhabited since earliest times. The Romans had a legionary fort nearby, and Scone, two miles to the north, was the capital of that old Pictish kingdom. Scottish kings were crowned there for 400 years until Edward I took the Stone of Scone to Westminster Abbey, where it still stands beneath the coronation chair.

Medieval Perth was a prosperous royal burgh, port and cattle market. One of the only buildings remaining from this period is St John's Kirk, founded in 1126 but rebuilt in the 15th century. Its carillon of 35 bells can be heard regularly. Other early buildings open to visitors include 15th-century Huntingtower Castle, Balhousie Castle – now home of the Black Watch Regimental Museum – and the Fair Maid's House, believed to have been the guildhall of the glovers, once Perth's most important craft guild. A previous house on the site was the home of Catherine Glover, heroine of Scott's novel *The Fair Maid of Perth*.

Perth's centre is flanked by two historic open spaces on the banks of the Tay. Originally water-meadows which marked the city limits, the North Inch and South Inch have provided recreation for the people of Perth since the days when golfers and archers had to share them with grazing cattle. One of Perth's four golf courses is still on the North Inch, as is the modern Bell's Sports Centre. The South Inch has a fun park with boating and paddling pools and crazy golf. More traditional sporting events include curling tournaments at the ice rink and race meetings at Scone. The river provides a variety of pastimes, from sailing to salmon-fishing, whilst for walks it is hard to beat Kinnoull Hill, just outside the city.

☆STAR ATTRACTIONS

Caithness Glass

Visitors can watch Caithness paperweights being made from the viewing gallery here at the factory of Caithness Glass. The visitor centre contains a collectors' gallery, and there is a factory shop.

☎(0738) 37373
Located: on Inveralmond Industrial Estate.

Open: Mon–Sat 9–5, Sun 1–5 (11–5 Easter–Sep). Glassmaking Mon–Fri only.
Admission: free.
P. ⌷ (licensed) & shop

Fairways Heavy Horse Centre

Two miles out of Perth, between Kinnoull Hill and the Tay, this is both a breeding and a working establishment for Clydesdales – one of the most popular breeds in the days of the working horse. Newly born foals can sometimes be seen, and horse-drawn wagon rides are available for visitors. Video films feature the horses at work, and various horse-drawn implements such as ploughs and reapers are on display. At weekends a blacksmith can often be seen at work.

☎(0738) 25931
Located: in Walnut Grove, Kilfauns.

Open: Apr–Sep daily 10–6.
Admission: fee payable.
P. ⌷ 🕭 & shop

Perth Museum and Art Gallery

This imposing classical building near Perth Bridge combines an excellent collection of fine and applied art with good displays of natural history and local history. Memorabilia of Perth's glovers' guild and various finds from archaeological digs in the area are among the exhibits. Special events and temporary exhibitions are held frequently.

☎(0738) 32488
Located: 78 George Street.

Open: Mon–Sat 10–1 & 2–5.
Admission: free.
P. shop ✶

The Round House

Perhaps Perth's most curious building, the Round House was built in the 1830s as a waterworks. Its tall chimney, topped by a Grecian urn, served the steam engine that enabled pumps to draw water from filter beds on Moncrieffe Island in the Tay. Today the Round House is Perth's tourist information centre. Its audio-visual programme is a good introduction to the sights of Perth and the surrounding area.

☎(0738) 38358
Located: in Marshall Place.

Open: all year daily.
Admission: free.

PITLOCHRY, TAYSIDE   Pitlochry Power Station, Dam and Fish Pass   Map 8 SE78

Anyone who has ever wondered where electricity comes from will be fascinated by a visit to Pitlochry Power Station. One of the nine hydro stations in the Tummel Valley, Pitlochry offers the public an amazing chance to view its workings. There is also an exhibition and an audio visual presentation. The massive dam created Loch Faskally, where fishing and boating are available. A viewing gallery underground at the Fish Pass allows visitors a chance to see the salmon leap upstream as they head for the spawning ground.

☎(0796) 3152

Open: ✱Exhibition, Easter–late Oct, daily 9.45–5.30.
Admission: ✱30p (children 8–16 15p).
Shop ✸

PITMEDDEN, GRAMPIAN   Pitmedden Garden   Map 15 NJ82

The main feature at Pitmedden is the fine 17th-century Great Garden, originally laid out by Sir Alexander Seton, complete with fountains, pavilions, sundials and elaborate floral designs. Also in the grounds of this 100-acre estate, is a museum of farming life and a woodland and farmland walk.

☎Udny (06513) 2352

Open: Gardens & grounds all year daily 9.30–sunset. Museum May–Sep daily 11–6 (last admission 5.15).
Admission: Museum & garden £1.60 (children 80p). Garden only 90p (children 45p).
&
National Trust for Scotland

POOLEWE, HIGHLAND   Inverewe Garden   Map 14 NG88

It is hard to believe that this magnificent garden was once a bleak and barren Highland peninsula, but this was indeed the case little more than 100 years ago. Now, against a backdrop of spectacular mountain scenery, you can enjoy its shrubs, trees, herbaceous borders and colourful displays of bulbs. Many of the plants are rare varieties and some are even sub-tropical species.

☎(044586) 200
Located: 1 mile north on A832.

Open: all year daily 9.30–sunset. Visitor Centre open Apr–late Oct Mon–Sat 10–5 (6.30 summer), Sun 12–5 (6.30 summer).
Admission: £1.80 (children 90p).
P. (10p) ☕ (Apr–mid Oct) &
National Trust for Scotland

QUEEN'S VIEW, TAYSIDE   Tummel Forestry Commission Centre   Map 14 NN85

This view of the Tummel Valley and the loch was a particular favourite with Queen Victoria when she toured Scotland in 1866. An exhibition and audio-visual programme shows various aspects of local history and industry. Outside the centre there are the remains of a Roman ring fort and all around are interesting forest walks.

☎Pitlochry (0796) 3123

Open: end Mar–end Oct 10–5.30.
Admission: free.
P. (adjacent) & shop ✸

SCONE, TAYSIDE   Scone Palace   Map 11 N002

A must for any history lesson, Scone Palace is famous as the crowning place for the Kings of Scotland. In 1296 the Stone of Destiny (the Coronation Stone) was seized by Edward I and taken to Westminster Abbey, but Scottish kings were still crowned here until 1651. The present palace dates mainly from 1803, but incorporates part of the building of 1580. Inside, you'll find a notable collection of French furniture and some fine needlework that was done by Mary, Queen of Scots. The grounds contain one of the finest Pinetums in the country, and there is an adventure playground for youngsters.

☎(0738) 52300

Open: Apr–early Oct, Mon–Sat 9.30–5, Sun 1.30–5 (Jul & Aug 10–5).
Admission: House & grounds £2.50 (children £2). Grounds only £1.20 (children £1). Family £9
P. ☕ (licensed) ⊼ & shop

Scotland's Lochs

Each year great numbers of people make the decision to cross the invisible border that stretches between the Tweed and Solway Firth and to visit Scotland. They come for all sorts of reasons – for touring holidays, for activities, in search of history and to observe the wildlife. But above all people come to enjoy and 'lose' themselves in the wildly beautiful and dramatic scenery; to get away from it all among Scotland's great mountains, forests, glens, its tumbling crystal rivers and waterfalls and, above all, its deep, dark lochs. The Scottish lochs – some great and some small – provide just about all the holiday ingredients that any visitor could possibly wish for. From the south, Loch Trool lies amid 135,000 acres of the Glen Trool Forest Park and is just one of a series of lochs and waterfalls. Further north, between Moffat and Selkirk, the three mile long St Mary's Loch, set among the green hills of Ettrick Forest, was thought sufficiently beautiful by Wordsworth to gain mention in his poetry. Not all the Scottish lochs are in wild and isolated places. Linlithgow is overlooked by its ancient town and the majestically towering ruins of a fine 15th-century palace. Loch Leven, just north of Kirkcaldy, is famed for its delicious salmon trout. Each year anglers from all over Europe take part in its international trout angling competitions, while during the winter, when its waters have set to ice, it is used for the sport of curling. On an island in the middle of Loch Leven, which can be reached by boat, are the ruins of Loch Leven Castle. Above all others, Loch Lomond, backed by gentle hills to the south and harsher mountains to the north, is a place that seems to symbolise Scotland for so many: This beautiful stretch of water, more than 20 miles long and studded with small islands, is the largest lake in Great Britain. It offers excellent salmon trout, pike and perch fishing and is also popular for yacht and dinghy sailing. There are nature trails around many of the lochs just waiting to be explored, while for the less energetic, pleasure steamer trips are often organised on larger lochs such as Loch Katrine and the infamous Loch Ness. Wherever there are lochs, there tends to be an abundance of interesting and often rare wildlife and, if you happen to be near Loch Ness and you're very lucky, maybe just a glimpse of the occasional monster!

For places to visit in the area check the location atlas at the end of the book.

Remote Loch Eribol is a sea loch on the north coast of Scotland.

SELKIRK, BORDERS   Bowhill   Map 12 NT42

A day at Bowhill offers something for everyone in the family. The beautiful home of the Scott Clan Chief with its outstanding art collection, including Sir Walter Scott's proofs, and its lovely setting. The grounds feature an adventure playground – bound to be a winner with the kids – as well as woodland and riverside walks and pony trekking.

☎(0750) 20732
Located: 3 miles west of Selkirk off A708.

Open: House & grounds early Jul–late Aug Mon–Sat 1–4.30, Sun 2–6. Grounds May–Aug 12–5 (except Fri). Riding centre all year.
Admission: House & grounds £2.50, grounds only £1.
P. ⌑ ⊼ & shop

for SKYE see opposite page

SOUTH QUEENSFERRY, LOTHIAN   Dalmeny House   Map 11 NT17

Enjoying a magnificent situation overlooking the Firth of Forth, Dalmeny House is the ancestral home of the Earls of Rosebery. Amongst the great wealth of fine furniture and works of art is the Rothschild Mentmore collection of French furniture, porcelain and tapestries. There is also a fascinating exhibition of pictures and items associated with Napoleon. The grounds of the estate reach the shore and offer some fine walks.

☎031-331 1888

Open: *beginning of May–Sep, Sun–Thu 2–5.30 (last admission 5pm).
Admission: *fee payable.
P. ⌑ &

SOUTH QUEENSFERRY, LOTHIAN   Hopetoun House   Map 11 NT17

Scotland's finest Adam mansion, Hopetoun House is the home of the 4th Marquess of Linlithgow. Much of the beautiful furniture and hangings are original, dating from 1760, and there are portraits by Rubens, Rembrandt and Canaletto. Fallow and red deer and St Kilda sheep roam the extensive grounds and there are stunning views across the Firth of Forth. There is an educational day centre and a stables museum which features an exhibition on 'Horse and Man in Lowland Scotland'.

☎031-331 2451
Located: 2 miles west of South Queensferry on an unclassified road.

Open: Easter, then May–mid Sep daily, 11–5.30 (last admission 5pm).
Admission: £2.50 (reduced rates for children & senior citizens).
P. ⌑ (licensed) ⊼ & (ground floor & gardens only) shop & garden centre

for STIRLING see page 176

STRANRAER, DUMFRIES AND GALLOWAY   Castle Kennedy Gardens
Map 10 NX15

These fine 17th-century and later gardens enjoy national acclaim for the splendid collection of azaleas, magnolias, embrothiums and rhododendrons. The pinetum here was the first of its kind in Scotland. Situated on a peninsula between two lochs and overlooked by an elegant castle, it is now the home of the Earl and Countess of Stair.

☎(0776) 2024
Located: 3 miles east of Stranraer on A75.

Open: *Apr–Sep, daily 10–5.
Admission: fee payable.
P. ⌑ ⊼ & shop & plant centre

for THORNHILL see page 177

Symbols

☎	telephone number
P.	parking on the premises
⌑	refreshments available
⊼	picnic area
&	accessible to wheelchair-bound visitors
🐕	no dogs
*	indicates 1987 details

The Romantic Isle

There are several ways of getting 'over the sea to Skye' – from Mallaig to Armadale or from Glenelg to Kylerhea, but most people opt to board the ferry at Kyle of Lochalsh and take the five minute trip to the pretty little port of Kyleakin. Of all the Scottish islands, Skye – just 50 miles long and steeped in myth and legend – is perhaps the most beautiful. Spectacular mountain scenery, old castles and crofts and pretty, often white-washed waterside cottages are sometimes surrounded by swirling mists and the most brilliant sunsets often take place. This is also the Scottish island that probably offers the most for the visitor to see and do. The great Cuillin Hills, to the south of the island, offer some of the very best climbing to be found anywhere in Scotland. There are also centres for pony-trekking on the island and ample opportunities for those who like river, loch or sea fishing. A number of boat trips – both around Skye and to other islands nearby – are on offer; surely one of the best ways of becoming familiar with this area and to catch glimpses of the abundant wildlife that has made its home here. Many of Skye's small towns have old castles, crofts, museums or some other place of interest to hold the visitor's attention, and much of the island's history is connected with Bonnie Prince Charlie who came here as a fugitive from the English after the Battle of Culloden in 1746.

☆STAR ATTRACTIONS

Dunvegan Castle
The massive Dunvegan Castle has been the seat of the MacLeod Clan for 700 years and claims to be the oldest inhabited dwelling in Scotland. Certainly the village grew up around its castle. Once this moated castle was only accessible by boat, but now a bridge makes access easy for visitors. The castle contains all sorts of treasures, including a lock of Bonnie Prince Charlie's hair and the Bratach Sith – or Fairy Flag – believed to have magical properties.

☎(047022) 206
Located: at Dunvegan.

Open: Easter–Oct Mon–Sat: mid May–Sep 10.30–5.30, otherwise 2–5. Closed Sun.
Admission: £2.50; gardens only £1.
P. ⌂ & (gardens only) shop

Clan Donald Centre
Forty acres of glorious woodland gardens and nature trails are the setting for the dramatic ruins of Armadale Castle, overlooking the Sound of Sleat. This is a lovely place for walking (there are guided walks available too) and it is rich in wild flowers and banks of rhododendrons in season. An exhibition in the restored part of the castle tells the story of the family who owned this castle – the Clan Donald. The restored stables now house a fine restaurant where visitors can enjoy 'Taste of Scotland' food, and there is also a craft and book shop.

☎Ardvasar (04714) 305 or 227
Located: at Armadale, ½ mile north of Armadale Pier

Open: Easter–Oct daily 10–5.30.
Admission: ✳£1.20 (children and senior citizens 80p).
P. ⌂ licensed & shop ⴕ

Skye Museum of Island Life
A most unusual museum which consists of five thatched cottages that demonstrate what the old croft houses that were common Highland dwellings a century ago were like. Inside is a fascinating collection of old tools, implements and the like used by Highlanders at that time. Also on display is an intriguing collection of old letters, papers and pictures.

☎Duntulm (047052) 279
Located: at Kilmuir.

Open: mid May–Oct, daily (except Sun) 9–6.
Admission: fee payable.
P. & shop

Historic Gateway to the Highlands

Both the townscape and the history of this lovely old burgh have always been dominated by its castle. Perched on a sheer crag, it looks down over narrow streets and historic stone buildings to the meandering River Forth far below.

For many centuries Stirling was the lowest bridging point on the Forth. This has ensured its castle a colourful history as guardian of the main route to the Highlands. In its early days it was repeatedly and bitterly fought over by English and Scots, the English suffering crushing defeat in two famous battles nearby: Stirling Bridge in 1297 and Bannockburn in 1314. From 1370 to 1603 Stirling Castle was the home of the Stuart kings. Scottish monarchs were born, crowned and married at Stirling, and the town continued to witness some of the more momentous events of Scotland's history.

Even after 1603, when James VI of Scotland also became James I of England and moved his court to London, Stirling's commanding position ensured that it saw action in the Civil War and in the Jacobite Rebellions of the 18th century. Only in the past 200 years has it had a more peaceful existence. For a long time the castle was a barracks, but today it is visitors who benefit from its lofty position, enjoying views that stretch far into the Highlands. Nearer at hand, beyond the river and the town, the ruins of Cambuskenneth Abbey can be seen. Here Robert the Bruce held his first Scottish parliament, in 1326. Views to the north take in the great rock of Abbey Craig, crowned by the Wallace Monument. This striking 220ft stone tower was built in the 1860s in honour of William Wallace, hero of the Battle of Stirling Bridge.

Historic buildings in the town include the 15th-century Church of the Holy Rude, where James VI was crowned in 1567. Next to it stands Mar's Wark, a remarkable ruin, built by the Scottish Regent, the Earl of Mar, in the 1570s, but never completed. Nearby, in Broad Street, are the Tolbooth – the early 18th-century town hall and jail, topped by a distinctive clock-tower – and the Mercat Cross, a reminder of the days when Broad Street was the site of Stirling's thriving market.

☆STAR ATTRACTIONS

Stirling Castle

The Renaissance architecture of the castle buildings may be a surprise to visitors expecting an austere medieval fortress, but most of the main buildings in the castle precinct date from the 16th century when it was a royal residence. The Royal Palace was built by James V, father of Mary, Queen of Scots, and the adjacent Chapel Royal was rebuilt by James VI on the site of the 12th-century chapel. Part of the castle now houses the Museum of the Argyll and Sutherland Highlanders, where regimental silver, medals and uniforms are on display. Adjacent to the castle is a visitor centre where Stirling's history is brought vividly to life by drawings, photographs and an audio-visual presentation.

Smith Art Gallery and Museum

A series of special events and temporary exhibitions marked the reopening of the main gallery here in 1987 after a major restoration. The museum's permanent collections range from works of art to natural history exhibits, with a special display on the story of Stirling from William Wallace to the present day.

🏛Regimental Museum (0786) 75165,
Visitor Centre (0786) 62517
Located: Upper Castle Hill.

Open: Castle: all year daily (except 1–4 Jan), Apr–Sep 9.30–5.15, Sun 10.30–4.45; Oct–Mar 9.30–4.20, Sun 12.30–3.35 Regimental Museum: Easter–Sep 10–5.30, Sun 11–5; Oct Mon–Fri 10–4. Visitor Centre: *all year (ecept Jan) 9.30–6, Sun 10.30–5.20 (closes 1 hr earlier in winter).
Admission: Castle: *£1.50 (children & senior citizens 75p). Family ticket £3. Regimental Museum: free. Visitor Centre: free, but charge for audio visual.
P. ⌂ shop ⑂ (in Regimental Museum)
Ancient Monument
🏛(0786) 71917
Located: 40 Albert Place, Dumbarton Road.

Open: Apr–Oct Tue–Sat 10.30–12.30 & 1–5, Sun 2–5; Nov–Mar Wed–Sun 2–5, (Sat 10.30–5).
Admission: free.
& shop ⑂

THORNHILL, DUMFRIES AND GALLOWAY   Drumlanrig Castle   Map 11 NX89

The lovely grounds of Drumlanrig Castle are the setting for an exciting adventure playground with aerial runways, high slides and a Wild West Fort. There are woodland walks as well as formal gradens; a visitor centre with exhibitions and a working crafts centre. The pink sandstone castle contains one of the world's greatest art collections.

☎(0848) 30248
Located: 4 miles north-west off A76, on west bank of River Nith.

Open: end Apr–late Aug daily, except Fri. Sun 2–6, other days 1.30–5 till end Jun, then 11–5. Last entry 45 minutes before closing.
Admission: House & grounds £2.50 (senior citizens £1.75, children 5–16 £1, under 5 free). Grounds only £1.
P. ⌂ ⟊ & shop ✗ (except park)

TRAQUAIR, BORDERS   Traquair House   Map 11 NT33

Famous as the oldest continuously inhabited house (10th-century) in Scotland, Traquair has been visited by 27 Scottish and English monarchs. The handsome Bear Gates in front of the house were closed in 1745 and will not be opened again until a Stuart is on the throne. This does not, however, mean that visitors are not welcome – they just enter through a different gate. The house contains many fine treasures and has strong associations with Mary, Queen of Scots. Real ale is brewed here in the 18th-century bewery and there are five craft workshops. New maze and children's play area.

☎Innerleithen (0896) 830323
Located: 1 mile south of Innerleithen, on B709.

Open: *Easter–mid Oct, daily 1.30–5.30; (opens from 10.30 Jul–mid Sep). Last admission 5pm.
Admission: fee payable.
⌂ (licensed) ⟊ & (ground floor & gardens only) shop ✗ (except in grounds).

UDDINGSTON, STRATHCLYDE   Glasgow Zoo   Map 11 NS66

An unusually spacious open-plan zoo with a comprehensive collection of birds, mammals and reptiles. Many rare and endangered species are flourishing here. Other activities include a children's showground, an education centre and fine walking areas.

☎041-771 1185

Open: all year, daily 10–5 (or 6pm, depending on season)
Admission: £2.50 (children & senior citizens £1.40, children under 3 free). Family ticket £6.50.
P. ⌂ ⟊ & ✗

WANLOCKHEAD, DUMFRIES & GALLOWAY   Museum of Scottish Lead Mining
Map 11 NS81

To really get a taste of lead mining in the 18th-century you must enter the Visitors' Walkway – a 1½ mile-long tour of a lead mine with its display on mining and social history. A Miners' Reading Society library was founded here in 1756 and there is also a collection of local gold, silver and minerals. A fascinating outdoor museum includes beam engines, a smelt mill and but-an-ben cottages.

☎Leadhills (06594) 387
Located: on B797 at northern end of Mennock Pass.

Open: Easter–end Sep, daily 11–4. Last tour of mine 3.30pm.
Admission: Visitor Centre & cottages 70p (children 5–16 30p); mine 50p (children 5–16 20p).
P. ⟊ & shop

Index

MAP OF REGIONS

SCOTLAND

Aberdeen

Dundee

Glasgow · Edinburgh

Newcastle upon Tyne

Carlisle

NORTHERN ENGLAND

Leeds · Hull

Liverpool · Sheffield

Colwyn Bay

Stoke on Trent

CENTRAL ENGLAND & EAST ANGLIA

Norwich

WALES

Pembroke

Oxford · Chelmsford

Cardiff · Bristol

SOUTH & SOUTH EAST ENGLAND

Maidstone

WEST COUNTRY

Southampton

Brighton

Exeter

Truro

Key to Atlas

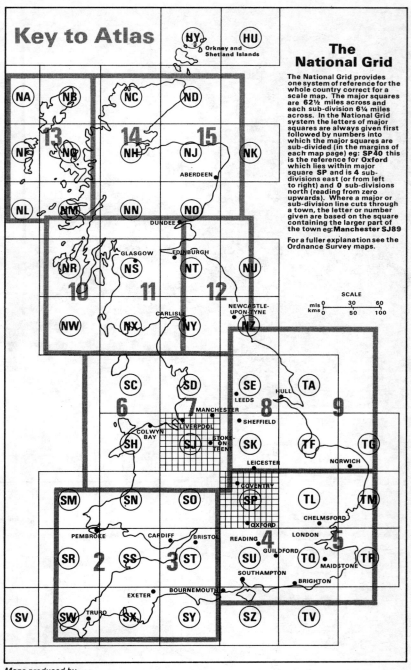

The National Grid

The National Grid provides one system of reference for the whole country correct for a scale map. The major squares are 62½ miles across and each sub-division 6¼ miles across. In the National Grid system the letters of major squares are always given first followed by numbers into which the major squares are sub-divided (in the margins of each map page) eg: **SP40** this is the reference for **Oxford** which lies within major square **SP** and is 4 sub-divisions east (or from left to right) and 0 sub-divisions north (reading from zero upwards). Where a major or sub-division line cuts through a town, the letter or number given are based on the square containing the larger part of the town eg: **Manchester SJ89**

For a fuller explanation see the Ordnance Survey maps.

SCALE

mls 0   30   60
kms 0   50   100

Maps produced by
The AA Cartographic Department
(Publications Division), Fanum House,
Basingstoke, Hampshire RG21 2EA

This atlas is for location purposes only:
see Members' Handbook for current road
and AA road services information.

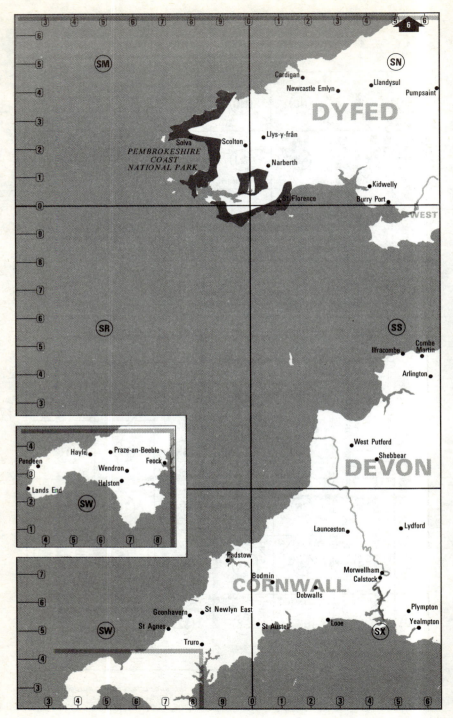

2

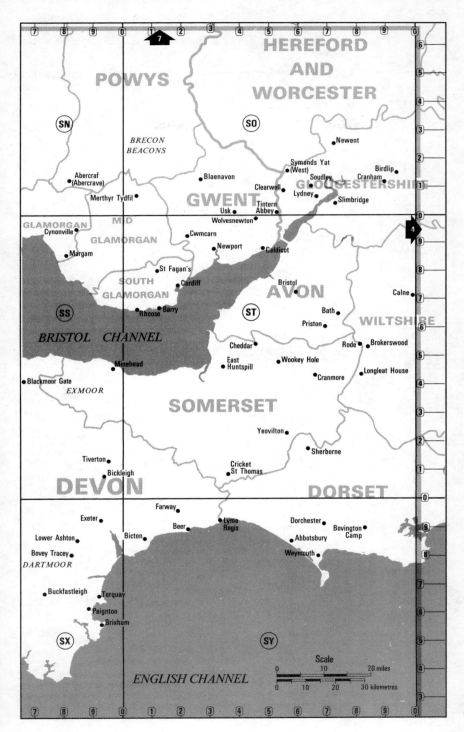

3

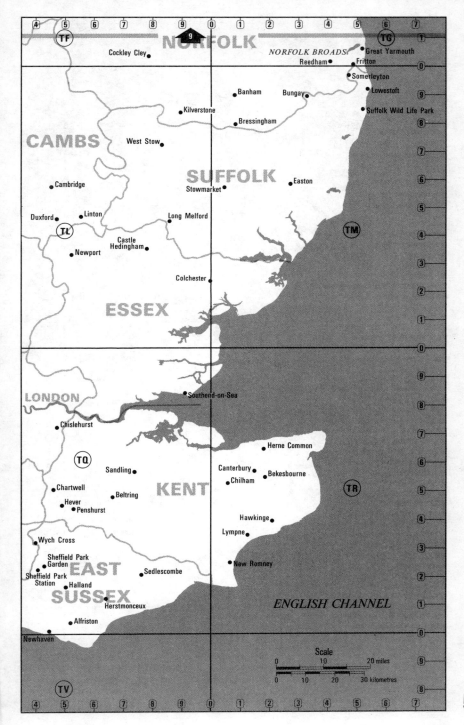

NORFOLK

9

TF

Cockley Cley

NORFOLK BROADS Great Yarmouth
Reedham • Fritton
Somerleyton
Banham Bungay Lowestoft
Kilverstone Suffolk Wild Life Park
Bressingham

TG

CAMBS

West Stow

SUFFOLK

Cambridge Stowmarket Easton

Duxford Linton
TL Long Melford
Newport Castle
Hedingham

Colchester

TM

ESSEX

LONDON

Southend-on-Sea

Chislehurst

Herne Common

TQ
Sandling Canterbury Bekesbourne
Chartwell Chilham
Hever Beltring KENT
Penshurst

TR

Hawkinge
Wych Cross Lympne
Sheffield Park
Garden EAST Sedlescombe New Romney
Sheffield Park
Station Halland
SUSSEX
Herstmonceux ENGLISH CHANNEL

Alfriston

Newhaven

TV

Scale

0   10   20 miles

0   10   20   30 kilometres

5

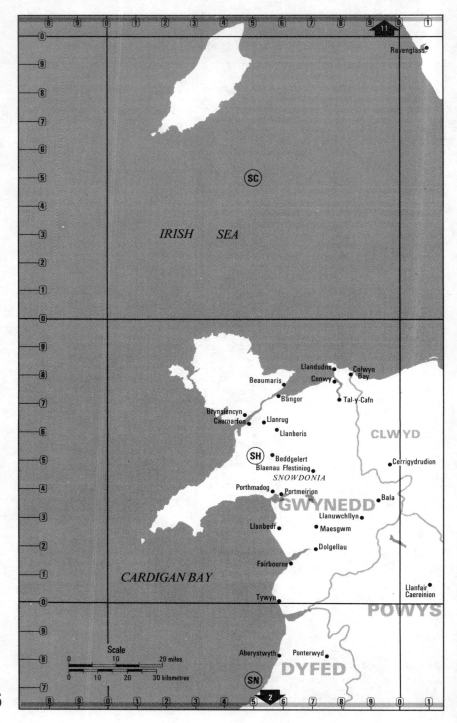

6

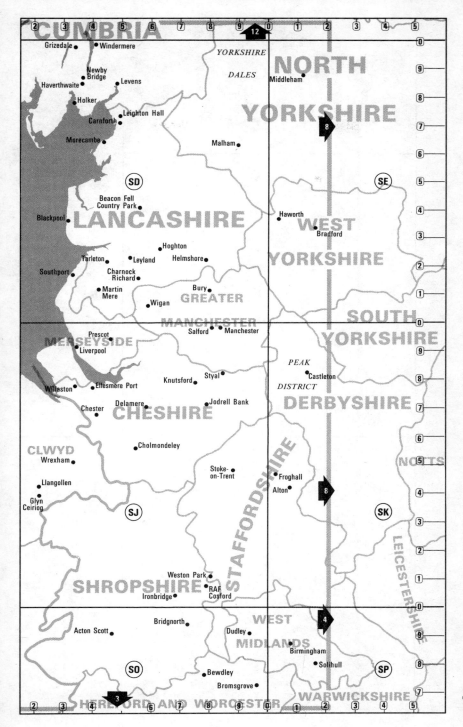

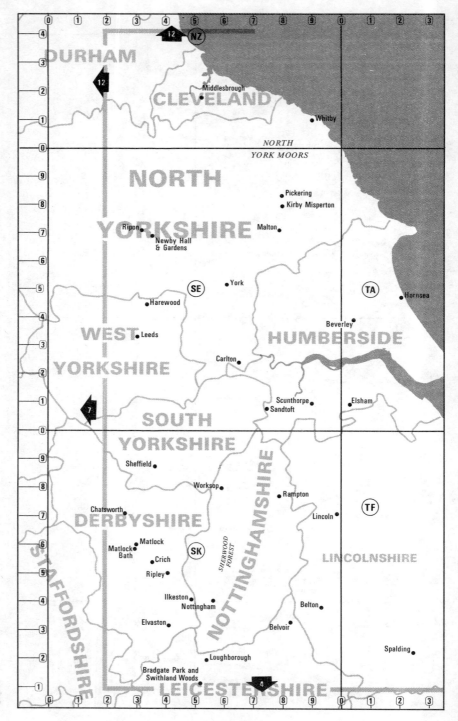

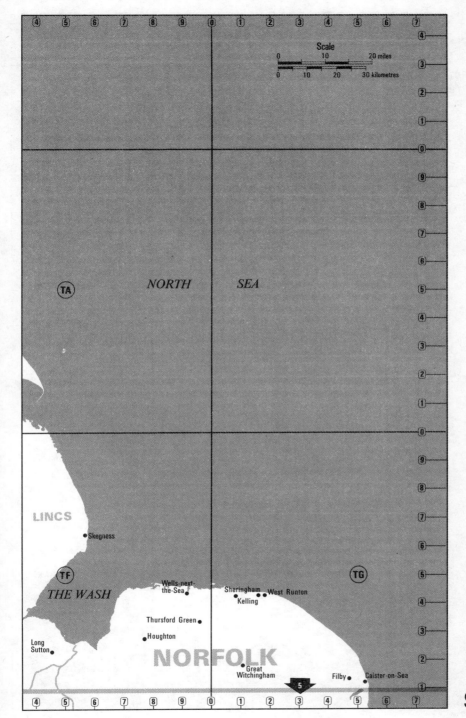

Scale

0   10   20 miles

0   10   20   30 kilometres

NORTH   *SEA*

TA

LINCS

• Skegness

TF

THE WASH

Wells-next-
the-Sea •

Sheringham • • West Runton
• Kelling

TG

Thursford Green •

• Houghton

Long
Sutton •

NORFOLK

• Great
Witchingham

Filby •

Caister-on-Sea •

5

9

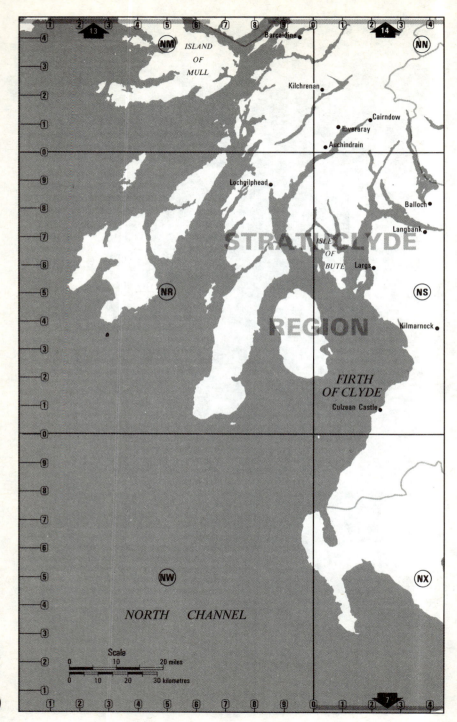

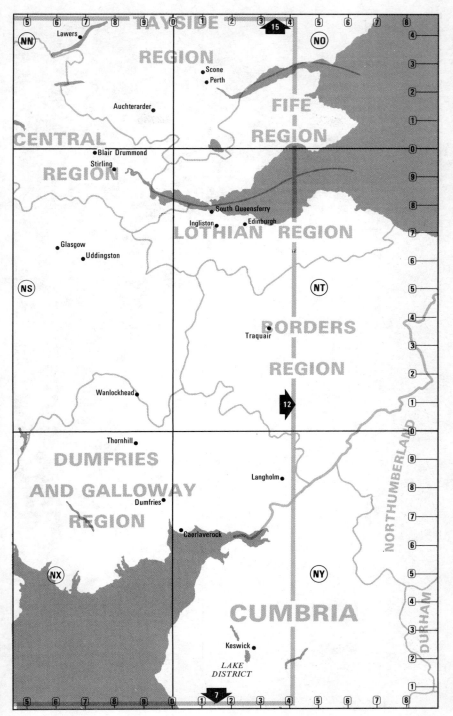

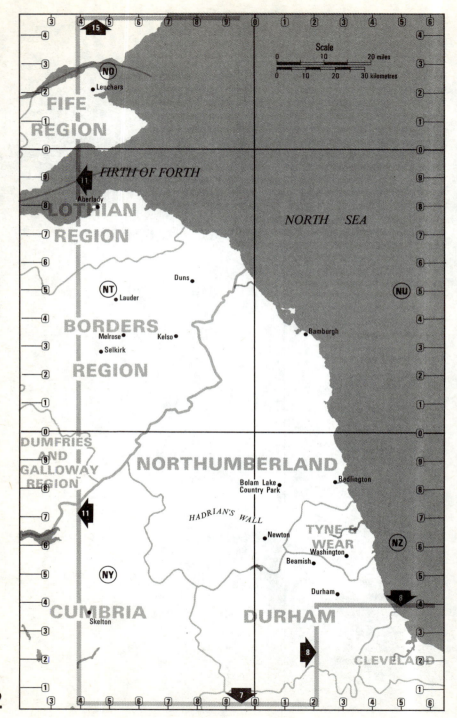

Scale

0   10   20 miles

0   10   20   30 kilometres

FIFE REGION

NO

• Leuchars

FIRTH OF FORTH

11

Aberlady •

LOTHIAN REGION

NORTH   SEA

NT

• Lauder

Duns •

NU

BORDERS

Melrose •   Kelso •   Bamburgh •

• Selkirk

REGION

DUMFRIES AND GALLOWAY REGION

NORTHUMBERLAND

Bolam Lake •   Bedlington •
Country Park

HADRIAN'S WALL

11

TYNE & WEAR

• Newton

NZ

NY   Washington •

Beamish •

Durham •

8

CUMBRIA   **DURHAM**

• Skelton

8   **CLEVELAND**

7

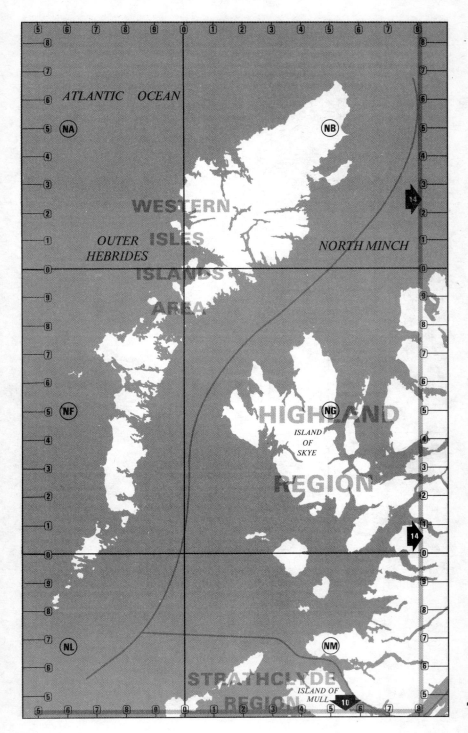

ATLANTIC OCEAN

NA

NB

WESTERN

OUTER
HEBRIDES

ISLES

ISLANDS

AREA

NORTH MINCH

NF

HIGHLAND

ISLAND
OF
SKYE

NG

REGION

14

14

NL

NM

STRATHCLYDE

REGION

ISLAND OF
MULL

10

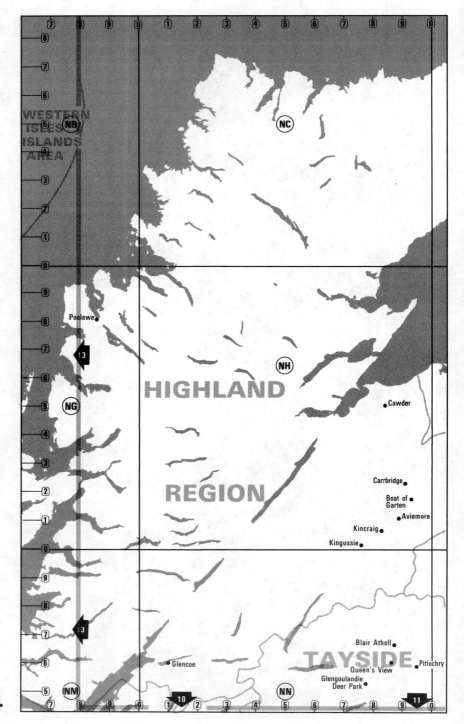

14